Dick Bosman
on Pitching

PRAISE FOR *DICK BOSMAN ON PITCHING*

"Dick Bosman was a very good pitcher and a great pitching coach; he has taught me so much about the art of pitching. He also knows about golf and cars and kids. It's all in this book. I loved it."—Tim Kurkjian, ESPN

"A true professor of pitching, Boz has a natural gift for teaching, whether it's educating a genuine prospect or an aging broadcaster. He's certainly impacted my baseball knowledge in a positive way."—Phil Wood, host of *Nationals Talk Live* and commentator on Mid-Atlantic Sports Network

"Long known to baseball insiders as a pitcher's pitcher, Dick Bosman now shares his thoughtful insights with a wider audience. A must-read for not only baseball fans but any reader wanting to understand better the complicated, demanding, yet beautiful game of baseball."—Lee Lowenfish, author of the award-winning biography *Branch Rickey: Baseball's Ferocious Gentleman* and collaborator with Tom Seaver on *The Art of Pitching*

"Dick Bosman has led one of the most spectacularly underrated baseball lives in the history of the game. From its beginnings on a farm in Kenosha, Wisconsin, to a productive stint on the mound during baseball's most glamorous era to an innovative and ongoing tenure as a pitching coach, this career is more than book worthy. Long-time DC baseball expert and author Ted Leavengood thoroughly details Bosman's journey, not only focusing on his career but also on Bosman's passion, the art of pitching."—Dave Marran, retired sports editor, *Kenosha News*

"Follow the ideas detailed in this book, and you are well on your way to understanding what it takes to pitch at the highest level. One of the reasons that every generation gets better than the one before is because people like Dick Bosman share with the world what they have learned from their experiences."—Dr. Bob Rotella, sports psychologist and author of *Golf Is Not a Game of Perfect*

"Dick Bosman's life in baseball has endured so long because of his love of the game, the fact that he's better at it than most, and his innate knowledge and understanding of its intricacies that he's happy to pass along. That's Dick Bosman in a nutshell, and in *Dick Bosman on Pitching*, Ted Leavengood pulls back the curtain and shows readers how Bosman grew his love of the game into a career, reinventing himself along the way and paying it forward as he helped the next generation learn and appreciate baseball the way he has."—Pete Kerzel, managing editor, MASNsports.com

Dick Bosman on Pitching

Lessons from the Life of a Major League Ballplayer and Pitching Coach

TED LEAVENGOOD
DICK BOSMAN

ROWMAN & LITTLEFIELD
Lanham • Boulder • New York • London

Published by Rowman & Littlefield
A wholly owned subsidary of The Rowman & Littlefield Publishing Group, Inc.
4501 Forbes Boulevard, Suite 200, Lanham, Maryland 20706
www.rowman.com

Unit A, Whitacre Mews, 26-34 Stannary Street, London SE11 4AB

British Library Cataloguing in Publication Information Available

Library of Congress Cataloging-in-Publication Data

Names: Leavengood, Ted, author. | Bosman, Dick, author.
Title: Dick Bosman on pitching : lessons from the life of a major league
  ballplayer and pitching coach / Ted Leavengood, Dick Bosman.
Description: Lanham, Maryland : Rowman & Littlefield, [2018] | Includes
  bibliographical references and index.
Identifiers: LCCN 2017030215 (print) | LCCN 2017053932 (ebook) | ISBN
  9781538106624 (electronic) | ISBN 9781538106617 (hardback : alk. paper)
Subjects: LCSH: Bosman, Dick. | Pitchers (Baseball)—United
  States—Biography. | Baseball coaches—United States—Biography. |
  Pitching (Baseball)
Classification: LCC GV865.B676 (ebook) | LCC GV865.B676 L43 2018 (print) |
  DDC 796.357092 [B] —dc23
LC record available at https://lccn.loc.gov/2017030215

Printed in the United States of America

Contents

Foreword

One of the greatest joys in life during the past 40 years has been the time I have spent with major-league and minor-league pitchers and their pitching coaches and managers, and helping them learn how to pitch successfully at the highest level. During that time, I have spent many hours with Dick Bosman discussing how to combine the art and science of pitching so that pitchers can gain solid, individualized fundamentals they can then take into game situations, trusting in their skills. It takes a talented, knowledgeable, and canny coach to consistently help pitchers succeed at the highest level. From my experience in baseball, Dick Bosman is one of the best. He truly "gets it."

Some may ask what I mean when I say Dick "gets it." First, Dick has a positive, optimistic approach that involves a consistent process, one that, if adhered to, leads to success. He understands that he has to get players to "buy into" his process and live it for a sustained time period. But Dick also understands that he must believe in his players' abilities and potentials as much as they believe in his process. Dick knows that a pitcher's perception of his own talent may be even more important than how much actual talent he may possess. Belief and faith in one's self when it is time to pitch will ultimately play a huge role in how successful a pitcher becomes.

At the major-league level, a pitcher must see himself making the batter miss or hitting pop flies or ground balls. If they cannot see themselves doing this against the best in the game, it will not matter how good their "stuff" looks in the bullpen or at lower levels. This is the game within the game. This is where pitching becomes more art than science. Some see pitching as consisting solely of technique and speed. Others think it is all in the mind. The truth is somewhere in between. The problem is complicated by the fact that no one can take a picture of what is going on inside a pitcher's head when he is throwing. Thus, it is easy to pretend that what goes on inside a pitcher's head does not exist, even though pitchers know what takes place. I do not know for certain if the difference is in the mind, the heart, the soul, or the human spirit or will, but I do know it is the stuff inside that separates pitchers at the top levels from those elsewhere.

Most observers tend to think the mind starts above the shoulders and everything below the shoulders is the body, treating the two areas as separate entities. But you cannot pitch without getting the mind and body to work together as one because they are intimately connected.

Dick Bosman understands that to succeed you must have a true passion for pitching. You must be willing to prepare physically and mentally for every hitter and every situation. Dick knows that to succeed, a pitcher must be strong enough to deal with disappointment and setbacks. He recognizes that at the major-league level a pitcher can make great pitches and still get hit. Dick helps each pitcher understand that a good pitch is the one thing you can own and control. He wants a pitcher to control what he can and stop trying to control what he cannot—like a big-league hitter sometimes hitting a really good pitch.

Many times I have watched Dick support a pitcher by saying, "Welcome to the big leagues, the hitters are real good also. Just keep making good pitches and stop worrying about outcome." He teaches every pitcher that *he* has the ball. The pitcher owns the ball and the mound—but only if he has his mind in the right place. He must have a clear plan and picture. Clarity, trust, and commitment give a pitcher power. And doubt and fear when it is time to throw will make a pitcher weak. By doubting himself, a pitcher gives away his position of strength. Pitchers with confidence and a clear plan and mind-set attack the hitter and get ahead in the count, and stay ahead; adhering to that principle gives them power and a huge advantage.

By following the ideas detailed in this book you will be well on your way to understanding what it takes to pitch at the highest level. One of the reasons every generation of ballplayers gets better than the one before it is because people like Dick Bosman share what they have learned from their experiences, and the same mistakes do not have to be repeated.

—Dr. Bob Rotella, sports psychologist and author
of *Golf Is Not a Game of Perfect*

Acknowledgments

Dave Marran, former sports editor for *Kenosha News*, deserves special thanks. He has been a constant source of help with this book. As an old and trusted friend of Dick's, he pointed me in the right direction numerous times as the project got underway. Thanks are due to Reverend Ed Winkler and his wife Nina of Charlottesville, Virginia, for reading the manuscript and other acts of moral support; to Phil Wood for his corrections to the manuscript; and to Chris Shebby for reading the manuscript as well. Thanks to Brent and David Bolin, George and Mary Clark, Rob Clayman and Carol Miller, Dr. Joel Cohen, Melinda Frederick and Rich Lerner, Marc Hall, David Hubler, Mike Lynch, Carroll Minnick, Ron Newmeyer, and Jon Witty, who have helped at one time or another, most for many years. Thanks to the Bob Davids SABR Chapter members, especially Pete Cottrell, D. Bruce Brown, Mark Pattison, David Hughes, Eric Johnston, Mike Shapiro, and Mike Grieb. Thanks to Christen Karniski and Jessica McCleary at Rowman and Littlefield for their patience and expertise. Thanks to my wife, Donna Boxer, for her unwavering support and editorial genius. Thanks to my daughters, Julia Leavengood-Boxer and Claire Leavengood-Boxer, for their inspiration and many years of ballpark memories.

—Ted Leavengood

Thanks to my wife, Pam, the light of my life, who is truly the straw that stirs the drink. To my mom and dad for their love and support. To Andy Smith, who made it fun. To Frank Howard, who next to my dad is the best man I've known. To Billy Klaus for sticking with me when things looked bleak. To Ted Williams for teaching me how to pitch from the neck up and Sid Hudson who as a pitching coach was the only teacher I ever had. To Ken Aspromonte for believing in me. To John Koons Jr. for his friendship and providing me with the opportunity to start my coaching career. To Donald Malan and Mike Harris for saving my sanity in the early days in the car business. To Syd Thrift and Ken "the Hawk" Harrelson for taking a chance on an unknown coach. To Buzz Capra and Chuch Hartenstein. To Jim Marshall for his guidance and advice. To Doug Melvin, who hired me three times but only fired me once. To Greg Biagini and Johnny Oates, who led by example every day and for nine years let me be the pitching coach. To Larry Hardy, Tom Foley, and Jimmy Karr, Head Professional Kingsway CC. To Mitch Lukevics, a man's man—if you can't work for him, you can't work for anybody. To Bob Rotella for his wisdom and advice. To Neil Allen, a dear friend and the best pitching coach I've ever been around. Thanks to Ted Leavengood for getting this project started and to the staff at Rowman and Littlefield for finishing it in such fine form. Lastly, thank you to the countless numbers of aspiring pitchers I have had the pleasure of working with over these many years who have helped me arrive at my philosophy on how to teach what Tom Seaver calls "this search for perfection we cannot totally achieve."

—Dick Bosman

I

A FIERY COMPETITOR

1

Baseball and Cars

For high school players, it was the end of the 1962 baseball season in Wisconsin. The final pitch of the state championship game had been thrown, and for Mary Bradford High School it was a disappointing 2–0 loss. But a whole new world of baseball beckoned to George and Nella Bosman, who sat at their kitchen table looking in all seriousness at their son Dick, who had pitched the state championship game for Mary Bradford High. There had been long conversations with Dick about signing a contract to pitch for a major-league team. Everyone knew it was a weighty step they were preparing to take. "When you sign on that line, you are their property," George Bosman told his son.[1]

Despite the gravity of the conversation, excitement bubbled just beneath the surface. The vision of pitching in the majors had been shared by George and Dick Bosman for half a dozen years and now it was taking shape, a real thing sitting in front of them in the form of Paul Tretiak, the scout for the Pittsburgh Pirates. The Bosman family had no idea what the future might hold for their son Dick, but the proposition before them had been carefully tailored to their needs, and they were ready to act.

As thoughtful as the Bosmans were trying to be, only Tretiak had a realistic idea about the likely progression for a talented kid signing with a major-league team. He had seen Bosman throw numerous times but wanted a second opinion. With parental permission, he had taken Dick to Burlington, Iowa, the prior week to have him throw in front of the manager for the minor-league team there. At the end of the session, the manager told Tretiak that Bosman could pitch for his team that night if he wanted to. "Your career can start right here," Tretiak told Bosman, as he recalls.

Tretiak had followed this road himself, playing in the majors after World War II for eight seasons. He played second base for the Yankees and Cubs, and had been a friend to Whitey Ford. Tretiak had followed his playing career with one as a major-league scout and coach. He was a baseball lifer, someone who would be around the game until the day he died.[2]

The aggregate knowledge Dick offers to young pitchers has accumulated from the many baseball savants he has known and the countless baseball situations he has observed on the most personal level. That knowledge becomes a philosophy of pitching, one that is like a single game on the mound that evolves to meet the moment, one that is fluid and changing.

He could not know how long Dick Bosman would be in the game. He could not know that Bosman himself would have a baseball career that would span five decades and that the most profound contributions Bosman would make would be as a pitching coach for four teams. Bosman would become what his teammate in Washington, Jim Hannan, called a "very good pitching coach."[3] More importantly, he was a coach that young pitcher Ben McDonald—his protégé for the Baltimore Orioles—would call "not only a good pitching coach, but a good friend."[4]

Paul Tretiak knew only how much potential Dick Bosman had. He did not know if the young man would find mentors to mold that potential into major-league success or whether Bosman would be a teachable student of the game. Tretiak knew there were many twists and turns on the way to the ultimate goal, and he knew how precarious the road could be. But it had to start somewhere, and Tretiak believed Bosman would be well-served to start as soon as possible.

The excitement about Dick's prospects had built steadily during his senior year at Mary Bradford High School. As a junior, he had pitched and played first base, slugging 13 home runs. He was the second starting pitcher on that team but became the ace as a senior. The scouts began showing up as he piled up one impressive win after another and the high school team remained undefeated. The scouts were there from his hometown Milwaukee Braves and the Cincinnati Reds.

Tretiak wined and dined the Bosmans more than his competition, and there was a comfort level between the Pirates scout and the Bosmans that did not exist with the others. George and Nella believed he had the most interest in their son, and they had concerns where baseball would take Dick. Was it a legitimate career choice or just a dream? George Bosman was a practical man who wanted something that made sense for his son. But the issue was settled when the Bosmans—members of the Christian Reform Church who took their faith seriously—insisted to Tretiak that their son could not play baseball on Sundays. They wanted that in writing as part of the contract. When Tretiak included language to that effect in the documents that Dick was to sign, the decision was made.

Dick knew there would be a day of reckoning on the issue of Sunday baseball. He was aware of only one major-league player, Johnny Vander Meer, who early in his career refused to pitch on Sundays. He doubted he could do the same, but he wanted his parents to be comfortable with the decision, so he deferred to them. He was a minor as well and needed his father's approval to play professionally, but Dick was ready to take the leap into the future and for a $7,000 bonus he signed his first professional baseball contract at that kitchen table in Kenosha, Wisconsin. Bonus money for young prospects was far more modest in 1962 than in the decades that followed. One of the elite prospects that summer, Jim Palmer, would sign with the Orioles for $50,000, far more than many major-league players made annually.

A baseball career was a long-shot deal. Few made the grade, but when there was real money attached to the dream, it was hard to turn it down. There was one more caveat linked to Bosman's contract. Dick had no doubts about the direction he wanted to go, but he wasn't sure he was completely ready. He wanted the rest of the year for himself. He did not want to pitch for the Burlington Bees that summer. He asked Tretiak to give him until the following spring to start his career. Tretiak said he was wasting a year of his major-league career but agreed.

The reason Bosman often gave for the delay was wanting to try college. He attended the University of Wisconsin at Parkside that fall, but in truth, as he said, "I was in love and reluctant to leave home. I wasn't worth a darn as a student." It was just part of the process of saying good-bye, and soon enough, he revealed, "I found out that girl wasn't for me," admitting, "It was a wasted year." But he pitched for a semipro team in Kenosha to stay in shape and worked at a factory just across the Illinois border to make enough money to gain a sense of financial independence.

Home had been a good place for Dick, and his reluctance to leave was easy to understand. When Dick signed his contract, there was a new baby sister who had just taken up residence with the Bosmans. Dick was the oldest of the children, but he had three sisters now. There was Diane, the baby, who would know little of baseball or softball except what she would put together in scrapbooks. And then there were Virginia and Barbara, who would always remember. They were two and four years younger than Dick, respectively.

They were a large and close-knit family. Uncle Clarence lived just 250 yards up 52nd Street, a "good three wood" from the family. Another relative was the Kenosha fire chief, and another would become mayor. The Bosman family was woven integrally into the fabric of the community, and baseball had always been part of that connection.

Uncle Clarence was the brother of Dick's grandfather, and he had been a fast-pitch softball player of some reputation for many years. George Bosman and his brother Clarence both had considerable talent with a softball. Each man had perfected the underhand whip action, which sent the sphere hurtling through the air at speeds to rival anything a professional baseball pitcher could manage.

George was the first to see the potential in his son and the first to dream of Dick pitching in the majors. When Dick was 11, he had asked his father if he could go into town for Little League tryouts. There was little question what the answer would be. After he saw his son pitch for the first time, George could see that his boy threw harder than the rest of the kids. The following year, when Dick was 12 and in his last season of Little League, his father taught him how to throw a "spinner." It was, in effect, a slider, the same pitch that would take Dick all the way to the big leagues 10 years later.

Wisconsin was hardly the perfect place for developing major-league talent. Bosman said of his senior year in high school, "We had snow outs, freeze outs, rain outs. By the time all was said and done, we were lucky to play 12, 15 games in a season." But there were many factors that went in his favor as well. Some of the obvious ones—like his father's love for the game—and others—like growing up on a farm—outweighed the negatives.

"Some of the apples were good for eating and some were good for throwing," Dick remembered of the orchard next to his father's 10-acre farm. Whether it was chucking tomatoes from the farm at his friend Jim Renick or apples from the orchard, there were plenty of ways to build arm strength for a kid raised on a farm.

The Bosman connection to the land was a strong one. Grandfather Richard Bosman farmed a 500-acre tract of land in Wheatland, Wisconsin, 25 miles west of Kenosha and the shores of Lake Michigan. He leased the land because men like him who had survived the Great Depression were leery of owning it. The Bosman family lived on his grandfather's farm when Dick was born on February 17, 1944. But two years later, they bought a place closer to town, a 10-acre tract of land just outside Kenosha.

It was still a farm on which they planted soybeans, corn, and tomatoes. But according to Dick, "Intuitively my father knew that if he did not go to work for someone that had a union so that he could accrue a pension, he was never going to be able to retire." George found work driving for Yellow Transit Freight Lines, which had a hub in Kenosha. He did not drive long haul on the road. "He drove locally because he wanted to be home at night."

The new place wasn't a grand old farm in the same sense as the one on which he had been born, but the place on 52nd Street was big enough for Dick to think of it as a farm. There was annual plowing of the fields and a large garage in the field where they stored and worked on their tractors and trucks. "I learned to drive a tractor by the time I was eight or nine," Dick remembered.

Whether it was the chores on the farm or throwing apples and tomatoes, when Dick joined his first Little League team, he had a stronger arm than any of the other boys his age. He was also guided by the tradition of George and Clarence Bosman, who only played softball after the chores were done but were good enough at getting a softball past the opposing hitters to wonder how much talent they really had. They had enough knowledge of the game that when George saw that his young son Dick could do much the same with a baseball as he and his uncle could do with a softball, he began to see a future that men and boys of that era dreamed about.

And then there was Dick's mother, who drove him throughout the wider Milwaukee metropolitan area to his games. "I did not have a driver's license when I was 14, 15 years old, and my dad was busy working. It fell to my mom to get me to all of those games," he reflected. She was the one in the stands much of the time, as she stayed and watched her son's games, watching him chase his dream from early on. "There was never a complaint on her part."

After Little League there was Babe Ruth League Baseball, run by the city of Kenosha, and the Mary Bradford High School coach, Andy Smith, managed one of the teams and encouraged the more talented players to try out for the high school team. He worked with the best kids from Babe Ruth League teams and guided them through their baseball experience. By the time they reached Mary Bradford High, he knew what kind of talent each young boy had.

There were only two high schools in Kenosha, Saint Josephs, a Catholic school, and Mary Bradford. Most of the kids on those teams had been playing against one another for several years. Andy Smith had been working with Dick Bosman from an early age and was a significant influence on Bosman's development as a pitcher and person until he graduated and signed with the Pirates.

Smith saw what the scouts did: a kid who was a little stronger, a little bit bigger, and could put a little more on the ball than his peers. That ability did not wilt as Dick got older and the competition got better. By the time he reached Mary Bradford High, his baseball world had expanded beyond the boundaries of Kenosha, as the team had begun to play further afield in the area between Milwaukee and Chicago. He was pitching against teams from Racine and Waukegan as the season progressed.

In 1962, Mary Bradford High remained undefeated behind Dick's strong right arm. Then there were the playoffs, which Dick remembered as consisting of only four games before the championship finals of the Wisconsin State Tournament. With the tournament so close to both Chicago and Milwaukee, it attracted attention from major-league scouts, and it was difficult for a hard-throwing kid to fly under their radar. It was an easy drive to see what all the fuss was about, so by the time the Mary Bradford team was in the Wisconsin state finals, there were plenty of scouts in the crowd.

"I pitched my heart out," Dick remembered of the game. "It could have gone on all night because we weren't going to score any runs. But our short-stop threw a ball away, and we lost the game 2–0." Although he lost the game, Bosman won the right to continue his career in baseball, which proved the more lasting trophy of them all.

As important as baseball and softball were in the Bosman household, there was another sporting venture that demanded almost as much attention and one where speed was just as important. Cars were magic in the early 1960s, and racing them at high speed could bring almost as much excitement as an extra-inning game for the state championship.

It started for Dick when he was 14 years old. There was an old 1937 Chevrolet that sat wasting in the barn next door to the Bosman family home. They bought the car for almost nothing. "It was a brown car with mohair seats in it," Dick remembered. The car had been sitting for quite a while, and the motor was frozen from disuse.

"Dad showed me how to take the cylinder head off, and then he poured kerosene on top of the cylinders," Dick related. They worked the cylinders loose and put the head back on, and Dick's father pulled the old car down the long drive from the garage with the tractor. Dick let out the clutch as his father had instructed, but he had forgotten to turn the key on. "As soon as I turned the key that thing lit off, and I ran right into the back of the tractor. We were laughing, but I was excited too that we had gotten that motor running."

Bosman and his friend Jim Renick learned to drive a car by running the old Chevy in the fields behind his parents' house on a small track they created. But they never drove it on the streets. It was not until Dick was 16 that he got his first car for use on the road. It was a 1951 Chevrolet four-door sedan that a cousin was selling. George Bosman paid $75 for the car, and although it was not new in 1960, it was deemed street worthy.

Dick began working on it with much of the knowledge he had gained from the old '37. It had three gears on the column when he got the car, but with parts scrounged from the junkyard he installed a three-speed floor shift and dual exhausts. "It did not go all that fast, but it made a lot of noise," Dick remembered. They marked off a quarter mile on 52nd Street outside their house and began drag racing. The street was only a two-lane road, not the main artery it is today. They

> There has to be that spark, that fire within that can set an old engine running or a fine pitching talent on a path toward the majors.

did not have the expertise or the money to add horsepower to that Chevrolet engine. "We did not know that much about it . . . and we could not afford a head gasket," Dick recalled.

It was just another way to compete, but it was also a tremendous rush to get a car going fast in a hurry. As he spent more time racing, he came to understand how expensive a proposition it was. The other drivers were getting sponsorships if they wanted to pursue racing seriously. He did not take that step but also could not walk away from the sport, relating, "In my fantasy heart of hearts, I always thought I might want to drag race professionally." In pursuit of this idea he spent the better part of the bonus money he got from the Pittsburgh Pirates on speed equipment.

It was straight line racing, not "roundy-round," although that was something of interest to Bosman as well. But his focus was on dragsters, if only because it was easier to find a place to match up against someone else. "Great Lakes Dragway, which is still running . . . is where we would go," Dick related. They watched the best of the racers from Milwaukee and Chicago. But it was getting behind those massive engines that intrigued Bosman, one that was practically sitting in your lap, as he remembers it.

Several drivers let him race their cars, and he "got up to some pretty good speeds," topping out at 215 miles per hour, according to articles at the time.[5] But it was a serious endeavor and not one to be taken lightly. "Those things were belching fire and smoke at you, and might blow up."[6] It was apparent from his experiences on the track just how perilously close to the edge those drivers were operating. Maintaining control of the machine could be difficult, and it was not something to do just for fun. It was a serious business that required the full attention of anyone doing it.

Bosman continued to race during the offseason well into his professional baseball career. When he became part of the Washington Senators minor-league organization, they expressed concern about the hobby. Bosman's father George had been opposed to his son's interest in racing from the first time he altered the old 1951 Chevy. "He was never in favor of me getting into a car and trying to make it go as fast as possible," Dick revealed.

But the deciding moment came when a dragster Bosman was racing caught fire and the only thing that stood between the young pitching prospect and a career-ending injury was his flame-retardant suit.[7] When Bosman stepped away from that inferno, he left drag racing as a serious venture. He knew that racing was its own career and if he could not give it the kind of attention it needed it would be best not to pursue it at all.

A sigh of relief could be heard both in the Washington front office and at the old kitchen table when Bosman decided that baseball was going to be enough to get his adrenaline going. He drove hard and threw hard because he was an intense competitor in whatever he was doing, one with that extra motivation, maybe even the swagger, that it took to make it to the top. Whether throwing a fastball or spinning a tight slider, it was that added effort and last dollop of confidence and desire that would help him become a major-league pitcher.

2

Learning to Pitch

The Pirates sent Dick Bosman a Greyhound bus ticket to take him to his first professional baseball camp in Kingsport, Tennessee. But George Bosman would have none of it. His son was not riding a bus all the way south. George, Dick, and sister Virginia packed up the car and made the long trip to Tennessee. No matter what route you took to Kingsport, it was not a major destination point unless you were trying to make a minor-league roster for the Pittsburgh Pirates.

Dick had few expectations about the experience. What he found in the first week was a diverse group of young kids like himself. "There were a lot of 17-, 18-, 19-year-old kids, many of whom had never been away from home before. We were playing baseball every day for the first time," Dick remembered.[1] For many of those gathered at the Pirates camp, the sessions were actually a tryout. Having signed a contract with bonus money attached to it, Dick's status was relatively secure, but this was not the case for most of the rest in camp at the beginning.

For Dick Bosman, baseball is not just a game. There is nothing more important than winning, regardless of what you are doing. That fiercely competitive spirit makes every game, every season as new and important as the first time.

Pirates officials would read out a list of names of players to be cut before lunch each day. By the time the afternoon practice began, those kids were gone. It was hardly the well-organized camp that a team in recent decades would conduct. Branch Rickey III was the general manager in charge of the operation, and Al Kubski was the manager. "We talked baseball, but he was almost like a babysitter," Dick recalled. "There wasn't a lot of coaching. It was more a time of evaluation."

"A lot more goes into it today," Bosman said, comparing the Pirates camp in 1963 to the modern Major League Baseball operation, which oversees a well-managed system to feed talent up the hierarchy of player development. He is now intimately involved in the process and knows how from early in the spring training camp until the Amateur Draft in June, the Tampa Bay Rays—Dick's current major-league organization—put together the rosters of the minor-league teams that comprise the organization.

A much larger group of scouts and evaluators are charged with not only helping the team pick the "best available talent in the first five rounds," according to Bosman, but also "filling out the rosters of the minor-league teams." In the later rounds of the draft, the team works just as hard to make certain there is a shortstop and third baseman at the lower reaches of the organization. Sometimes that concern can trump the idea of the best available talent.

In 1963, Dick Bosman was part of a very different world, and although he may have had higher status as a player signed to a contract, there was no real road map as to how to develop his talent or where he fit into the organization's plans for the future. It was sink or swim for the most part, and the ones who wanted it the most progressed at the end of each season. Dick worked in relief that first season, tossing only 46 innings in the six-team Appalachian League in the 68-game season of Rookie League play in 1963. He had a good degree of success throughout the course of the season, with 66 strikeouts and a respectable 3.52 ERA.

Kubski called Dick into his office at the end of the season and said, "We're going to put you on the Columbus roster." Columbus was the highest level of play in the Pittsburgh organization at the time. Bosman did not know what the sudden promotion meant, but he was told that the Pirates were trying to protect him from the upcoming Rule 5 Draft. According to the rules as they then were structured, a team could only select him in that draft if they were willing to play him at a higher level than where he was lodged at the time. The rule was intended to prevent a team from stockpiling players at lower levels.

For Dick it meant that any team that selected him would be required to bring him to their major-league camp the following spring.

When Dick left for home at the end of the season, he believed his career with the Pirates was secure. In late fall of 1963, however, the Bosman family got a letter from the ownership group of the San Francisco Giants telling them that his contract had been purchased by that team. Having been told by Kubski that he was safely ensconced with the Pirates, he called Paul Tretiak to find out what had happened. The Giants had seen Bosman pitching against their Salem Rebels affiliate in the Appalachian League and liked what they saw. Tretiak told him only, "Congratulations, you are going to major-league camp in Casa Grande, Arizona, with the San Francisco Giants." It was only then that he understood that he would be playing somewhere new in 1964.

The key for Dick was his first chance to play alongside major leaguers in the spring. In February, Bosman made plans to travel to Arizona. He had done nothing special to get ready for his second year as a professional. "They gave me no workout plan or anything like that," Bosman said, contrasting the limited conditioning he undertook with the extensive training the modern-day player undergoes, making their career a 12-month regimen that requires a workout routine for much of the offseason.

> The most important aspect of any athletic endeavor is getting into the best possible physical condition. It doesn't happen overnight. It is a grind.

For his first big-league camp, Bosman flew to Phoenix, Arizona, before continuing on to Casa Grande, where San Francisco held forth in the spring. An older-model bus with "San Francisco Giants" painted on the side picked him up from the airport in the evening and carried him through the darkness toward Casa Grande. The Giants were copying the blueprint of the Los Angeles Dodgers in designing a plush spring training complex that included a golf course, a team motel exclusively for players, and other appealing amenities. It was in the middle of the Arizona desert that Bosman was first introduced to such big-league players as Willie Mays, Willie McCovey, and Juan Marichal.

Alvin Dark was the Giants manager, and Dick would play for him at the major-league level in Oakland late in his career. Jack Sanford was a proven member of the Giants rotation who befriended Dick, teaching him the rudiments of how a major-league camp operated and what was expected of a rookie.

For the first time, George and Nella Bosman came to see their son play professional baseball that spring. It was the big leagues, and everyone was excited. Dick left them tickets for exhibition games, and they were no doubt happy to see that the next team on the schedule was from Chicago. Dick did not last long at the major-league complex, but before being sent out he told Dark he had not gotten a chance to pitch. Dark promised to remedy the situation, and the next day Bosman made the trip to Mesa, Arizona, for the game against the Cubs. Dark inserted Bosman into the game in the eighth inning on a hot, dry Arizona afternoon.

The Cubs were still being led by one of Dick's heroes, Ernie Banks. He was facing a lineup, even in the eighth inning, that included hitters the likes of Ron Santo and Billy Williams, as well as Banks. Bosman was not getting anyone out as he stood on the mound beneath an unrelenting Arizona sun. Giants catcher Del Crandall came to the mound and said, "I don't know what you're doing kid, but you need to figure this out, cause I'm dying back there." Bosman found a way to get out of the inning, but he knew with certainty that he was not ready for the big leagues. He was happy to report to the minor-league complex the next day.

Bosman spent the 1964 season in Lexington, North Carolina, in the Class D Western Carolina League. "It was exactly where I needed to be," he admitted. Ray Miller, who went on to become a highly successful pitching coach with the Baltimore Orioles, was his roommate. Max Lanier was the manager, and his son Hal played for the Giants. The level of organization was a notch above the Rookie League play he had experienced the prior year with the Pirates, but there was no more well-developed plan for Bosman's career than there had been with Pittsburgh.

Major-league teams at the time did not deploy pitching or hitting coaches to minor-league teams, especially at the lower levels. Each organization had a minor-league roving instructor who visited with a team, watching the action and working with players in an attempt to provide instruction. Bosman was still primarily being used as a reliever, and he went to Lanier and asked him about his status as a bullpen pitcher.

"Am I ever going to get a chance to start, Max?" he said as an honest query.

"Well, are you a starter?" Lanier asked, as if he had little idea where he should deploy Bosman to best effect.

"I can be," Dick answered.

"Well then, you're starting tomorrow," Lanier responded.

Bosman started nine games that season but continued to be used as a swingman for the most part, coming into games whenever needed, even closing. He compiled a 3.21 ERA in 129 innings. It was a good season overall, and again he had more strikeouts than innings pitched. But it would be the last season he would be able to say that, as his career was about to change.

There was a more serious transformation looming when that summer his father called to tell his son that a letter had come from the local draft board. The Bosmans had just returned to Kenosha from watching their son play when they found the letter waiting for them. Ray Miller had gotten his draft notice as well, and the two young men drove to take their draft physicals together.

Dick let the Giants know he was on the verge of being drafted. The Giants told him that at the end of the season he and Ray should come to Phoenix, where the team would get them enlisted in the National Guard. It was a long drive across country. Ray started in Baltimore, where he lived at the time, and picked up Bosman in Kenosha before heading to Phoenix. They began basic training that fall. Neither man knew exactly what they were getting into, but they soon had a drill sergeant in their face and there was no special treatment for minor-league baseball players. "They were training us to go to war," Dick reflected. His skills as an auto mechanic came into play more so than those with a baseball, and he became a heavy artillery repairman whose future seemed to include working on the huge howitzers aimed at the North Vietnamese along the demilitarized zone. He was sent to the Aberdeen Proving Grounds in Maryland for further work on heavy artillery, and suddenly baseball was a fading memory.

By the end of his military training in Maryland, it was early 1965, and Dick was scheduled to ship out for Vietnam. The war was escalating there from a back-burner skirmish with only 25,000 American "advisors" in 1964, to a full-blown conflagration that would see more than 500,000 soldiers patrolling the jungles of South Vietnam. By the end of 1965, there were almost 200,000 American soldiers in Vietnam, mostly young men like Dick and Ray.

It was the luck of the draw that Dick was able to stay stateside. "They cancelled my battalion's orders at the very end. We stayed and the rest of those guys I had trained with went to Vietnam," he recalled. "The whole battalion did not go," and he believes to this day that the decision had nothing to do with his status with the Giants. He added, "A lot of those guys I trained with and was friends with did not come back. And that haunts me to this day."

His status in a nondeployed National Guard unit allowed Bosman to report to spring training within a few weeks of the decision about who was going to war and who would stay behind. But the Giants had failed to protect him from the Rule 5 Draft. Whether it was his uncertain status as a soldier or some other reason, Bosman would never know. But once again, he was with a new team, chosen in the Rule 5 Draft by the Washington Senators. He reported to camp with his new team in Lake Wales, Florida, in February. It was in this new organization that he would encounter Sid Hudson, whose influence on how Dick pitched and how he learned the art of pitching was game-changing.

His assignment for the 1965 season was in the Eastern League, where he pitched for the York White Roses and Billy Klaus, the manager. Once again there was only the manager and a trainer to comprise the team staff. But Sid Hudson was the minor-league roving pitching instructor, with whom Bosman had worked in spring camp. Dick was overmatched against the Eastern League hitters, many of whom—like George Scott—would play in the majors. "They hit me pretty good," he remembered about the first part of that season playing Double-A ball.

Hudson worked to change the way Bosman approached the game. Dick gave up being the hard thrower who could strike out more than a batter an inning, because he was overmatched against the best hitters. Hudson stressed the importance of keeping the ball down and getting ground-ball outs.

"I was used to going to two strikes on guys and throwing a fastball or slider and striking somebody out," Bosman said. "But those guys in the Eastern League were much more selective, and if you made a mistake, you paid for it." The first half of the season, Bosman was paying a higher price for mistakes, which reduced the value of striking batters out. The second half of the 1965 campaign was a turning point for Bosman, and while the strikeouts were no longer piling up, he was getting better results overall.

As the season ended, Dick went to Billy Klaus to ask for his help in finding him a slot in the Fall Instructional League (FSIL) in Florida with the Senators. His luck held. Bosman went to Florida instead of home to Wisconsin. The Senators' FSIL team played at Al Lopez Field in Tampa. It was two months of intensive train-

> Senators pitching coach Sid Hudson convinced Dick that he had to be more than just a hard thrower, and Bosman's path to the majors quickened when he began consistently keeping the ball down and getting easy ground-ball outs.

ing, not quite boot camp, but they played a lot of baseball in a short period of time.

Bosman concentrated on Hudson's every word during those months. It was more emphasis on "killing worms in front of home plate," he remembered, as he tried to "gain control of the hitters that way rather than by striking them out." The highlight for Dick was combining for a no-hitter with another young Senators pitcher, Don Loun.

Gil Hodges, the manager for the Senators, was watching that game and liked what he saw. As a result, Bosman was invited to the Washington major league camp in the spring of 1966. He was one of the final cuts from the roster, and the team again sent him to pitch for the York White Roses. York was just a short bus ride from Washington. More importantly, when Dick reported, this time it was with a more refined slider, which Hudson had helped him sharpen and tighten. He was now the "sinker–slider" pitcher, which he would be known as for the rest of his career.

"I never learned a changeup," Bosman recalled. But it wasn't for lack of effort. "He [Sid Hudson] tried so hard to teach me a changeup," Dick added. There was little of the sophistication then about how to throw that pitch. There were none of the many grips that Bosman has been teaching for several decades and now teaches to young hurlers with the Tampa Bay Rays. "If I had known then what I know now, I'd have had a changeup," Bosman declared. Instead, he had to be content with changing speeds on his sinker and slider to extend his repertoire.

Bosman was able to get away with a two-pitch arsenal for his entire career and thrive with it. But in the ensuing decades, pitchers would need to adjust as the game changed. In 1966, pitchers dominated the game. The infamous "Year of the Pitcher" in 1968 was on the horizon. Dick Bosman's many years in baseball would occur mostly on the other side of that divide. In the coming years, hitters steadily got bigger, faster, and stronger. Pitchers would have to find new ways to get them out. It would take more than an expanding arsenal of changeup grips, but that was part of altering their side of the game, which pitchers would need to do in coming years. Dick Bosman the pitching coach would learn far more about the art of pitching than he had during his time on the mound.

Bosman was not concerned with the larger picture at the time, just how to get batters out enough to pitch in the majors, and he was knocking on the door as the 1966 season began. When Bosman was sent down at the end of spring training, Senators manager Gil Hodges said to him, "You have a good 30 days and I will get you back here."

In truth, the Washington Senators pitching staff was woefully thin. The rotation had three slots, occupied by Pete Richert, Mike McCormick, and Phil Ortega, but after that they were depending on young guys like Bosman to come through. The best young arms in the system, according to Senators relief pitcher Dave Baldwin, were Jack Jenkins, Barry Moore, and Dick Bosman. They were considered the "can't miss" prospects who threw hard. Bosman had the best control of the three, Baldwin remembered, which made him the most likely to achieve success in the majors.[2]

Bosman picked up where he had left off the prior September and had a good 30 days. True to his word, Hodges and the Senators called him up at the end of May. He still remembers where he was when he got his call to report to the Senators. It was a rainy morning in Pawtucket, Rhode Island, where York was playing a series against the Boston Red Sox affiliate. He left Pawtucket for Washington and would spend the next few days watching his new major-league team play the Red Sox before heading to Fenway Park, where Bosman made his first major-league start on June 1, 1966.

Dick remembers how small the stadium felt, how close the fans were, and, of course, how close the Green Monster was in left field. But he focused on the job at hand and did not let the fans rattle him. He gave up only a single to Carl Yastrzemski in the first inning and made it through the first three innings without giving up a run.

"Geez, I can do this," he remembers thinking.[3] He gave up two runs in the fourth inning to tie the score at 2–2. He was learning something important with every pitch. Bosman reflected, "I was already starting to figure out that if I made my pitches, by and large, I was going to get outs. If I left pitches out over the plate, they were going to get hit hard."

Bosman pitched into the eighth inning and left with his team ahead, 4–3. The Senators would win the game by a margin of 6–3 to give Bosman his first major-league win. The rest of his tenure in Washington that season did not go as well. Four days after his first start, he failed to get out of the fifth inning against the Chicago White Sox. Two days later, he was brought into the ninth inning against the Orioles and could not retire a single batter. He recorded two losses in only three days. By the end of the month his ERA stood at 8.84.

He managed another winning performance, again in Fenway Park against the Red Sox, this time with Jim Lonborg as the opposing pitcher. He went seven strong innings and allowed only a single run to win his second game. But again, Bosman was ineffective in the games that followed and was shipped out at the end of July, returning to York, where he would pitch for most of the rest of the season, save a single game after being called up in late September.

"It was pretty darned traumatic," Bosman said, thinking back to that first season in the majors. He roomed with Ken McMullen, the Senators' young third baseman, with whom he could talk about the game and his precarious status in it. But the most dominating presence in the Washington clubhouse by far was Frank Howard. "He was the steadying influence through it all," Dick said about Howard. "He taught us how to be big-leaguers. He always carried himself with class . . . and taught us how to carry ourselves whether we lost or we won." Bosman and Howard have maintained a close friendship that dates to that first call-up for Dick.

> "You learn by doing," Bosman stated with certainty. "It's all in the doing. You have to go out and do it, and then repeat it until it is wired in."

Bosman knew he needed more seasoning, and the Senators did as well. He reported to Hawaii in 1967, to start the season, and spent most of the year there. He pitched better than he had at any point in his career, logging 196 innings and pitching to a 2.76 ERA. Pitching in Washington in 1966 taught him the importance of locating the ball.

"You learn by doing," he stated with certainty. "It's all in the doing. You have to go out and do it, and then repeat it until it is wired in." Bosman did not have the benefit of modern technology to break down his mechanics.

There was hardly any mention of the word *mechanics*. All he had was the knowledge that he needed better control of where the ball was going. He needed to make better pitches more consistently, and the only way to do it seemed to be making good pitches over and over again until his brain knew only one approach, the right one.

This time when he got the call to return to Washington, he was much more confident about his place in the game. The roster for the Triple-A Hawaii Islanders was packed with such veterans as Gene Freese, Willie Kirkland, and Jim Mahoney, all of whom imparted knowledge of the game at the major-league level. But Bosman was the best talent on the team, and it wasn't even close.

"We coached each other," Bosman reflected. Wayne Terwilliger was the manager, but Dick learned as much from the veterans. When Bosman finally got the call in 1967, he was ready. He got in seven starts at the end of the 1967 season for the Senators. He won three of them and pitched to a 1.75 ERA. "I did not have a bad ballgame," he recalled. "I shut out the White Sox and knocked them out of the pennant race."

The 1968 season was going to be different, not only for Bosman, but also for baseball as a whole. It was the "Year of the Pitcher," when Bob Gibson had an ERA of 1.12 and Luis Tiant and six others had ERAs that fell below 2.00. Bosman was intent on proving he belonged with that group. In 1967, his ERA was notable, even if he only pitched a limited number of innings. He thought he was ready to take the next step in his career.

The Senators were almost respectable in 1967, and having young guys like Dick Bosman, Joe Coleman, and Barry Moore gave fans reason to hope for the future. But there was bad news as well. Gil Hodges left for the New York Mets, where he would make history with the Miracle Mets of 1969. He took his pitching coach, Rube Walker, and the rest of his staff with him. It left the Senators in the lurch, and they had to build a coaching staff from the ground up, starting with Jim Lemon, who proved ineffective as manager. He did manage to make one decision that would be helpful for Bosman, bringing Sid Hudson along to become the Washington pitching coach. Hodges's departure undercut the steady progress the Senators had been making under his leadership.

"We were a bad club," Bosman said. "It was not a good atmosphere." Bosman had a season that reflected the organization's malaise and dysfunction.

He was in the starting rotation until he had a bad game and then he was back in the bullpen. "It was like a tryout camp," he recalled. The promise that the Senators had shown in 1967 was gone, and the same was true for Bosman. The good news from 1967 flew out the window left open by Hodges.

"But the groundwork was being laid for years to come," Bosman said of the 1968 season. Jim Lemon was fired at the end of the year, and change was in the air. There was so much wrong with the Washington Senators. The city did not have a wealthy ownership group to bankroll the team, and it showed. The weakness was begging to be exploited, and a foul predator was circling. Something new was about to land in Washington, something unforeseen that would greatly change the Washington Senators and Dick Bosman.

3

The Head Game

Hall of Fame player Ted Williams said on many occasions, "Pitchers are the dumbest sons of bitches in the world."[1] He liked to rankle pitchers, to get under their skin and push them to the limits of their tolerance. When Bob Short, the new owner of the Washington Senators, announced on February 21, 1969, that he was bringing in Ted Williams to manage the Senators for the upcoming season, the move was greeted with enthusiasm by everyone except the pitching staff.

There was legitimate concern that whatever he might do with the hitters would be undone by his ill-tempered management of the pitching staff. But Dick Bosman and everyone else knew that staying the course was not an option. Something had to change, and Ted Williams would certainly provide a new direction for the team. In the days after the press announcement, excitement began to build among both Washington fans and players, even the pitchers.

> There is a fineness to pitching that many do not comprehend that is essential. "It is the fine line between working hard on the mound and working nice and easy, and letting the batter get himself out," advises Bosman.

The Senators were an expansion team that had never taken hold. They had provided a training ground for manager Gil Hodges, who built the team slowly and provided a brief glimmer of hope until he left. Then the team sank to the bottom in 1968. The hiring of Williams to manage the squad was a loud statement from new owner Short that things were going to be different on his watch. He wanted to make noise, and there was no better way than to hire one of the greatest hitters of the twentieth century to manage his new team.

Hodges had overseen Bosman's first two years in the majors and been a positive influence on the career of the young pitcher. Now there was Williams, who was almost larger than life, and his influence on Bosman would be proportional to that reputation. The announcement that a figure like Ted Williams had been hired to replace Jim Lemon was met with considerable enthusiasm by Bosman. "It had to be better than where we were at in 1968," he declared.[2]

Bosman had found the swingman role for the 1968 Senators extremely frustrating. His talents were being underutilized, and those in charge were unwilling to change things despite clear evidence the current situation was producing horrible results. Throughout the 1968 campaign, the Senators clubhouse had been fraught with divisiveness as cliques formed and recriminations floated back and forth about who was to blame for the mess the team was in. Dick believed his career had taken a bad turn when he joined the Washington Senators.

When he heard the news that Williams had been named as the new manager, Dick was not only elated about a famous player taking charge, but also certain that whatever change the new manager brought with him would be an improvement. He hoped more than anything that Williams would give him a fair chance at the starting rotation.

Williams had been offered other managerial posts but always turned them down. Somehow Bob Short had found the right formula to lure the somewhat reclusive Williams away from his sport-fishing gig with the Sears Corporation to manage a last-place club. Money was at the heart of Williams's decision. His salary was pegged to be $65,000 annually, enough to place him in the upper tier of player salaries at the time. But it was the ownership stake in the club that Short provided his new manager that convinced the irascible Splendid Splinter to take the job.

Four days after the announcement, Williams made his first appearance in Pompano Beach, Florida, at the spring training facilities of the Senators. The largest press contingent to ever darken the corridors of the Pompano complex waited breathlessly for the famous man to speak. Williams loved to be the center of attention, and his new job put him back on the map, back in front of a crowd. He did not disappoint.

"I may turn out to be a horseshit manager, but . . . I am going to be the last man out on that field every day if that will help," he told the press throng that day. The press was enthralled by the new story line, and his players were in awe of the great man. They were hardly alone. Even the players in the opposing dugout were susceptible to the magic and allure of Ted Williams. During the spring season, stars like Pete Rose and Johnny Bench approached Ted for autographs during exhibition games.[3]

Williams immediately began talking hitting. It was what made him famous. He was the last player to hit .400 for a season. He was in Cooperstown for his ability to hit a baseball. Thus, it was natural to think he might be able to coax something more from the anemic Washington Senators offensive machine. His greatest hope for success was in twisting more out of Frank Howard's mammoth talent, but there were other big men, other projects to consider—such as Mike Epstein.

The more surprising historical point is what he cajoled out of the Washington pitching staff. It has been said often that every hitter on the 1969 Senators roster improved, and the success that Frank Howard, Eddie Brinkman, and Mike Epstein experienced under Williams's watchful eye was awe-inspiring. But there were almost as many notable success stories on the pitching staff as well. The greatest step forward was taken by Dick Bosman, who finally began to realize the vast potential that had been bubbling just below the surface for three years.

After reading about Williams's hiring in the Milwaukee newspapers, Bosman packed his bags into his new Camaro for the drive to Florida. He picked up Senators catcher Jim French in Ohio, and they did not stop for anything more than gas until they reached Pompano Beach early the next morning. They had come along together through the Washington minor-league organization as batterymates. Bosman was 25 years old; French was 27. Both were young enough to drive through the night, swapping stories to keep one another awake at the wheel. They were also both of an age that they looked forward to meeting a baseball legend of their youth like Ted Williams. When they arrived, they went directly to the hotel to check in. It was in the hotel lobby that Bosman first encountered Williams.

Bosman and French walked into the hotel lobby shortly after 7:00 a.m. to find Ted Williams standing with Washington coach Nellie Fox. Fox noticed the two players when they came in and immediately called them over to introduce them to their new skipper. After shaking the great man's hand, they explained to him that they had not slept all night, hoping to catch up on their sleep before reporting to the field later that day.

"No. You guys will feel a lot better after you get in a good workout today," Ted informed them, letting them know that his expectation would be to see them at the field when he got there later in the morning. They put in a full day's work that day, and the spring was off to a tough start. Bosman worried that Williams would judge him on his performance from the previous season, which had hardly been his best. "It always makes it tougher on a guy to make a club when you have a guy who doesn't know you at all," Dick worried.

Dick got hit hard in his first spring training outings and began to worry that he might not make the club going north. But Ted saw something in his young pitcher despite the early struggles. "You've got a chance to be pretty good, but you've got to learn to use what you've got," Williams told him.[4] "When do we start?" was Dick's response.

Pitching was something that Williams left to his coaching staff for the most part, and one of his best managerial choices was retaining Sid Hudson. Bosman was pleased to find his mentor still with the team, as was the rest of the staff. Williams had history with Hudson. Sid had finished his career with the Red Sox, playing three seasons with Ted from 1952 to 1954.

"Sid, I have known you a long time. You've got all this experience. I'll just turn it over to you," Hudson remembered Williams saying years later.[5] Bosman became one of Hudson's most successful projects as a pitching coach, but it may have been the extra incentives Williams provided that pushed Dick over the top.

Bosman was not afraid of the hard work. He remembers running that spring in his Kangaroo leather spikes until his feet ached, but he had learned a strong work ethic from his dad. It was more than just the willingness to work hard. Bosman fit well into the Ted Williams model of pitching success because the Senators manager was urging his hurlers to throw the slider. It was the pitch that had most confounded him as a hitter. Bosman was a sinker–slider pitcher, so he was already on board with that part of his manager's program. For Bosman, it was just a matter of working with Hudson to tighten the slider and spot his sinking fastball more effectively.

The other part of pitching that was so essential to Ted Williams was the cat-and-mouse game between hitter and pitcher. The pitch-by-pitch drama is at the very heart of baseball, and its magic underpins the greatness of the game. Williams had studied the theatrics of the game long and hard, and become an unparalleled master. He constantly demanded that his hitters in the dugout focus on the subtle nuances of what the pitcher was doing and how he was going to pitch the batter.

> Ted Williams scolded his hitters for always looking for the fastball, but it is a lesson a good pitcher learns early. Hitters sit on the fastball and tailor their swing to it. Only the good ones can hit a good changeup, cutter, and slider. Those are the pitches Dick Bosman emphasizes in his teaching.

"Hey bush, what's the next pitch going to be?" Williams asked the neophytes. Fastball was the most common response, which only brought a knowing smile to the great master's face, believing he knew more about the next pitch than the pitcher he was facing.

"See, that's why you jaybirds will never learn to hit. Always looking fastball," he retorted.[6]

For pitchers, the basic game was turned on its head. Williams's constant patter about hitting helped the moundsmen analyze the equation from the other side. "What's the hitter trying to do; who is he; and where is he in the lineup?" Those were the questions Bosman learned to ask in 1969.

Every game situation was slightly different and required the pitcher to apply his baseball intellect to that specific hitter and what the opposition wanted to accomplish at that point in the game. For the pitcher, the issue was how to use his "stuff" to "take away the hitter's strengths and force him to yield to the pitcher's strengths."

Listening to Williams dissect game situations was a unique learning tool for a young pitcher like Bosman because it gave him essential insights into the mind of the hitter from one of the best. Dick learned to throw his slider "at any time, in any count." From early in the season, Bosman tried to establish that fact in the hitter's mind. Bosman was going to be throwing sliders whenever he wanted, regardless of the hitter's preference.

More and more, he learned to "use the slider early in the count," until, in his own words, "I had them looking for it on the other side of the plate. Then I could use my fastball late in the count." As the game progressed and hitters began to see the pattern, he would turn it around, throwing the fastball early and the slider away late in the count.

> The pitcher must apply his baseball intellect to the specific hitter he is facing and know what the hitter wants to accomplish in the situation and how to use his "stuff" to take away the batter's strengths, forcing him to roll over on the low and away breaking pitch or pop up the high, inside fastball.

Even when the hitter was ahead in the count, 1–0 or 2–0, and "looking for something he could pull," he said, "I am not coming in there to them in their power zone and let them hammer something middle in. I am going to throw them something away and force them to hit it the other way or roll over on it and hit a ground ball." Accomplishing the feat required confidence and tight control of his limited pitch repertoire. Bosman's control had set him apart from other young pitchers coming through the Washington farm system, and it was becoming even more refined as he worked out with Hudson and Williams in the spring of 1969.

Williams came to know Bosman's approach so well that when Dick was on the mound he would tell others in the dugout exactly what his pitcher was going to throw in a given situation. "This one's gonna be a slider over here, or that one's gonna be a fastball over there. It was uncanny how well he could do it," Dick related. That knowledge evolved throughout the course of many conversations between Williams and Bosman that spring in Florida.

Bosman could almost visualize the chessboard that existed in the 60 feet, six inches separating the pitcher from the batter. He was an ardent disciple of mental preparation for each game and the task of figuring out "how I can get this guy out with the stuff I have today." Dick was as keen a student of the game as any pitcher in camp that spring, according to Sid Hudson. Said Hudson, "He had a good attitude, and he really worked at it. He'd try anything you suggested to him."[7]

The intensity of that spring was a sharp contrast to spring trainings of the past. What was happening in Pompano Beach, according to Bosman, was a "full renaissance of baseball in Washington, DC. Ted Williams spoke baseball every minute of the day and night when he was awake. He drew crowds." The crowds were why Bob Short had paid the money to bring Williams out of retirement. It may have been a secondary consideration whether Ted could be a successful manager, whether he could get along with the players and coaching staff. But Williams, for all his foul language and quick temper, was a remarkably keen student of the game, one who loved baseball dearly and tried to immediately bring his prodigious baseball intellect to bear on his newest job in baseball: managing the lowly Washington Senators.

Williams knew he did not have the necessary experience for managing every situation in the entirety of a nine-inning game. He said as much to Senator's coach Wayne Terwilliger, "Twig" as he was known. He told Twig he would be counting on his coaching staff to cover those aspects of the game. Williams understood the game that was played between pitcher and hitter as well as anyone living at the time, but he was candid in acknowledging his need for help in many other areas of managing a team in his first season. He had sound and experienced voices in Nellie Fox and Wayne Terwilliger.

Dick and others believed that Williams made an early mistake by hiring Joe Camacho as his bench coach even before he came to Pompano. Camacho was a former Cleveland Indians minor leaguer who had played with Rocky Colavito and Herb Score. Williams had become friends with Camacho and put him in charge of his summer baseball camp for youngsters in Massachusetts.

According to Bosman, the much better choice would have been Nellie Fox, who had far more dugout experience in major-league game situations. Terwilliger had plenty of experience as well. Twig had been manager of the Senators' Buffalo team playing at the Triple-A level. Either he or Fox would have been preferable to Camacho, but Williams trusted Camacho, who had a history of providing honest advice and counsel to Williams, even when the famous man was at his worst. The situation during games was not always perfect, but it was significantly improved from where the team had been the prior season. Fox and Terwilliger got their messages across most of the time, and Williams was willing to listen more often than not.

The rest of the pitching staff was generally in awe of Williams and paying close attention, as Bosman did. Senators reliever Casey Cox said years later that he inverted the basic message from his manager to hitters. Hearing Williams say, "Get a good pitch to hit, bush," made Cox realize it was his mission to throw the patient hitter as many strikes as he could and get ahead in the count. He and Bosman both became more consistent in hitting the lowered strike zone, which began in 1969.

Bosman was hardly aware that Major League Baseball had changed the rules, lowering the mound and shrinking the strike zone for the 1969 season. He and his brethren were preoccupied with the moment-to-moment reality of pitcher versus hitter. Even more, Dick's immediate concern was trying to make the club, not whether the mound was higher or lower. Learning an umpire's strike zone was a game-to-game and an inning-to-inning affair anyway. It was the smart pitcher's job to pay attention at that level, and there was little time for anything more.

Nonetheless, Cox and Bosman adapted to the new reality of a tighter strike zone far more effectively than others on the Senators staff and in the American League. For example, 22-year-old Joe Coleman would be part of the backbone of Washington's rotation in 1969, but he would also issue 100 walks in 247 innings. Those numbers were in stark contrast to his rookie season, when his high, riding fastball had played well with the strike zone as it was called in 1968. The young, hard-throwing moundsman would not, or could not, adapt his pitches to the new strike zone. Coleman's lack of control was a constant source of contention between the young hurler and his hot-tempered manager.

Bosman's 39 bases on balls in 193 innings was by far the best on the staff and may have been one of the first reasons that he and Williams established an early rapport. Jim Hannan, who had shown great promise in 1968, with 10 wins and a 3.01 ERA, was unable to decipher the new strike zone. Barry Moore experienced similar problems. Only Bosman and Cox learned to keep the ball down consistently.

However, when judging the pitching staff as a whole, Williams was able to get more from his hurlers than anyone would have thought possible. Joe Coleman was only 21 years old, but he had established himself as the ace of the Senators staff in 1968, along with veteran Camilo Pascual. In 1969, Coleman would log 247 innings.

Williams used his bullpen more than almost any other team that season. Until Bosman established himself as a starter, there was an ongoing experiment from week to week to see who would stick in the rotation. After Bosman and Coleman, Casey Cox would be the most important arm at Williams's disposal that season, and he would pitch 171 innings in a swingman role.

After an up and down spring, it was enough for Dick that he had made the roster as the team headed north. He was one of the last pitchers to make the roster, but he was making the trip to Washington to start the season on the same flight with Ted Williams.

Bosman was not happy to be starting the 1969 season in the bullpen, but he got a chance to start almost immediately during the first week in April. The Orioles hit him hard in his first two starts, and he was back in the pen. Then he pitched eight and two-thirds innings of scoreless relief at the end of the month and got another shot at starting. The next time out, against the Cleveland Indians on May 2, Dick had one of his best games and changed the trajectory of his career and his life in baseball.

Bosman allowed only a single hit in nine innings that day. He threw a complete-game shutout to win by a 5–0 margin. In the second inning of the game, Cleveland first baseman Tony Horton blooped a single over short-stop Eddie Brinkman for the only hit in what could easily have been a more notable masterpiece. "Holding an ice pack to his pitching elbow," Bosman recalled the pitch after the game for the press, saying, "It was a high fastball, just where I wanted to put it."[8] It broke the bat just a few inches above the batter's hands but found a hole.

Sid Hudson called it a "masterpiece," adding, "A pitcher cannot pitch much better than that."[9] It established Bosman's role with Williams. Dick remembered the end of the game, stating, "Ted Williams was standing there on the dugout steps with an especially knowing look on his face, like, 'I knew you could do that.'" Williams had told Bosman that "he could be that guy," and now there was irrefutable evidence that the new manager had been right all along.

Dick built on his new status as Williams's favorite starter with another good outing against the White Sox in early May. It was the second game of a Sunday doubleheader, and Bosman went eight innings, winning by a score of 3–2 to push his record to four wins and two losses. But when he got up Monday morning, his shoulder hurt so badly he couldn't brush his teeth. He called the team trainer, Tommy McKenna, who said he needed to talk to Dr. Resta, the team doctor, as soon as possible. After X-rays were taken, Dick was diagnosed with a strained deltoid muscle. Dr. Resta said, "I'm going to shoot you up with some cortisone and put you on the disabled list."

Dick was scared. Just when the pieces were starting to fit, just when he was earning Ted Williams's confidence, he had his first serious injury. As with everything else, he worked hard to get back. After deep heat and rehab with McKenna, he was pronounced ready to throw again and sent to Buffalo, where the team's Triple-A affiliate played. Buffalo was not an ideal place to pitch. "It was awful," according to Dick. The manager was Hector Lopez, who had played with Bosman in Hawaii, a player's paradise when compared to Buffalo. Dick told Lopez he preferred not to pitch, but near the end of the required rehab stint Lopez needed him. It was in Tidewater, Virginia, and Lopez told Bosman he had no one to pitch in relief that night.

Sure enough, Lopez called for him in the seventh inning. Bosman felt good warming up in the bullpen and even better on the mound. "But I got whacked," he remembered. But his arm felt good, and he rejoined the Senators on a road trip in Minnesota. After almost a month of inactivity, Dick took the mound again on June 17, in Washington. It was only a relief stint in the ninth inning, and Dick remembers facing Al Bumbry that evening. He threw him a masterful backdoor slider that struck Bumbry out and led to a perfect inning of work.

"It may have been one of the first of those I ever threw," he recalled. It was not a pitch that a kid just up from the minors could master and was another sign that Bosman was learning by doing. He rejoined the starting rotation the next time through and never looked back for the rest of the 1969 season.

The next four weeks were his best stretch as a starting pitcher after coming up from Hawaii at the end of the 1967 season. From June 22 until a poor outing on July 27, Bosman allowed only five earned runs in 44 innings. The team was hot throughout that stretch as well, winning six in a row to begin the month of July. Bosman replaced Camilo Pascual in the rotation during this run, which was quite difficult for the old warrior. "My coorve ball. I dunno, I do not get over the plate," Pascual told Shirley Povich in an article that outlined the pitcher's many accomplishments.[10]

Bosman was now looking more and more like the ace of the staff. His ERA sat at 2.14 to begin July. The Senators were headed for Boston and a much anticipated Fourth of July weekend series against the Red Sox, Ted Williams's old team. The skipper was back in his beloved Fenway Park, and his Senators team were nipping at the heels of the Red Sox for third place in the American League's six-team Eastern Division. The Fourth of July game at Fenway had been designated for the unveiling of Major League Baseball's "All-Time Great Team," to be announced in pregame festivities. As the player names were called out one by one, each legendary figure came out to take his place on the foul line at Fenway.

Ted Williams's name was called, and the Fenway faithful rose in thunderous applause. As icing on the cake, he was named the "Greatest Red Sox Player" ever to put on the uniform as well.[11] His old teammates Bobby Doerr and Joe Cronin stood beside him as he accepted the award. There had been many years when Ted's relationship with the fans in Boston had been difficult at best, but it had all been forgotten as the "Kid" waved his cap to the adoring multitude.

There was baseball to be played, however, and nothing could have given Williams more pleasure than beating his former team. The holiday doubleheader provided plenty of opportunity, and Frank Howard got things off to a great start with his 28th home run of the season to spark a 5–1 win in the opener. Washington lost the nightcap but still had a winning record for the first time in many years.

There was another doubleheader against Boston on Saturday, July 5, one that was split by Washington as well. A single game was scheduled for Sunday, and for the rubber match Dick took the mound with his manager's pride at stake. The Red Sox had a tough batting order, with Carl Yastrzemski at its heart. There was Reggie Smith and George Scott, both tough outs who had played against Bosman in the Eastern League. But Bosman was the ace that day, and he threw a nine-inning, complete-game shutout. He kept the ball low all day with the heavy sink that challenged the opposition to get any lift on it. In the ninth inning on a hot day, he faced Tony Conigliaro for the final out and was breezing to such a degree that with two strikes he threw a rare side-arm curve. Conigliaro rolled over on it and hit a weak ground ball to end the game. Bosman did not walk a batter. He even chipped in a RBI single in the 5–0 win.[12]

The month of July cemented Bosman's role as the undisputed staff ace. The rotation consisted of Joe Coleman, Jim Hannan, Barry Moore, and Bosman, with Casey Cox filling in as a starter when the doubleheaders backed up the rotation. Dick failed to win a game in July after the Boston series but lowered his ERA to 1.99 by the end of the month.

The best pitcher in the American League that season was Jim Palmer of the Baltimore Orioles. Palmer would go on to lose the World Series to the Amazin' Mets. His ERA sat at 1.96 at the end of August, just a few digits less than Bosman's. Mike Cuellar, also in the Orioles rotation, was the only American League pitcher who was even close to Palmer and Bosman, with a 2.43 ERA. The race for the ERA title would be a two-person affair.

August 1969 may have been the best month of Bosman's career. Every time he took the ball he gave his teammates a chance to win. They pushed their record above .500 and kept it there, playing the best baseball any expansion Senators team had ever accomplished. They were tight on the heels of the Tigers and Red Sox for the top half of the American League East. Dick's best friend, Frank Howard, was having his own career year and was in a race for the home run title with Reggie Jackson and Harmon Killebrew. Suddenly it was a great time to be a Washington Senators fan.

From August 1 until the end of the season on September 30, Bosman won eight straight games. He went from a record of six wins against five defeats to 14–5. There were no more shutouts, just good, sound baseball almost every time he took the mound. He was having fun and hardly even knew how he was doing it.

A reporter asked him, "How are you doing this?" Dick remembered. "I don't know, but don't wake me up," was his response. He was "in the zone." He related, "My concentration was very, very keen every time I went out there."[13] Dick had little understanding at the time as to what the phrase meant, but as a pitching coach it has become more important to know what to tell his young hurlers about how to maintain their best effort.

"How do good guys get in it and stay in it?" is the most commonly asked question about being in the "zone." Sports psychologist Bob Rotella is a dear friend of Bosman's, and although Rotella is more focused on golf than baseball, there are "solid comparisons between standing on the 18th tee trying to win a golf tournament and standing on a major-league pitching mound in a key situation."

The way Dick sees it today, when you are locked in on success, your mind is calm. Your mind visualizes successful things. In 1969, driving to the park, he remembered, "I could visualize Harmon Killebrew swinging and missing at a slider, Tony Oliva rolling over on a slider and hitting a weak ground ball, or Bobby Allison hitting a popup on a high fastball . . . all positive things one on top of another." Jim Palmer said that at his best, "He can almost see where the ball will go before he has thrown it."[14] Rotella believes this visual projection of success is about trusting in and "being arrogant about how good you are." In 1969, Dick was just starting to get that swagger, just beginning to see himself as being among the best.

Bosman was blazing a path to the top for the first time. He had never had a season like 1969, so he was taking it one game at a time. He was "just totally immersed in the process of each game. Totally immersed in the process of each hitter. That is the only way you are going to do anything like that," he asserts now and believes nothing has changed to this day. "When I play a round of golf, I do not total up my score until the end of the round. I may know where I stand more or less, but I don't add up the first nine so that I know what I need to score on the back nine. I am just playing it shot by shot," he states.

> Any pitcher worth his salt knows what his best pitch is against every batter, whether it is early in the count or late. He knows how he got them out in games past, and when he is on his game, when the stars have aligned, he can visualize getting them out in the next game and then go out and do it almost exactly the way he pictured it beforehand.

He did not even know that he was closing in on the ERA title in 1969, or at least he was not keeping up with what Cuellar and Palmer were doing. In the final two months of the 1969 season, it was just pitch-by-pitch and game-by-game as they came down to the end of the campaign hoping for something magical.

Bosman and the Senators began to get recognition for what was going on at RFK Stadium in late 1969. At the end of August, *Sporting News* opined that Washington had the most balanced pitching staff in the American League.[15] There were five pitchers projected to have double-digit wins by the end of the season and five with ERA's lower than 3.00. The team ERA finished at 3.45, fifth overall in the American League. The

> The radar gun approach to pitching is scout-driven and overvalues the fastball. The trick is to finesse the hitter, to keep him off balance at all times. To accomplish that task requires preparation, knowing what each batter can handle and what he cannot. The fastball is only a small part of the game, and radar gun readings do little to indicate the success a pitcher will have against major-league hitters.

pitching was one of the key reasons the team won 18 games in September and pushed the expansion Senators to their best finish ever, at 86 wins and 76 losses.

The last three-game series of the 1969 season was, fittingly enough, against the Boston Red Sox. Washington was three games behind them, and a sweep of the final series with Boston at RFK would push the Senators into third place, ahead of Ted's former team. But it was not to be. Bosman won the next-to-last game by a score of 7–2, and the performance moved him ahead of Palmer in the race for the lowest ERA, but Williams's immediate goal of beating out the Red Sox for third place fell by the wayside.

Frank Howard wanted to hit .300 and mash 50 home runs but fell just short on both counts, finishing with 48 home runs and a .296 average. Both were career highs and were greatly influenced by the presence of Ted Williams. But the biggest difference for Hondo was garnering 104 walks that year. He had managed only 54 the prior season.

Part of the surge in walks for Howard may have been the strike zone, but most of it was listening to Williams telling him to "get a good pitch to hit" every time he went to the plate. In 1970, Howard would lead the league in walks, with 132. He went from leading the American League in strikeouts in 1967, to leading in walks, thanks to the influence of Williams as his manager and de facto hitting coach.

The 1969 campaign saw numerous career years enjoyed by Washington Senators players. Mike Epstein tapped into his size and power for the first time to hit 30 home runs. He even hit a respectable .278 and established himself as not only a legitimate major-league player, but also a potential star. Ken McMullen boosted his average notably, and Del Unser had a fine season in center field.

The most remarkable turnaround may have been that of slender shortstop Ed Brinkman. He learned to hit after failing to make the Mendoza Line in either 1967 or 1968. Brinkman's sparkling glove was essential to the success of Dick Bosman. Dick's strategy of getting worm burners required capable infielders. By making a hitter of Brinkman, Williams was able to get a Gold Glove–caliber player into almost every game to help his pitching staff.

Bosman remembered that Brinkman and McMullen made him "believe in his style of pitching," stating,

I induced ground balls to the left side of the infield, and unless they were hit hard, those guys were going to be able to get to it and the batter was going to be out. Ken McMullen was a blue-collar kind of defender. He wasn't spectacular, but he made the routine play and was excellent at making the barehanded pick-up coming in from third base and throwing the runner out.

Bosman believes to this day that both men were "great assets to have on the field."

Largely due to his influence on players like Ed Brinkman, Frank Howard, and Dick Bosman, Ted Williams won the Manager of the Year Award from *Sporting News*. There was a general consensus that the Senators could only improve during the offseason. Bosman's perch atop the Senators staff as ace was just part of a new sense that even the pitching was turning a corner. The performance of the Washington staff in 1969 was a key element for those who believed in a budding future for the team.

There were nagging issues, however, and maybe they said more about the future than anyone wanted to hear. Unresolved in 1969 was the relationship between Joe Coleman and Ted Williams. Both were feisty individuals who were unlikely to back down or change their stripes at another man's urging. Coleman's inability to forge a bond with his manager would have unfortunate consequences for the team at the end of the following year.

But at the end of 1969, Ted Williams was riding high. He sought to expand his influence with Bob Short during the offseason with an eye toward building a team capable of more substantial success in the nation's capital. Short had no general manager after firing George Selkirk when he bought the team at the end of 1968. He had informed the press that he would serve as his own GM.

Ted saw a vacuum that needed filling and began to lobby for trades that would help mold a better team for the 1970 season. Minnesota Twins owner Calvin Griffith liked outfielder Brant Alyea, who Williams saw as a one-hit wonder. Ted counseled Short to jump on Griffith's offer of young third-base prospect Graig Nettles for Alyea. Williams could not believe their luck and urged Short to move quickly lest Griffith hear the truth about Alyea from someone.

Williams wanted to trade Mike Epstein as well and had two excellent reasons for doing so. The first was his skepticism that Epstein could repeat his success, which was to prove prescient. Bosman believed a benefit of such a trade would have been to move Howard from left field to first base. Hondo was a fine first baseman who presented infielders with a huge target at first base, one who could move around the bag with the athleticism of the All-American basketball player he had been at Ohio State University.

The second reason to trade Epstein was to bolster the pitching rotation. Pitching talent was woefully thin, as Williams well knew. He had a keen eye for baseball talent and a savvy knowledge of "makeup," the personal character that allowed talented players to become stars. He urged Short to hire scouts to assess talent, proposing Minnie Minoso and Camilo Pascual to scout Latin America, where an increasing number of star players were making an impact on winning teams.

Short listened to nothing Williams had to say. He began avoiding Williams for fear he would be cornered into listening to yet another tirade about Alyea or Epstein. At the winter meetings after the 1969 season, Short was offered such young talent as Tug McGraw and Nolan Ryan for Epstein, but Short wanted marquee players with recognizable names that would sell tickets. Short had neither the knowledge of the game to be his own GM nor the good sense to listen to one of the best baseball minds in Ted Williams.

The one trade Short made at the beginning of the 1970 campaign was dispensing Ken McMullen to the California Angels for Rick Reichardt and Aurelio Rodriguez. Williams learned of the offer from announcer Shelby Whitfield and was so angry that Short was going to refuse the trade that he was in open rebellion. The trucking magnate could not afford to lose his marquee manager and finally relented, agreeing to the deal. The die was cast, however, and Short's lack of sound baseball knowledge and the crushing debt he had used to buy the team would spell doom in the coming seasons.

For Dick Bosman, Ted Williams's tenure in Washington would be the best three seasons of his career. Beginning in May 1969, and stretching until the last game at RFK, the baseball contained within those bookends represents a body of work that would be the pinnacle of achievement for Bosman as a major-league pitcher. Dick was only 25 years old at the beginning of the 1969 season. So much would happen during those three years. He would get married and mature as a man and a player. But the real stepping-off point began with the naming of Ted Williams as Washington's manager.

In 1969, there was so much promise for the future. Men had landed on the moon in August, and after winning 14 games, Dick Bosman was hopeful he might be just starting to reach for the stars himself. But Dick knew that his manager had been lucky in 1969. When Ted Williams made a decision about a pinch-hitter or bringing in a pitcher from the bullpen, it worked. He had a Midas touch that season. Maybe it was luck, or maybe it was being in the "zone," where the swagger of being Ted Williams was good enough. Whether it was luck or swagger, the aura of invincibility surrounding Williams as manager would not hold.

4

Opening Day Starter

In spring training 1970, Dick Bosman reported to camp in Pompano Beach in good shape. He had married Pam Yates, a native Washingtonian, the previous year. Pam Bosman was a flight attendant from the Northern Virginia suburbs outside Washington, DC. Ted Williams teased Bosman that married life would put pounds on him during the offseason. He bet his star pitcher that he would report to camp weighing more than 205 pounds. Bosman won the bet, reporting in February at 204 pounds.

In 1970, staying in shape for a major-league pitcher consisted of working out at the gym and getting a friend to take a mitt and catch fastballs and sliders. There was no scientific approach to building specific muscle groups and maybe even less knowledge about a proper diet. Teams were not inclined to invest in the health of their players. It was an aspect of the game that had gone largely unchanged throughout the history of baseball.

Tom Seaver, who was a contemporary of Bosman's, would write in his book, *The Art of Pitching*, "During my 18 years in pitching, the emphasis on conditioning, weight training, and flexibility is one of the most dramatic changes I have seen."[1] It was during the first decade of player free agency, when major-league teams were forced to invest large amounts of money in players, that their health became a notable issue. For Dick Bosman and Ted Williams in 1970, the issue of conditioning began with reporting to camp at weight and a program of running, running, and more running. Seaver's extensive regimen of targeted exercise and stretching routines would not become commonplace for another decade.

The offseason provided few reasons to think about baseball and plenty of distractions. Bosman had given up dragsters but found a new and related passion for snowmobiling. He sold and raced them in Kenosha, where there was no shortage of snow. The hours of a small business owner were grueling. He often worked 10-hour days and sometimes more during the height of the winter season.

In late January came the inevitable realization that it was almost time for baseball, that there were only a few weeks to shed any excess pounds and start working out seriously to get ready. Bosman wanted to have a great campaign in 1970. He signed a contract for a significant raise in February, agreeing to $27,000 for the season. He told William Gildea of the *Washington Post* that we wanted to "earn his money," and for Bosman that meant "winning 20 games, hurling 250 to 300 innings, and helping Washington move up in the standings."[2]

Getting in shape was essential if Dick was going to have any chance of achieving the ambitious aims he had articulated to Gildea. Twenty wins was realistic given Bosman's success in 1969 and the belief by many that the team itself was capable of taking another step forward. For Bosman, however, articulating his expectations in the press was indicative of the swagger and confidence he felt about the new season. He no longer was seeing himself as a pitcher that needed to prove himself, but as one who had achieved success. Now he was projecting that success forward into the future. Part of that projection was built on a practical and thoughtful system he used to prepare himself both before and during the baseball season.

Bosman was a prodigious note-taker, meticulous about everything from preparing to get into a dragster to taking the mound. He had begun charting everything about opposing batters the prior season, as well as his own pitching patterns and pitch-by-pitch tendencies. "Early in my big-league

> Pitching mechanics need to be as simple as possible because the rest of it—the mental side of the task—is so complex. The modern pitcher must craft a strategy for each game, each batter, and be able to improvise moment to moment, then repeat that operation more than 30 times in a season.

career, I had a hard time remembering how I got people out," he recalled. "I've got to write this stuff down," he told himself.[3] There were too many good hitters, and if Bosman was successful getting them out with a specific approach, he wanted to remember how he had done it. "It just became a habit of mine to write stuff down on whatever was at hand during the game," he revealed.

Bosman transferred those notes periodically into a notebook, where he condensed and organized them. In 1969, taking those notebooks out and seeing himself getting the best hitters out with specific pitches in particular locations was part of getting ready for the upcoming season. He began to think about how the new season was going to work, visualizing getting Harmon Killebrew out on that same side-arm curveball from 1969.

Bosman was ahead of his time. There are no indications that other pitchers in 1969 were taking a similarly analytic approach to their craft. Videotape was just beginning to be used by a handful of teams. It would be a decade before Bill James would begin to make his first inroads into Major League Baseball with his thoughtful analysis of the game and many years before computer analytics became commonplace. It was Bosman's application of a smart, reasoned approach to pitching that would make him an excellent pitching coach, one that would have an impact not only on the pitchers with whom he worked, but also the game of baseball overall.

The 1969 season was Dick's first sustained success, his breakout season, and he wanted to be able to recreate exactly how he had done it, rather than stumbling through a process of reinvention. His somewhat cerebral preparation was another angle on his profession, which originated with his father. When he got a chance to visit home when the team was in Milwaukee or Chicago, his father's parting words to him were always, "Be smart out there. Don't just pitch instinctively, think about what you're doing." Bosman's father approached his own fast-pitch softball game that way. It wasn't about striking out every batter but "outsmarting the hitter." For George and Dick Bosman alike, the pitcher was the smart one. Ted Williams could think whatever he liked about the fraternity of moundsmen, but Dick Bosman knew that pitching required intellect, as well as a strong arm.

Ted Williams never had been considered good managerial timber because most assumed the game came easily to him. Even great talents like Williams are far more than instinctual in their approach. Ted worked at his craft, studying his own batting stance and swing. And he was relentless in his study of pitchers. A big man like Frank Howard might be able to hit the ball farther than an Eddie Brinkman, and a tall, lanky lefty like Sandy Koufax might be able to throw harder than Dick Bosman, but success was seldom won on physical talent alone. For a few years in Washington, Williams was a good hitting instructor for banjo hitters like Eddie Brinkman and sluggers like Frank Howard alike.

Williams had a grudging respect for guys like Bosman, who relied on location and command. They were called "finesse pitchers," and Williams said Bosman was "one of the three best finesse pitchers."[4] He included two of the top hurlers in the American League, Mike Cuellar and Dave McNally of the Baltimore Orioles, in the group. According to Williams, a finesse pitcher relied less on his ability to overpower the hitter and more on his knowledge of the opposing hitters and his capacity to locate pitches and exploit the batter's weaknesses. Dick Bosman not only used his understanding of batters in game situations to get them out, but also he had a notebook that cataloged these situations for the best hitters in the American League. Bosman took visualizing success to a new level and made it part of his process for achieving the ambitious objectives he had set for the 1970 season.

One of his goals was to pitch the home opener in Washington, which in 1970 was still called the "Presidential Opener": the first game of the season, which featured the president of the United States throwing out the first pitch from the box seats near home plate. Said Dick, "If you are a member of the Washington Senators organization, you aspire to have that honor, to pitch the Presidential Home Opener. It is recognition that you are their best pitcher." He had seen Camilo Pascual, the long-serving ace of the staff, take that honor in 1968 and 1969. Now he was "that man," the one Ted Williams fittingly enough named to start the first game of the season.

> Early in his career Bosman began keeping a notebook of game situations and what worked for specific hitters he knew he would face again. Today's pitchers have the same information available from computer databases, and the best pitchers, the ones most suited for the starting rotation, will use some form of data-driven mental preparation for every game they throw.

A spring training injury threatened to derail his status as the Opening Day starter, when during pitcher's fielding practice, Bosman reached down to field a bunt and felt something "pop." Although his hamstring was severely strained, Dick vowed to be ready to pitch the home opener. It was still early enough in the spring for him to grind his way back. He was able to go five innings in one of the last spring games against the Cincinnati Reds, but the leg needed extensive wrapping for support and the overall effect was less than optimal.

Although President Nixon was a devout fan of the Washington baseball club dating to his years as vice president in the 1950s, he could not make Opening Day in 1970, and sent his son-in-law, David Eisenhower, in his stead. The Senators had lost the first game of the season for eight consecutive years and were facing a tough Detroit Tigers team led by Mickey Lolich. The 1970 Tigers still included many of the same players who had won the 1968 World Series. Bosman's hamstring was a big part of the untold story for Opening Day. The taping of the affected area made it difficult for him to move, much less repeat his mechanics, and he walked nine Tigers in the five innings he pitched. Washington lost another Opening Day game, this time to Lolich's Tigers by a score of 5–0.

The hamstring was better the next time out, and Dick won three games in April 1970, throwing a complete-game shutout against his hometown Milwaukee Brewers on April 29. But the first half of the season was mediocre by the ambitious standards Dick had set for himself. At the end of June, he had only seven wins against seven losses after beating the Red Sox in Boston to end the month. For the first few weeks of April, the momentum of the 1969 season seemed to carry the Senators, but by the end of the month it was gone. The pitching was the weak link, just as Ted Williams had told Bob Short at the winter meetings.

One problem was Joe Coleman, who was still struggling with his skipper, who seemed never to have anything good to say about him. Coleman, wilting under the criticism of Ted Williams, pitched even more poorly than in 1969. Casey Cox could not repeat the success he had the prior year, and by the beginning of July, halfway through the 1970 season, the Senators were six games below .500.

The second half of the season always brought out the best in Bosman. "I like the heat. It keeps me loose," was his only explanation. His command was much better in the second half. In 1969, he had walked only 39 batters during the entire season. He walked 49 by the end of June 1970. For a pitcher with two pitches, successful outcomes depended on command, and it was not until the second half of 1970 that Dick found the groove and began locating the ball much the way he had throughout 1969.

"The difference of two or three inches on the plate was huge in getting a guy out . . . but the command of the slider was even more important," he explained. Yet, even when he was not putting the ball where he wanted, Bosman would not give in to a hitter. "I just wouldn't do it," Dick declared. In an early August game, he began locating his slider almost to perfection and would remain "in the zone" until the end of the season.

Proof came in a Thursday afternoon game on August 13, against the Minnesota Twins at RFK Stadium. Jim Kaat, still the ace of a very good Minnesota team, was the opposing pitcher, and both men had their best stuff that day. Cesar Tovar led off the game with a bunt single to third, but Dick struck out Tony Oliva and Harmon Killebrew to end the inning. The Twins did not manage to put another player on base until the sixth inning, when Kaat managed a walk. He was erased immediately on a double play.

Kaat was nearly as good, allowing only an unearned run in the bottom of the first inning, but Bosman made that run stand for nine innings, as the Senators won the game, 1–0. "I was pretty damned efficient that day," Bosman reflected, looking back from the distance of 46 years. He believed he may have had better stuff that day than any other game in his career, and there were some good ones yet to come.

Dick beat Kansas City, 2–1, at the end of the month in a complete game to give him back-to-back complete-game gems, pushing his win total to 14. His ERA stood at 2.98, falling below 3.00 for the first time that season. Standing in the moment, when everything seemed to be going so well, his goal of a 20-win season still seemed within reach. He had only seven starts left in which to win six games, but he knew he was visualizing those six extra wins and anything was possible. When George Minot of the *Washington Post* asked Dick whether 20 wins were still possible, Bosman reminded the writer that he had won eight starts in a row in 1969.

His first start in September was against the Cleveland Indians and Sam McDowell. It may have been Bosman's best start after the one-hitter against Jim Kaat. He gave up only a single run in nine innings and fanned eight without walking a single batter as the Senators won by a 4–1 margin. The Cleveland game elevated Dick's win total to 15 games, a mark not met by any Senators pitcher since Pete Richert in 1965.

Bosman considered Richert a "mentor," someone who had gone out of his way to show him the ropes in 1966, when Bosman had come up from the minors for the first time. Richert had been the staff ace that year, and he followed his 15-win season in '65 with 14 wins in 1966. Like Bosman, he was the best pitcher on a last-place team in the American League. Richert was traded to the Orioles in 1967.

Dick's next two starts would end the speculation about 20 wins. He lost to the Yankees and Tigers but remained as competitive as ever. He pitched another gem, this time a complete-game shutout against the Orioles. The win, in the middle of September, ran his record to 16–9. It was and remains the best mark by any pitcher for the expansion Washington Senators during the difficult years that marked the franchise's history in Washington. Only Richert and Claude Osteen had managed 15 wins in a season after the team began play in 1961. It was good company Bosman was keeping.

It would be more than just a personal high-water mark; it would be the pinnacle for the team. They were in last place in the American League East, but their record was 70 wins against 78 losses. In 1969, the team won nine of its last 11 games to close out the season 10 games above .500. Bosman thought they still had another run in them, but some of his teammates were ready to go home. Bosman's 16th win on September 17 would be the last by the club. They lost the final 14 games of the season. Bosman was on the mound for three of those games.

The losing, the being the best pitcher on a bad team finally got to Dick after the team was beaten on September 27, by the Boston Red Sox. Bosman's frustrations poured forth in an interview with Minot. "I came ready to pitch that season," Dick remembered. But by the end of the 1970 season he understood that some of his teammates had lost that sense of urgency. "The guys are laying down on the job," he told Minot in the locker room that afternoon. "There are just a few of them, but they have let the season go down the drain."[5]

One day that stands out in Dick's memory was a start he was scheduled to make on a rainy day, when many of the players were sitting in the clubhouse watching a Redskins game. There was far too much talk among many of the players in favor of the baseball game being cancelled so they could see the end of the football game. "This is a day I'm going to pitch," Dick recalled. "And they want to watch *football?*" Minot's article appeared in the *Washington Post* on September 28. "Bosman Raps Mates" was the headline splashed across the sports page.

That evening the Alexandria Club of Grandstand Managers held its annual banquet. The group was the most well-recognized fan club in the region, and their annual event honored the two best players on the team at the end of each season. Frank Howard was announced as Player of the Year and Dick Bosman Pitcher of the Year.

Dick worried as he entered the banquet room that the story in the morning papers would spark recriminations from some of the fans and maybe the coaches who were in attendance that night. But one by one, the coaches and staff came over and shook his hand. "Well said," was the common refrain from the coaching staff until the one notable exception made his way across the room. Ted Williams told Bosman he should have remained silent. Bosman responded, "I was only telling the truth," and the two men let it be.

Exasperation was a natural reaction for someone as competitive as Bosman. "Some may not have the guts to say it, but I do,"[6] Bosman told Minot in the heat of the moment, establishing himself as the heart of a team that seemed to have lost its fire. Bosman was clearly not talking about his roommate that season, Frank Howard, or others like Eddie Brinkman who were game to the end. He assured them of that the next day in the clubhouse. It was not so different for Bosman than for Ted Williams. Dick was all baseball from the moment he stepped onto the field until he left that stadium at the end of the day.

Looking back on his fiery approach to the game, Bosman recounted with pride the remarks of Orioles slugger Boog Powell when the two men were at the end of their careers and playing together for the Cleveland Indians in 1975. Bosman and Powell were looking back on their careers and their many matchups against one another as they drank with Cleveland teammates in a local pub. "I'll tell you one thing about Bosman," Powell offered. "He'd rather bite the head off a rattlesnake than give you a good fastball to hit." "That's exactly the way I felt too," Bosman remembered. "I wouldn't give in to nobody."[7]

Boog Powell was articulating the competitive essence of the game, when the pitcher stares toward the plate and the batter back toward him. The two men were fierce protagonists playing for two teams at different ends of the American League hierarchy. Whatever pitch caused the batter the most consternation, that was the pitch Dick was going to throw. Bosman would throw one slider after another if the batter looked uncomfortable with the pitch. To win consistently against such talented sluggers as Boog Powell meant you had to have the ability to put the ball where you wanted it. "The fine detail of being able to locate that ball" was essential.

Bosman's repertoire may have been limited, but he had a little something different for key situations. "I threw some sidearm too, which Ted was a big advocate of," he commented, "because if you have the batter with two strikes, he is very uncomfortable if you show him something different. I threw a sidearm curve and a side-arm fastball, and I had pretty good results with those pitches."

Williams even advocated the knuckleball to Bosman during spring training 1970. Dick tried the pitch during an exhibition game against the Cincinnati Reds. He reflected, "Pete Rose is up and there is a man on third and one out, and I go to two strikes to Rose, so I throw the knuckleball to him. He grounds out to second and drives in the run. As he runs past the mound he says to me, 'you didn't win the ERA title throwing that shit.'" But when Bosman was on, when he was hitting his spots with the slider, Williams could only look on with pride, because Dick made the batter prove he could hit *Bosman's* pitch, not theirs. There were many days when opposing players, even the good ones like Boog Powell, rarely laid a finger on it.

The frustration that Bosman expressed at the end of the 1970 season about the Senators organization was about to get worse. The Washington sports pages blared forth heartbreaking news just days after the banquet. Bob Short had blown up the team and done so in his own inimitable style. He was not listening to Ted Williams or anyone with knowledge of the game. Short had often spoken of his desire for big-name players, the ones that would bring out the crowds. He did not even wait until the postseason had officially begun to pull the trigger on one of the worst trades in baseball history.

Bob Short traded his starting shortstop and third baseman—Eddie Brinkman and Aurelio Rodriguez—as well as Joe Coleman, his most promising young pitcher. Short gave up three crucial players from the 1970 team and got Denny McLain from the Detroit Tigers, along with an aging third baseman in Don Wert, a rookie outfielder in Elliot Maddox, and a rookie pitcher in Norm McRae. In an early article for the Society for American Baseball Research's *Baseball Research Journal* in 1978, Bill James developed a system for evaluating the equity of baseball trades by establishing an objective value for each player. The ideas contained in the article presaged such later analytic player evaluation systems such as Wins above Replacement (WAR). Using his early system, James concluded that the McLain trade was the worst he had encountered.[8]

McLain's celebrity status was no longer linked to his 30-win season in 1968. At the time of the trade, he was defined by his nefarious activities away from baseball. Short had wanted to trade for McLain before, but Williams and others had discouraged him. Short finally got the deal he was looking for. It might not have made much sense to fans or pundits, but Short got one thing out of the deal he desperately needed, an estimated $200,000 in cash from the Tigers. He announced the deal just a few days before the World Series began to gain maximum press coverage.

McLain was not the pitcher who had won 30 games in 1968. His 1970 season was a nightmare by any standard. His descent into chaos began when on February 23 of that year, the cover of *Sports Illustrated* featured a photo of McLain with a bold headline that read, "Denny McLain and the Mob, Baseball's Big Scandal."[9] The article contained allegations that had the potential to rival the Black Sox Scandal of 1919, because the inside story outlined McLain's involvement in a gambling ring that had bet on baseball, including one game in which McLain had pitched.

Commissioner Bowie Kuhn suspended McLain shortly thereafter. The suspension was to run for six months, or the first half of the 1970 season. Kuhn proved to be something short of Kenesaw Mountain Landis, the legendary first commissioner of baseball. McLain had asserted his innocence vigorously to Kuhn, who gave credence to the idea that McLain was the "victim of a confidence scheme."[10] Members of the press and even his teammates were surprised that a more severe sentence had not been forthcoming. McLain took the mound again for the Tigers in July 1970, but on August 28—less than two months later—he was suspended for the rest of the year for carrying a firearm on the team plane. For the portion of the season when McLain was active, he was ineffective. He posted a 4.63 ERA and won only three games for the Tigers. He was damaged goods, and most inside the game knew it.

Bosman believes that Williams began to lose interest in the Senators when it became clear there was no chance to field a winner in Washington. The McLain trade was the last straw. There was no way to instill a winning spirit on a team that lacked the ability to put sound players on the field at every position. The disaster that was to be the 1971 season began with the loss of 14 straight games in September 1970, but that snowball became a landslide when McLain joined the show.

"When things starting going south in the middle of 1970, I had this fear that things were headed back to where they had been in 1968," Dick recalled. But the situation in 1971 would far surpass any of the "backbiting and dissention in the clubhouse" that Bosman had endured in 1968. McLain became a one-man wrecking crew set loose in an already difficult situation. Bosman was interested in only one thing—winning ballgames—but that was going to be more difficult in 1971, especially without the talented infielders who scooped up the proliferation of ground balls that indicated Bosman was on top of his game.

In Brinkman's place was a 22-year-old rookie named Toby Harrah. Harrah had been a top draft pick and was well-regarded, but in 1971 he would hit only .230 and commit 23 errors in the field. At third was Dave Nelson, who was a better hitter than Harrah, but he was not the equal of Aurelio Rodriguez with the glove or the bat. Coleman would win 20 games for the Tigers, and Brinkman and Rodriguez would be mainstays on a Tigers team that would finish second in the American League East in 1971 and first in 1972, when they would face an Oakland Athletics team led by Reggie Jackson.

Bosman was still dreaming of winning 20 games and doing all he could in the offseason to ready himself for the task. Bob Short may not have known much about the game of baseball, but he paid well. Dick got an increase in salary to $35,000. He believed he was worth $40,000 but took the offer. The money was commensurate with his place on the team. He was named Washington's Most Valuable Player at the Baseball Writer's Banquet, held in January at the Shoreham Hotel.

The Presidential Home Opener was an emotional moment for the Washington Senators in 1971. A just-released prisoner of war in Vietnam threw out the first pitch instead of the president. Bosman's second Opening Day start went far better than the prior year. He threw a complete-game shutout at the Oakland Athletics and their star pitcher, Vida Blue. The last time, and only other time, the Senators had won the Presidential Opener had been under Mickey Vernon in 1962.

In the offseason, Bob Short had acquired former St. Louis Cardinals standout center fielder Curt Flood as an added draw behind Denny McLain. Like McLain, Flood had achieved a certain notoriety within the sport when he failed to report to Philadelphia as part of a trade for Dick Allen. Flood sat out the 1970 season to initiate what became a historic legal challenge to Major League Baseball's reserve clause. It was a courageous act, but it was painfully apparent in April 1971 that Flood was no longer the fine glove man who won world championships as a star with the Cardinals in 1964 and 1967.

Dick's next outing was indicative of what was to come. It was Sunday, April 11, and a doubleheader was scheduled at RFK Stadium with the New York Yankees. Bosman pitched the first game and was just as solid as he had been in the opener. Unfortunately, his fine effort did not result in a win. The problems began in the second inning, when Curt Blefary of the Yankees hit a sharp liner to left-center field. Flood did not pick up the ball immediately, and after a late jump on the ball he made a futile leap for the sinking line drive, leaving it to roll toward the wall. Frank Howard ran it down and quickly relayed the ball to Toby Harrah, the cutoff man, who then threw toward the plate.

The second ill-advised decision came when Mike Epstein cut off the throw for no discernible reason rather than allowing it to go through. Blefary crossed home without a play. Catcher Jim French opined in the press the next day that he believed had the throw gone through, they would have had Blefary at the plate.[11] Bosman allowed only three hits that day, but Washington lost the game to the Yankees, 1–0, the lone tally in the game being Blefary's hit that had been misplayed into a home run.

Denny McLain was the number-two pitcher in a Washington rotation that featured him and Bosman, followed by a revolving cast of unproven talents. The average ERA for the league was 3.48, and Washington managed only 4.15. The offense was as anemic as the defense was porous. Whatever talent existed on the club was undone by the rancorous atmosphere in the dugout. Ted Williams was an irascible firecracker whose fuse was always lit. He went off on players regularly. Flood and McLain became flash points for his anger early in the season, but Flood left the team for good in late April. McLain found numerous coconspirators, particularly among the position players.

The Washington clubhouse was not a pleasant place to work, according to Bosman.

The problem with McLain was not just his disruptive presence in the clubhouse. His stuff just wasn't that good anymore. If Bob Short had listened to Ted Williams and hired a few scouts, he might have known that Denny's "arm was shot and his velocity was way down," according to Bosman. When McLain returned from his suspension in 1970, he had needed repeated cortisone injections to relieve severe shoulder pain.[12] Whether or not Short had scouts, the issues related to McLain's shoulder were known throughout the league. Shelby Whitfield suggests in his book *Kiss It Goodbye* that Bob Short may have known McLain was damaged goods but traded for him nonetheless, expressly for the notoriety and to buy the loyalty of Detroit's ownership when he moved the team.[13]

In the end, McLain managed 216 innings in 1971, second on the team to Bosman's 236. McLain was largely ineffective, with an ERA of 4.28. which earned him 22 losses. "The guy was just an awful teammate," Dick remembered of McLain. "He was a disruptive force off the field, and on the field, he just wasn't going to be able to get a lot of people out." McLain *had* endured real tragedy. He lost a daughter in a car crash. For a man seemingly addicted to celebrity, his wife was a wonderful and down-to-earth woman, whom Bosman remembers as quite different than her husband. "She was one of the nicest people you would ever meet. But this guy was the worst teammate I had ever been around," Bosman commented. "He blamed Ted for his failing because Ted wanted a five-day rotation. Hell, he [McLain] couldn't answer the bell on a four-day as bad as his arm was."

The dysfunction that plagued the Senators in 1968 was pale in comparison to the trouble McLain brewed almost from Opening Day 1971. McLain flouted Williams's rules and encouraged others to do likewise. He formed a group called the "underminers," which held clandestine initiations of players into their group. McLain found enough support for his revolt to make Ted's job that much more difficult, and the Washington manager was constantly seething about some new rebellion McLain had instigated.

Against this backdrop, Dick was the same fierce competitor as always. He still wanted to win 20 games and, at the end of April, was turning in quality starts every time he took the mound. His ERA stood at 2.85. But that fine beginning was completely undone when he lost six straight starts in May.

His record fell to two wins against seven losses. He finally won another game on June 1, by a score of 6–5, against the California Angels. Even then he was forced to endure a 32-minute delay in the game after the lights went out at RFK Stadium. Many in the stadium that night wondered whether Short had failed to pay the bill on time. It was no idle musing.

Dick admitted that the losing streak had gotten to him, that he was "pressing, overthrowing, and trying to be a fastball pitcher" when he was a "sinker–slider pitcher."[14] His wife Pam was even varying his dietary regime in the morning before he pitched in hopes of shaking the jinx. Finally, as in prior years, he found his rhythm in the second half of the season. In August, Bosman won his last three starts to move his record to 10 wins against 13 losses. He was pitching for a team in crisis, and the unfolding drama affected everyone.

> Dick mastered the cat-and-mouse game between pitcher and hitter. When he was on his game, he knew exactly what the perfect pitch was for the situation, so much so that he could see the batter lunging for it, rolling over the top of the ball, and hitting a harmless grounder to Brinkman at shortstop.

From the beginning, there had been rumors that Short wanted to move the Washington Senators to the Dallas-Ft. Worth area of Texas. He had scheduled an exhibition game at the end of spring training 1969 in Dallas. It was an anomaly, one that caught the attention of many and was noted in the press. But in the second half of the 1971 season, there was more than just rumor. A June article in *Sporting News* stated that Short was not paying the rent on RFK Stadium to the DC Armory Board, which oversaw its operation. The Armory Board had threatened Short with cutting off the lights if he did not pay, which makes the early June electrical outage noteworthy.

When Short finally addressed the issues publicly, he admitted he was losing money. He announced that the team was for sale and said he was asking $12.4 million for the last-place squad. The New York Yankees were purchased by George Steinbrenner in 1973, for $9 million, so Short's asking price was wildly inflated by any standard. Commissioner Bowie Kuhn began looking for a buyer to keep the team in Washington. There were several who displayed interest, including Bill Veeck, Bob Hope, and the owners of a large supermarket chain in DC. One by one the American League owners found holes in the offers presented to keep the team in DC. A meeting was scheduled in Boston for September 21, to decide how to resolve the issue. There could be no move away from Washington without clear consensus from the rest of the owners.

Short quietly lobbied for his plan to move the team and found a solid core of owners who were sympathetic to his cause, but there were several teams adamantly opposed as well. The Senators played out the final two months of the season unsure whether they would open the 1972 season in Washington or Texas. Many of the players had roots in the Washington, DC, area, for example, Bosman, whose wife was from the Virginia suburbs. With Bob Short and Bowie Kuhn—the same dynamic duo that had brought Denny McLain to DC—running the show, there was little reason for confidence.

The growing uncertainty did not keep Dick Bosman from competing. He turned in complete-game wins against the Kansas City Royals in August and the Orioles to start September. Ironically, Bosman was scheduled to pitch on September 21, the day the American League owners met to decide the fate of the club. Dick pitched one of his best games of the season that day, going the distance against the Cleveland Indians and allowing only a single run for his 12th win of the season. It would be his last win in a Washington Senators uniform.

The following morning, September 22, the headlines told the story. "Short to Take Senators to Texas," read the *Washington Post*.[15] The vote had been more lopsided than anticipated. Only two owners voted to keep the team in DC, and 10 voted in favor of Short's motion to move to Dallas. The article noted that there were only four more games to be played at RFK Stadium.

Bosman heard the news on the television late in the evening as he and his wife prepared for bed. They were staying at his wife's parents' house, where they had moved for the last few weeks of the season. As the news settled in, they sat in stunned silence thinking of their marriage in Washington, DC, the many memories they had of life there, and their many friends. "There was shock. There was bitterness that the club didn't do better and that this had to happen," Dick recalled about his feelings that night. Washington was Dick's only team, and he had grown from a prospect into a valued major-league pitcher during his time there.

The next day, George Minot opined about the great names that had played baseball in Washington throughout the years. Above the article appeared the pictures of Sam Rice and Walter Johnson, perhaps the most storied of them all, but Minot listed Goose Goslin, Bucky Harris, Joe Cronin, Mickey Vernon, and others, who he described as ghosts that would walk the streets of DC until the team returned.[16]

There were two highly respected names on the 1971 roster who belonged on Minot's list. Frank Howard and Dick Bosman, who would take the field on September 30 for the last game, were the longest-tenured players on the team. Both were fan favorites whose careers had provided drama and hope during the last years in Washington, and they felt more deeply the impact of the impending move than anyone else. There were a few other players with roots in the community, but none like Bosman and Howard. Hondo said in a press article that he was "disappointed as hell to be leaving Washington." He talked about the highlights of his career that had occurred in the city and concluded by saying, "I'm a DC boy."[17]

The last game of the season was against the New York Yankees, and Mike Kekich had the start against Bosman. It was more than fitting that it was Dick Bosman's turn in Ted Williams's five-man rotation. It seemed fated that Dick should pitch the final game in the 71-year history of baseball in the nation's capital. There were 14,460 fans on hand for the final game, but they made themselves heard as though there were many more. In center field they sent a long banner streaming down toward the playing surface that read simply, "Short Stinks." When the banner was unfurled, fans rose to applaud its sentiment. Somewhere on the concourse inside the stadium, an effigy of Short hung with a noose around its neck.

New York jumped on Dick for four runs in the first two innings, and he left the game in the fifth inning with the Yankees on top, 5–1. But in the sixth inning, Frank Howard ignited a four-run rally with a home run. The fans leapt to their feet to watch the ball's long journey and screamed their approval as Howard trotted around the bases, waving his batting helmet to the crowd, a huge smile on his face. When he crossed home plate he told Thurman Munson, "Thanks for the gift."[18] Howard believed that Kekich grooved the pitch, saying he was a dead fastball hitter and all Kekich threw him were fastballs.

The Senators scored two more runs to take the lead in the final game, 7–5. In the top of the ninth inning, with their team leading and only one final out to go, the fans could stand it no longer. They came pouring out of the stands, swarming the playing surface. Hundreds of fans rampaged the field, pulling up the bases and ripping up turf as souvenirs. They took letters and bulbs off the right-field scoreboard. The umpires stood watching from a safe distance and concluded finally that order could not be restored. The forfeit of the game by a score of 9–0 was announced, but no one was listening, as everyone was too busy looking for something to take home that might remind them what it had been like to have baseball in Washington.

The groundskeepers tried to protect the pitching rubber and home plate, and police appeared to stand guard with them, but the other bases disappeared. The crowd was jovial for the most part, although three people were arrested for disorderly conduct. Those that had not taken to the field found souvenirs along the concourse and in the seats. Fans could be seen uprooting entire seats from the concrete with tools they had brought for that explicit purpose. Many fans just sat in stunned silence watching the frenzied throng, savoring the last moments, trying to prolong the final minutes of baseball's long history in DC. The press ranged through the crowd gathering the stories of those in attendance. One older man shared his memories of watching Walter Johnson play at what had once been Griffith Stadium.[19]

There would be no more visions of baseball glory rising from the streets of Washington, DC. Like a luxury liner on a moonlit night sinking silently into the black waters, the lights of RFK Stadium began to go out one huge standard at a time. The police herded the last fans toward the exits. When the stadium was dark and the last fan gone, all that existed of baseball in Washington was the box score printed defiantly in the *Washington Post* the next day. There, the Senators had won by a score of 7–5, but history would record the game as another one lost to the Damn Yankees, this one by a score of 9–0. Either way, Dick Bosman took the loss and shared it with an entire city.

5

No-Hitter

There was no Presidential Home Opener in 1972, no patriotic bunting hanging on the stadium, just the angry voices of major-league players as they marched off the job on April 1, in the first baseball strike to ever halt official play. It was a giant first step, one that would be felt for decades in the game of baseball, but it was a tentative foot forward into the unknown that spring. The strike was ostensibly about funding the players' pension fund, but it was more about the growing lack of respect the players felt from ownership concerning their fledgling union.

In May 1970, the Major League Baseball Players Association (MLBPA) won official recognition as the union to represent the players with ownership. There had been small issues arbitrated in the first few years, but secure and adequate funding for their eventual retirement was the biggest issue for the players aside from the reserve clause. There was an existing pension agreement in place that had been negotiated in 1969, and MLBPA executive director Marvin Miller had spent the winter before the 1972 campaign trying to work out a new one. The issue was what share of television and broadcast revenues would be used to support the pension fund moving forward. The existing agreement was set to expire on March 31.

Miller proposed a cost of living increase that would mean a 17 percent increase in the owner's share, but since there was a surplus of $800,000 in the fund, he argued to the ownership that their increase would be mitigated substantially by applying the surplus. The owners said no and even reduced the existing offer they had on the table. Miller and the players believed they were being tested, that the owners thought it was time to break the back of the union. Miller traveled to the spring training camps in March, explaining the issues and asking for a strike authorization, which he got in every camp except that of the Boston Red Sox, where Tom Yawkey purportedly bought off his player reps.[1]

The owners met to discuss their stance on March 22. After the meeting, Cardinals owner Gussie Busch told the press that the owners "voted unanimously to take a stand." He added, "We're not giving them another goddam cent."[2] That red flag was waved in every training camp in Arizona and Florida, and rallied the players to take a stand. There was a problem, however. There was no strike fund, and the players were not paid during the offseason. Many players, like Dick Bosman, were cash poor.

Marvin Miller and MLBPA chief attorney Dick Moss scheduled one last meeting in Dallas—halfway between the Arizona and Florida training camps—to decide whether to strike. Miller was not sanguine about their chances and warned the players about what they were facing—the negative press and the weight of financial muscle behind the owners. The response by the players was one of surprising militancy. Tim McCarver of the Phillies, Reggie Jackson of the Athletics, and Ray Sadecki of the Mets were adamant about walking out. Their spirit was almost uniform, and the room quickly heated up as one team rep after another spoke out in favor of the strike. When the final vote was taken, there was only one vote against the walkout, and it was not from the Texas Rangers.[3]

Don Mincher was the Rangers' player rep at the meeting, and Dick Bosman was another union rep. Bosman was by the phone taking reports from Mincher and relaying them to the rest of the team. The newly minted Texas Rangers were scheduled to start their first season in Arlington, Texas, in only a few days' time. "If we did not draw a line in the sand, the owners were going to continue to bulldoze us," Dick recalled from his discussions with Mincher and Dave Nelson, who was another member of the Rangers deeply involved in the labor discussions. Bosman continued, "For guys like us who had been around the block a few times, it [the owners' funding demand] was just the last straw. It had been insult upon insult."[4]

After hearing that the vote in Dallas was for a strike, Dick spoke to Frank Howard about the issue before taking the floor to talk to the Texas players. He asked his friend if he would "stand up there with us" when Dick addressed the guys, some of whom were young and inexperienced but would follow the lead of the most senior player on the roster, especially one who was 6-foot-8. Dick presented the issues with Hondo standing beside him, and although some of the players were a little squeamish, they voted to walk out. They were talking through some of the logistics as to how they could arrange for everyone to get to Texas and continue working out at various sites throughout town when Bob Short, still the owner of the team, walked into the room.

Short explained to the group that he expected them to board the team bus and travel to Fort Lauderdale, where they were scheduled to play the Yankees in a spring training game. Howard stepped forward, separating himself from his teammates and placing himself front and center with Short. "Bob, our executive board has met and decided to strike," Hondo told Short. "So, until this pension thing is resolved, let's go men," he said, looking at the team. It was an authoritative statement delivered by the senior and most well-respected man on the squad. As Hondo walked out the door, the players slowly followed. Dick remembered telling Howard shortly thereafter, "Champ, I'm glad you did that. I'm not sure I could have walked out of there."

The players got in their cars and began traveling back to Dallas. Dick and Paul Lindblad made the trip together. Much as he and Jim French had done in 1969, they left in the early evening and did not stop until they made Dallas the next morning. Dick's wife Pam was already in Texas looking for an apartment for the couple. To complicate matters, she was scheduled to deliver their first child the same day the players decided to strike at the labor meeting across town. When Dick arrived at the apartment address the next day, he was greeted by his sister-in-law, who was there to help her sister with the baby when it arrived.

The players worked out at high school and college fields throughout town while they waited to hear what the owners would do. Miller had been correct about the tenor of the public reaction. There was almost uniform criticism of the players in the press. Dick had more pressing problems. Pam Bosman was late in delivering their baby, and they waited for the baby while also anticipating an answer from Bob Short and the owners. It was coffee and donuts in the mornings before going out to practice in hopes of staying in shape. Dick remembers that he and Pam were about out of money, and he was thinking about looking for part-time work when Miller and federal negotiators worked out a deal with the owners two weeks after the strike vote was taken.

Eighty-six games were lost from the schedule, which meant that some teams lost as many as six or seven games, but the 1972 season was restored and baseball began more or less as it would have. Dick and the rest of the team made plans to open the campaign in Anaheim against the Angels at exactly the point in the season when the strike ended. The players were not compensated for the off days of the strike. But no one really cared. The most important thing was that the union held.

When Short ordered the team to work, Hondo had led them out, and they had made it stick. The hard-line owners and Bowie Kuhn had tried to break the union but quickly found out they had a rebellion on their hands, one that would long endure.

When the team took the field in 1972, it was impossible to point to

> "Get ahead, stay ahead, use your head" is probably as good a short summary of Bosman's philosophy of pitching as can be put on a t-shirt, but the greatest substance lies in the third of the essential pitching commandments: Use your head.

any tangible differences between the Texas Rangers and the Washington Senators. They had a new home in Arlington, Texas. The ballpark was new to the players, but it was a retrofit and still lacked many of the amenities of a major-league stadium. The clubhouses were in center field. Originally known as Turnpike Stadium for its convenience to the new interstate, it had been built in 1965 for a minor-league team, the Fort Worth Cats of the Texas League. The seating capacity had been only 10,000 when the facility was built, but in 1970 it had been expanded to a capacity of 20,500 to attract a major-league team.

Other than the new stadium there were the new double-knit uniforms rather than flannels. But for the most part the players were the same. Bob Short had traded center fielder Del Unser to Cleveland for a young pitcher named Rich Hand, who would join Dick and Pete Broberg as a rotation stalwart. Broberg had shown promise during his rookie year in 1971 with the Senators. The one huge constant was Ted Williams. He was still the manager, although the famous man was just going through the motions and would depart at the end of the season.

In 1972, the Texas Rangers would lose even more games than they had as the Washington Senators. The number of fans that were drawn to witness the first season of the Rangers was almost the same as had come out of loyalty to see the last season of the Senators. Dick Bosman was still the ace of the staff, and he pitched the season opener against the California Angels on the road. Dick lost a heartbreaker to Andy Messersmith by a score of 1–0, when the winning run scored in the bottom of the ninth inning.

When the Rangers returned to Texas for the home opener, there was none of the fanfare of a Presidential Opening Day, and only 20,000 fans were in attendance. For Arlington Stadium it was a sellout, but there were far fewer fans than the crowds that almost always came to see the president throw out the first pitch of the season in Washington. Dick was not as sharp as in his first start but picked up the win nonetheless.

During the game, another drama was unfolding that would have far greater consequence for Dick Bosman. Pam Bosman was in labor the entire day and did not want to intrude on her husband's state of mind before the first game in Arlington. Dick was unaware of the situation during the game, and it was not until its conclusion that Bob Short informed him that his wife was about to deliver. The team arranged for a police escort to get Dick to Harris Methodist Hospital in Ft. Worth, where he arrived shortly before the birth of his daughter Michelle. Pam's sister was there to help with the baby because Dick was more busy than usual in the preceding weeks as he tried to wrap up the loose ends from the strike and get the season started. As important as the union was, Michelle Bosman would prove of greater consequence.

One issue going forward for Dick was that he no longer had Paul Casanova as his primary catcher. Casanova and Jim French had been on the other end of Bosman's best and worst games. Neither was known for his hitting, but both were excellent "catch-and-throw men," Casanova being the better of the two. French was a fierce competitor and a close friend of Bosman's, but both members of the Senators catching corps were gone in 1972. Casanova was traded during the offseason to the Atlanta Braves for catcher Hal King.

It wasn't the catcher's fault that Dick got off to another slow start in 1972. There was plenty of heat in Texas, so Bosman got loose much sooner than he had in DC, but still he struggled. In an early May matchup against Mickey Lolich and the Tigers, Dick allowed six runs in only four innings of work and was knocked from the mound in the fifth inning without recording an out. His ERA skyrocketed to 5.79, higher than at any time since his rookie season in 1966.

By the end of the month, however, something had clicked. Maybe Dick just had to throw enough innings to sharpen and tighten the slider, but in June he found his timing and was turning in quality starts every time he took the mound. Still, the team wasn't winning because they couldn't score runs. Dick's ERA stood at 3.54 in mid-June, but for the season the team would not even manage to score three runs per game, which did much to explain Bosman's 4–7 record at the end of the month.

Just when he began to pitch well, he experienced one of the worst injuries of his career. It was in the last game in June against the Oakland Athletics. "It was an errant curveball, one I probably never should have thrown and wouldn't after that, but a guy named Bill Voss hit a line drive back at me and I couldn't get a glove on it," Dick recalled. After the ball struck him in the knee, he picked it up and threw Voss out, but later in the clubhouse he knew things were not as they should be. "We had just gone to the double-knit uniforms, and it looked like there was a water balloon underneath my jersey down by my leg," he revealed.

Bosman made two more starts with the swollen knee. They were not good starts, but he went seven and one-third innings against Kansas City in a game the team won. Then in Baltimore he only lasted four innings, and Dr. Resta, still the team doctor, came from Washington and Dick asked him to look at the knee. Resta was shocked that Dick was still pitching. "This man is still pitching?" Dick remembered him asking. "There's a blood clot in there. This guy could die out there if a blood clot broke off of that."

Dick missed most of the month of July, taking blood thinners and limiting his activities for "20-some days." He made a start at the end of the month, but his stamina was not what it had been and he lasted only five innings. He would not make it past the fifth inning in his next three starts. His rehabilitation was not truly complete until the latter half of August, when he pitched six full innings and allowed only two runs against the Yankees on August 18, in Arlington.

From there Bosman found his rhythm. Unfortunately, it was not until the final game of the season that he was all the way back. He threw a complete-game shutout against the Chicago White Sox on October 1, with an uncharacteristic 13 strikeouts. Typical of that season, the Rangers managed to score a single run that day. Dick made it stand until he had won his eighth game on the last day of the season.

"I thought I finished the year pretty well," Dick recalled of that game. There were several other landmarks that were noteworthy at the end of the 1972 campaign. The Rangers finished the season with a two-game series in Kansas City. Dick did not pitch but remembers the celebrations to mark the final hurrahs for old Municipal Stadium in Kansas City. He had last pitched there in mid-August, when he lasted only five innings but gave up just a single run.

> No athlete believes they will be injured until it happens. The best defense against injury is proper conditioning. Pitchers that apply the essentials of conditioning as they have developed throughout the years are more likely to have long careers than those that place less emphasis on a developmental routine created by professionals.

In 1972, the Kansas City Royals were an expansion team that was formed after Charles O. Finley left the city and took the Athletics to Oakland. The Royals, like the Rangers, were playing in a preexisting stadium that had its own history. It was not until the final game, however, that the history of the stadium sank in with Dick and many on the field that day.

The park was known as Municipal Stadium in 1972, but it had once been called Muehlebach Field when it was home to the Kansas City Monarchs of the Negro Leagues, with the team playing there from 1937 to 1954. Satchel Paige, Jackie Robinson, and Buck O'Neil were just a few of the great Negro League stars to take the field there. That history was celebrated in the festivities before the game. It was announced that after the final game George Toma, the groundskeeper, would make a ceremonial removal of home plate, which would be installed in the new park as a way to bring the spirit and history of the old park along to the new stadium.

Before the game, Ted Williams announced he was done. His commitment to the endeavor had waned substantially. "He came late to batting practice,"

Dick said, as indicative of how much Williams had lost interest in managing a baseball team. On October 4, 1972, Ted managed his last major-league game. He and Bosman spoke at the end of the season in Kansas City. "It was behind closed doors," Dick recalled, continuing,

> I told him how much he had meant to me, and I remember him coming out of there and holding a team meeting and then going around and shaking hands with every one of those guys in that clubhouse. He was about as graceful in doing that as you could be. But that was it, the last game, and it was played at that stadium.

The final game at Muehlebach Field was a fitting end to Ted's long career in the game. One of the most remarkable personal traits of Williams was his support for African American players during his tenure with the Boston Red Sox. It was a transitional period for baseball, and there were often incidents that were unpleasant for those players who were integrating facilities that had previously been available only to whites, for instance, spring training hotels. Williams had once taken a hotel clerk to task for not showing proper respect to Jim "Mudcat" Grant at a hotel, and there have been other similar stories told about Williams's open friendship with blacks in the game. It made poetic sense that Ted would hang up his spikes for good in old Muehlebach Field.

Until 1972, Dick and his wife Pam had been spending offseasons in Kenosha. After they were married, his father carved off a parcel of his 10-acre property for Dick and his wife. Although they bought a home in the city of Kenosha, they used the land to construct a building that would become the showroom for Dick's new snowmobile franchise for Arctic Cat. The venture also included one of the out buildings that Bosman had once used for his car racing equipment. The snowmobile business began in 1969, but its grand opening was during the offseason in 1970, an event that had much fanfare.

Wisconsin congressman Les Aspin was on hand for the official opening. "It was really a big deal," Dick said of the event. Frank Howard and other friends and teammates came to the grand opening, even Denny McLain. But it was Howard who stole the show, signing autographs and helping fans get into snowmobiles. "He was such a great ambassador that many in the crowd probably assumed the dealership belonged to Hondo," Dick believes, looking back on that time.

Despite early success, the dealership was short-lived. For two seasons, there was plenty of business and plenty of snow. But even then, the snowmobiles sat in the showroom during baseball season, which meant Dick was paying interest on them. In the winter, after the Senators left Washington, there was almost no snowfall, and Bosman's business dropped off sharply. Perhaps it was preordained. Maybe Texas and snow just did not mix, but the same year Dick moved from Washington and was on the verge of becoming a father, business dried up as effectively as the snow and he was forced to sell the snowmobile franchise, losing substantial money in the bargain.

After 1972, Dick's offseason work shifted back to cars as he took a job working for Koons Ford in Washington. Ex-Redskins player Jim Carroll was his brother-in-law, married to Pam's sister. Carroll had taken over the Koons dealership in Annapolis along Route 50 and encouraged Dick to come work at Koons Ford at 7 Corners and learn the ropes so that he would have a similar position when his playing days were over. Dick believed Carroll's offer made considerable sense for someone with a great and long love of cars. He and Pam sold the house in Kenosha and moved in with her parents in Fairfax, Virginia, until they found a place of their own.

Dick was an enthusiastic apprentice in learning the auto business from the ground up. It fit well with those early years working on cars with his dad and his enthusiasm for drag racing. "I was carrying fenders from the parts department to the body shop. I unloaded semi-trailers," Dick remembered of the mundane tasks he performed as a novice learning the business. Being a management trainee at Koons was not firing off an old Chevrolet with his father, but it was in the same ballpark. Dick had found something he liked doing even if it wasn't baseball.

There were many changes going on in Dick's life in the off-season before 1973. He was a father and had many new offseason routines to manage. The Texas Rangers were turning the page as well. Frank Howard may have played too prominent a role in the strike and was sent to Detroit for cash in August 1972. Don Mincher was traded to Oakland in July. Both

> One of the biggest changes in the game of baseball since Dick Bosman's playing days is the emphasis on offseason conditioning. It is as important to maintain strength and follow a prescribed routine in the offseason as during the peak months of pitching.

men were at the end of their careers, but the timing just months after they had defied Bob Short was curious. There was one important new face in the Texas Rangers clubhouse to start the 1973 season, that of manager Whitey Herzog. Dick had no problems with Whitey, but the word got around to Dick during the spring that Herzog was not happy with his low strikeout totals. Whitey wanted someone who threw harder.

Even in 1972, Dick had been one of the few old hands still pitching for Bob Short and Ted Williams. Bosman, then 28, was the senior member of the rotation. Dick believed that guys like Pete Broberg and Bill Gogolewski had been rushed into the majors and would never learn everything they needed to know in their on-the-job training program, which Sid Hudson was forced to conduct in 1972. The strength of that team had been its bullpen, consisting of Horacio Pina as the closer, with Paul Lindblad and Mike Paul setting him up. Only Broberg and Lindblad were around to open the 1973 season.

The Rangers started the 1973 campaign in much the same fashion as the prior year. Dick was 29 years old, and he pitched his fourth consecutive home opener on April 7, in Arlington. It was a Saturday night game, drawing a standing room only crowd of 22,000. Bosman was always at his best on Opening Day, and he went six innings and allowed only two earned runs but lost by a 3–1 margin. In his second start, against the Kansas City Royals in their new stadium, Dick hurled a complete-game shutout, allowing only three hits and getting his first win of the season. The weather was awful, as a rare cold snap forced the two teams to have huge heaters in the dugout blowing throughout the game. Despite the cold, Dick was loose enough and the slider was breaking just right, whatever the temperature was.

Bob Short had tried to add offensive punch after the 1972 season and did so in his own inimitable style. For the 1973 season, he added two veteran outfielders in Rico Carty and Alex Johnson, both of whom had been successful in other venues and were available for almost nothing. Carty had been an established star with the Atlanta Braves, playing alongside Hank Aaron in the outfield and leading the National League in batting average in 1970, with a mark of .366. But he had injured himself in winter ball, and when he came back in 1972, Carty got into loud altercations with Aaron and others in Atlanta such that the Braves were more than willing to part with him. It was another opportunity for Short to obtain a highly publicized veteran with a reputation off the field that had begun to exceed the one on the field.

Alex Johnson had led the American League in batting average in 1970, but he was known as a difficult personality. Johnson weighed in more at the Denny McLain end of the spectrum of bad behavior than Carty. After winning the batting title, he fought a protracted and highly publicized battle with California Angels manager Lefty Phillips for the better part of the season. Phillips repeatedly cited Johnson's lackadaisical play and benched him numerous times, which served to aggravate the situation.

The argument escalated until the Angels suspended Johnson, and the matter became the subject of a prolonged arbitration process that won Marvin Miller early praise as one who backed his players regardless of what the sports press might be saying. Johnson won his hearing and was awarded more than $29,970 in back pay. He was quickly gone from California and then from Cleveland. Bob Short signed him shortly thereafter.

Dick Bosman remembers Johnson fondly. "He could flat out hit. But he was moody and had a temper. He did not like to talk to the press, so he kept an electronics book in front of his face after games so the press wouldn't bother him while they were in the clubhouse," Dick commented. According to Bosman, "He was on page four of that book all summer long." Since Bosman was the union rep, Whitey Herzog approached him about Alex Johnson and what the procedures would be if things got "out of shape." "What were the rules according to Marvin Miller if Johnson got belligerent?" Herzog asked Dick. That part of Bosman's relationship with Herzog was good.

What Bosman remembers best about Johnson is being in the Milwaukee airport one afternoon as the weather held up their flight. Dick was traveling with Pam and his daughter, and Johnson was beside them as they waited. Johnson spent several hours effortlessly entertaining Dick's daughter Michelle, who was no more than two at the time. Dick was struck by the complexity of his teammate and the underlying humanity that he kept so well hidden.

When they got back to Texas, Dick had almost no time to unpack before he got a call from Joe Burke, Bob Short's general manager, telling him that he had been traded to Cleveland. "Good Luck, Dick," was about all Burke said before he hung up. The phone call lasted less than 30 seconds, recalled Bosman. Dick told the press that he was excited about the trade. "I just want to pitch. . . . It's going to be great playing for this club," he said.[5] But Bosman remembers how difficult a transition it was in truth, stating, "It was like leaving a family." While many of the old faces were gone, it was still a place of comfort for him. There were still many of the players with Texas who had come up through the Washington Senators system. Coaches and clubhouse guys were familiar faces he had been seeing for years.

Dick had to get on a plane that afternoon and fly to Boston, where he would join the Cleveland team. Cleveland management expected him to start a ballgame for them in two days. It was the Texas Rangers' responsibility to pack his family's belongings and move them, but his wife Pam did the work rather than wait. "I walked into that ballpark in Boston, and I don't know a soul," is Dick's recollection. "It was tough emotionally to say the least." Ken Aspromonte was the manager, and one of the first things Dick remembers him asking was, "You're pitching tomorrow night. Are you okay with that?"

"It was a team that had more guys that had been around the block a few times," Dick remembered. Gaylord Perry was the ace of the staff, coming off a Cy Young Award–winning season. Dick was being counted on to slot in behind Perry in the rotation and provide the team a more competitive look. The team had Dick Tidrow as its third starter and a young Milt Wilcox, who would pitch for 16 seasons in the majors. Dick Bosman should have improved the club substantially. The offense had a young Chris Chambliss at first base, George Hendrick in the outfield, and a young Buddy Bell playing third base. Dick would be throwing to Dave Duncan, whom Dick called a "cerebral guy and a fiery competitor." There were ample reasons to be optimistic about the team.

Bosman pitched into the seventh inning in his first two outings and gave the team a chance to win, although they lost the first game, 2–1, and the next, 4–2. Then he developed tendinitis in his shoulder, and things spiraled downhill from there. He won only a single game for the Indians that season. The win came in July, after he flew to Washington to get cortisone injections from Dr. Resta, the former team physician for the Senators. There were several visits. Dick's wife Pam would drive him to the airport in the morning, and he would arrive at National Airport and take a cab to 18th and I Streets, where the office was located. "I would sit on a camp stool while Dr. Resta stuck that six-inch needle in me, and he would work it around in my shoulder. I'd be damn near writhing on the floor," Bosman revealed.

Warren Spahn was the Cleveland pitching coach, and when Bosman returned, Spahn only wanted to know whether he had gotten the shot. After an affirmative response, Spahn said, "You're pitching in three days." The shots worked well enough for a while. Dick had several good outings in July, but in August the pain was back and the shoulder was too weak to respond to treatment. He would pitch well enough for a few innings, but then the shot would wear off and he would get hammered. By late August, he was pitching out of the bullpen.

The 1973 season went down as the worst of his career. It was so bad that when he left at the end of the year, he was worried about making the club the following spring. Phil Seghi, Cleveland's general manager, was upset because trading for Bosman had made him look bad. What Dick remembers about a that long summer in Cleveland was the fans. "They never booed me," he said. The press supported him as well despite him being a major disappointment to the team. He finished the season with an ERA of 5.64, but the fans never let him know about it.

When he returned to Washington for the final time to see Dr. Resta, the physician gave him a routine of exercises to do to strengthen the shoulder instead of the needle. The workout routine consisted of lifting a five-pound weight in a way that was similar to what Dr. Frank Jobe would develop later for pitchers after shoulder surgery. Doing the repetitions with the five-pound weight was difficult, but over time he regained strength in the shoulder.

During the offseason, the Bosman family was living with Dick's in-laws again in the Northern Virginia suburbs of Washington. Dick's father-in-law got up early each morning and went running before going to work. Dick began accompanying him on these runs, and when it was time to report to spring training the next February, he was in excellent shape and the shoulder felt considerably stronger.

Before reporting to spring training for the 1974 season, Bosman had another several months where he invested in his after-baseball career by working at Koons Ford. Dick was still on track to become a manager of a dealership when he retired from the game. The 1973 season in Cleveland had been so bad, Dick worried the "after-baseball" future might come all too soon. When he reported to spring training, manager Ken Aspromonte gave him his support, telling him, "I'm going to do everything I can to keep you on this club. I like your attitude, and I know you're a winner," as Dick recalled.

Bosman started the 1974 season for Cleveland in the rotation behind Gaylord Perry and his brother Jim Perry, who the Indians had traded for during spring training. Dick was not sharp in that first outing and was back in the bullpen for two months. In April, Cleveland traded Dick Tidrow and Chris Chambliss to the Yankees for four pitchers, two of whom were Fritz Peterson and Steve Kline, who took Dick's turn in the rotation. The pitching staff was crowded, and Dick was worried he would be the odd man out, but he was healthy again and able to hang on.

"It was a rough year, being in that situation," he remembered. Gaylord and Jim Perry supported Dick throughout the worst times that season. "They always told me to hang in there and things will sort themselves out," he declared. It was while pitching out of the bullpen that Bosman had his second chance to pitch in a game forfeited because of a fan riot. The Texas Rangers were managed by Billy Martin in 1974, and Martin was always known for his pugnacious behavior, which often spilled over to his players. The boiling cauldron in the Texas clubhouse led to several incidents with the Cleveland Indians, the first of which began in Arlington, Texas, in late May.

> Every pitcher faces a numbers game, whether it is early in their career or late. There are a limited number of slots on any professional pitching staff, and when the situation is precarious, gamers keep their head down and redouble their efforts to stay in shape and maintain their focus on what they do best.

Cleveland traveled to Arlington for a series against the Rangers, and Rangers infielder Lenny Randle was quoted in the press prior to the game as saying he believed Cleveland pitcher Gaylord Perry would not get many people out if he did not throw a spitter. The next night, Milt Wilcox threw at Randle, and the ball sailed behind him, leaving little to the imagination. Several pitches later, Randle laid down a bunt that rolled down the first-base line, and as Wilcox came over to field the ball, Randle elbowed the pitcher in the head as he bent down to pick up the ball. "It was perfect Billy Martin strategy," Bosman remembered. "Lay down a bunt and when the pitcher came over to field it, steamroll him."

That incident drew players from both benches, and some guys, including Mike Hargrove, got into it pretty good, according to Dick, but Bosman mostly danced around with his former teammates. The Texas fans became involved in the scuffle, which set a marker that could not be ignored in Cleveland. One enterprising Texan stuck his head into the Cleveland dugout and was punched in the face by catcher Dave Duncan for his trouble. When asked whether he was concerned about playing in Cleveland the next week, Martin told a reporter after the game, "They don't have enough fans there to worry about."[6]

In response to the flagrant challenge from Martin, the Indians brass scheduled a promotion for the first night of the Rangers series in June where beer would be sold for 10 cents. Not surprisingly, the game was marked by copious consumption of beer. Drunk and rowdy fans made their presence known early in the game, running onto the field in various displays of nakedness. "The colleges had all let out for the summer, and the stands were full of kids," Dick recalled. "It was a full moon, and those kids could sneak anything they wanted into the ballpark back then: booze, marijuana, whatever." Sitting out in the bullpen, Dick remembers the strong smell of pot coming from the stands.

Dick pitched the fourth, fifth, and six innings, and it was shortly thereafter that the game took an ugly turn. A disputed call in the sixth inning resulted in Indians fans raining bottles and trash onto the Rangers players, some of whom rightly feared for their safety. Cleveland trailed throughout the game, but in the bottom of the ninth they mounted a rally and tied the game, 5–5, and had the go-ahead run on second base when a fan ran onto the field and tried to steal Rangers outfielder Jeff Burroughs's cap.

Texas manager Billy Martin saw a dark challenge in the drunken fan's playful attack on Burroughs, and he charged the field with a bat, his players coming out of the dugout behind him. At the sight of Martin heading toward the fan, others in the stands spilled forth over the railings in large numbers and surrounded the Texas players on the field in an ugly scrum, where Martin and his crew were losing ground and about to be overwhelmed. Bosman and his teammates saw the danger and went to Martin's rescue. It took far too long for order to be restored, and the umpires, who had been assaulted by fans as well, awarded the game to Texas by forfeit.

A few weeks after 10-Cent Beer Night, Dick was restored to the starting rotation. He started the first game of a doubleheader against Milwaukee and went five innings, giving up only a single run in a game ultimately won by the Indians. Gaylord Perry gave him confidence and told him, "Just go hard for six innings." He pitched twice more in July before starting the July 19 game against the world champion Oakland Athletics, led by Reggie Jackson and Sal

Bando. That game against Oakland would be the high point in Dick's long career.

It was by accident that many of his family members were in the stands that night. His parents, George and Nella, had driven from Kenosha with Dick's sister Diane for the game because George was on vacation. Dick's wife and daughter came out to the game with them. Gaylord Perry had lost the game the night before against Catfish Hunter by a 2–1 score. Watching that game drove home just how tough it was to score on Oakland and how great their lineup was.

Dick knew he had to be on his game against the A's. Besides, "You go into every game saying to yourself, 'I'm not going to allow any hits.' That's what you do. You give up a hit and you say to yourself, 'I'm not going to give up another one' . . . you give up a run and you tell yourself you're not going to give up any more runs."

Going into the game with Oakland, Bosman knew he had to be conscious of each pitch to every batter, focused and aware of every game situation. The game started out tight right from the start. Dick and Dave Hamilton, the Oakland starter, matched one another with prefect frames in the first two innings. Then in the bottom of the third, Cleveland first baseman Tom McCraw singled for the first hit of the game. Designated hitter Joe Lis followed with a home run to give the Indians a 2–0 lead.

In the fourth inning, with two out, Sal Bando hit a squibber back to the mound, which Dick fielded, hurrying his throw and sending the ball wide of first base. "It sailed on me," Dick said after the game. "It was my night all the way, even the error."[7] Dick quickly regained the upper hand by ending the inning with a strikeout of Reggie Jackson.

The Indians scored two more in the fifth, and Alvin Dark, the Oakland manager, brought in Blue Moon Odom to replace Dave Hamilton. Bosman went back out to the mound in the fifth inning and began a string of four perfect innings where he induced ground-ball outs for the most part. In the fifth inning, Cleveland shortstop Frank Duffy made one of two key plays to keep the Oakland score sheet clean. The best was when he went deep into the hole to throw out Joe Rudi. Then in the seventh inning, Buddy Bell made a diving stop at third base and threw out Bert Campaneris. "Charlie Spikes made a good play out in right field," Dick remembered of the late innings, "but Charlie made them all look difficult."

Dick went into the top of the ninth inning facing the bottom of the lineup. "I was a bit shook before the ninth inning," Bosman recalled. "I told myself that it is just [catcher] John Ellis and me. Concentration is the key to this game, and I really concentrated on the last three hitters."[8] Buddy Bell relieved some of the tension by coming over to ask Dick how he wanted to play the first batter, Dick Green. Said Bosman, "He asked me whether I wanted him to play in. I said no because he ain't gonna bunt there. If it is one or two to nothing, they might bunt. Four to nothing, they're not going to do that." Green tried to yank one past Buddy, who made the play to get the first out.

"Jesus Alou was the next guy, and he was a bad-ball hitter and I was really worried about him," Dick related. "I really, really worked to keep the ball down to him so he would hit the ball on the ground, and he hit one to [Jack] Brohamer for the second out." It was back to the top of the order for the final out, and the fiercely competitive Billy North was standing at the plate.

"I got two strikes on him," said Bosman, "the second of which was a foul ball well up into the left-field stands. I was going to throw him a fastball up and away, and then try to strike him out with a slider, but he swung and missed the fastball." North said it was Bosman's best fastball of the night. Whether it was or not, it was the final pitch in Dick Bosman's no-hitter, the best capstone possible for any major-league pitcher's career. It was an efficient outing, as Dick threw only 79 pitches and faced only 28 batters.

After the strikeout of North, the stadium erupted in applause. As the players left the field, the 24,000 fans, who had mostly stayed to watch a historic game to the very end, began to chant, "We want Bosman." Dick came out of the dugout for a curtain call and spoke to the crowd briefly, saying, "Thank you for your support and appreciation." His parents were still there, of course, watchful and proud. Dick's mother said of the final outs that Dick's father was probably more nervous in the final inning than Dick. Nella Bosman remembered that her husband went to get a cold drink before the ninth inning, but during the final outs he "could hardly get the soda to his mouth his hand was shaking so much."

Dick's family members made their way out of the stadium and to the car, where they waited for Dick with hundreds of fans streaming past, several of whom recognized them and asked if it was Dick's car. Remembering the Cleveland fans from the descriptions of "10-Cent Beer Night," Nella told them it was not, worrying that they might be a little "nutso."

Dick remembers the Cleveland fans differently. These were the same fans who never booed him in the worst of times in 1973, and "they were long suffering," like so many of the fans for whom Bosman pitched. Dick gave them something to cheer about in 1974, other than cheap beer. It was a return to form for Bosman, and the Indians were briefly in the thick of the pennant race. They were in first place in July 1974, when Dick had won his first game after returning to the rotation. But they slowly fell off the pace and finished fourth in the six-team American League East.

6

End Game

After the no-hitter, Dick finished up the second half of the 1974 season in the Cleveland rotation. He pitched well enough to win five games, while losing five. He had restored his shoulder to good health and, at 30 years of age, believed he still had several good seasons left in his career. When the Indians convened their spring training camp, there was a new manager to replace Ken Aspromonte. Frank Robinson, the Hall of Fame slugger who had been the American League and National League MVP during his career, was making history as the first African American manager in the major leagues.

Robinson told the media early in the spring that Dick Bosman was going to be relegated to a swingman role again. In response, Bosman told the press he was a starter, adding, "and I am most effective if I work regularly."[1] There was no ill will between the manager and his pitcher, just Bosman stating his case honestly. Dick had all the respect in the world for Frank, but there were just too many pitchers in Cleveland. At first Bosman was used sparingly, if at all. He got a start at the end of April as part of a doubleheader against the Orioles and went eight and two-thirds innings, allowing only three runs, but lost by a score of 3–2. Then, after two starts in May, he was traded to the Oakland Athletics along with Jim Perry for Blue Moon Odom and cash.

"I did not see it coming. Maybe I should have, but I just never did," remembered Dick.[2] Yet, unlike the trade from Texas to Cleveland, Bosman was enthused about this change. Oakland was coming off three consecutive world championship seasons and brimming with confidence and talent. It was the first time in Dick's career he would suit up with a realistic chance to play for a championship at the end of the season.

The news of the trade arrived in a most surprising manner. Pam Bosman was the one who took the call from Charlie Finley. Dick arrived at their apartment in Cleveland to find her engaged in conversation on the phone, a big smile on her face as she talked in animated fashion. She quickly motioned for Dick to take the call. He took the phone to find Finley, who explained the trade to his new pitcher, on the line.

Both Dick and Pam were upbeat about the possibilities from the very beginning. The closest thing to excitement for Bosman throughout the course of his major-league career had been "being 10 games over .500 with the Senators in 1969." He commented, "I don't think it had ever gotten any better than that, so you're darn right I was thrilled to get the chance. These were guys I had played against and knew pretty well. Heck, these were the same guys I had no-hit the previous season."

> Spinners, knucklers, spitters, and changeups. They all have a different feel and look when put in the hands of individual pitchers. That is the *art of pitching*, seeing what a pitch looks like when a particular pitcher throws it. The best way to gauge the nuances of each situation is to watch the ball as it spins toward the catcher's mitt. The sum of the observations Dick has made throughout the years inform what he brings to the game today as a pitching coach.

Dick remembers the clubhouse as being contentious, with loud personalities that often clashed. "But when they went out onto the field, it was about one thing, winning ballgames. And they did it the right way. With no one out and a man on base, they moved the runner over. They hit the cutoff man, they did all the things that a team is supposed to do. They just did it the right way." He continued, "And years later, when I would talk to young guys about how it was done, I use my time with the Oakland Athletics as the model."

The one thing that united the brawling Oakland clubhouse was their shared dislike for the notoriously tightfisted Charlie Finley. Bosman had heard about the insurance magnate from various players throughout the years, but he would not get a formal introduction until several weeks after the trade. "I had won four or five games for him by the time he said the first word to me after I arrived with the team," Dick recalled.

The cheapness of Finley's approach was apparent early on. "We never flew charter, just regular commercial flights for the most part," said Bosman. Dick remembers one particularly vexing situation where the team wrapped up a series in Baltimore on a Monday and had a doubleheader the next day against the Detroit Tigers. Finley only paid to get the two pitchers to Detroit on Monday night so they could get a decent night's sleep before the game. The team flew out of National Airport on Tuesday morning and only landed in Detroit a few hours ahead of game time. Finley cut every corner he could to save a buck.

Playing for Oakland brought out the best in Bosman, and he became an integral cog on a team looking to build on its three world championships. It was the same team that had beaten the Los Angeles Dodgers in the 1974 World Series, with the notable exception of Jim "Catfish" Hunter. The ace of the three-time champions, Hunter had been granted free agency at the end of the 1974 season because Finley had reneged on the part of his salary that required the owner to deposit money in an insurance policy for his star hurler. The monthly payments were never made. At one time, an owner could have gotten away with such an obvious infraction of the rules of commerce, but now the players had a union and an arbitration process that fairly adjudicated such matters.

Marvin Miller and the MLBPA took the case to arbitration, where Peter Seitz heard the arguments. He ruled that Finley had broken the contract, voiding it. Without a valid contract, Seitz ruled that Catfish Hunter was the first free agent. Hunter signed with the Yankees, and Oakland traded for Dick Bosman to fill his shoes, making him their union rep at the end of his first season.

It was not a straight replacement deal. There was no one in baseball who could take on the workload of Catfish Hunter, who had won the American League Cy Young Award in 1974. Bosman would start 21 games for the Athletics in 1975, however, and filled in capably behind Ken Holtzman and Vida Blue in the rotation. It was still the team of Reggie Jackson, Joe Rudi, Sal Bando, and Bert Campaneris. The other guys at the top of the rotation had 20-win seasons under their belt and were All-Stars. Bosman was proud to suit up every day.

Sportswriter Ron Bergman asked Dick several months after the trade where he would be pitching-wise if he were still in Cleveland. At the time, Dick's record stood at seven wins and only three losses, but he guessed, "I'd be around .500 . . . estimating it based on the way they [Cleveland] have played so far. Obviously, the difference pitching here is a hell of a bullpen. I've only had one complete game here."[3] Bosman would go on to have the best record of his career other than his 1969 and 1970 campaigns in Washington.

Alvin Dark was the manager and Wes Stock the pitching coach for Oakland, and they leaned heavily on one member of the bullpen. Rollie Fingers is in the Hall of Fame as one of the best closers in the game, and in 1975 he was set up by Paul Lindblad and Jim Todd, who were at the top of their game. There were numerous spot starters, for instance, Glenn Abbott, Stan Bahnsen, and Sonny Siebert, guys like Dick who were willing to do anything to pitch for a championship team that had a chance to win it all in October.

Only Vida Blue and Ken Holtzman were guaranteed regular turns in the rotation, as Dark used the other starters in a "unique" fashion, according to sportswriter Bergman. The division of labor could be seen at the end of the season in the tale of the tape. There were the four principal bullpen pitchers, each of whom logged more than 100 innings for the season. Dick was in that group numerically, with 122 innings for Oakland, although he started 21 games and came out of the bullpen only once after coming over from Cleveland. He was ostensibly the third starter, but Fingers threw almost as many innings as Bosman. All three late-inning hurlers for Oakland had 120-plus innings in 1975.

Dick won 11 games against only four defeats for Oakland and pitched to a respectable 3.52 ERA. He had a team that "always made the easy plays" behind him. He described the Athletics in the field as not flashy but incredibly steady and dependable. He had confidence that his worm burners were going to end up in a glove somewhere behind him, a feeling he had never before known in his career.

Bosman logged only one nine-inning game for Oakland, a five-hitter, which he won by a score of 4–3, after the A's made two uncharacteristic errors. He pitched into the ninth two other times, but in every other start

Dick Bosman's approach to pitching required a sound defensive club behind him, especially in the infield. Pitching quickly and efficiently kept his infielders focused and ready.

that season he was lifted in the sixth or seventh innings despite having a lead. Alvin Dark could afford to do that because of Rollie Fingers and company.

Shortly after Bosman joined the rotation, the team took over first place in the American League Western Division for good and coasted into the playoffs with a seven-game lead over the Kansas City Royals. They won 98 games and were set to begin the American League Championship Series against the Boston Red Sox on October 4. It was certain that Ken Holtzman would pitch in game one, followed by Vida Blue in game two. Dick was told he would be the starter for game three in the best-of-five series.

It was what Dick had played for his entire career: a chance at the postseason. It had looked as though he would never get the opportunity, but in game one, he was summoned from the Oakland bullpen with the team down, 7–0, to Luis Tiant. Holtzman had pitched into the seventh inning, behind by a score of 2–0. He gave up two doubles to push the Boston lead to 3–0, and with a single out, Alvin Dark went to his normally reliable reliever, Jim Todd, who could not record an out and allowed another run. Paul Lindblad came in and, with three errors made behind him, allowed another two runs. Hoping to bring the nightmarish inning to a close, Dark brought Dick into the game. Bosman pitched to Rico Petrocelli and, in short order, got him to pop to shortstop for the third out.

Oakland fared no better in game two at Fenway Park the next day. Vida Blue was knocked from the mound in the fourth inning, and Alvin Dark brought in Rollie Fingers to pitch in the sixth inning. He pitched four innings, allowing three runs. There were many who second-guessed Dark's decision to use Fingers so early in a game where he was already behind, but the fallout accrued to Bosman and his hopes of starting game three.

Oakland was down to Boston, two games to none. There was an offday before game three that would rest the bullpen, and Dick assumed he would start the next day as he sat in front of his locker talking to All-Star outfielder Billy Williams. Mainly Dick was thinking over what he would do the next day. He was not nervous. He was confident he could comport himself in the high-pressure situation, but as he sat visualizing the various Red Sox hitters he had been facing throughout his career and how he would pitch them the next day, he saw pitching coach Wes Stock walking in his direction. He knew exactly what Stock was going to say.

"I don't want to hear it," Dick remembers telling Stock before his pitching coach opened his mouth. "I am pitching tomorrow and that is it."

"No, I'm sorry," Stock said slowly. "Charlie wants to pitch Holtzman."

There was no arguing the final verdict with Stock. Bosman's one chance to shine under the big lights evaporated. There would be no visualizing success on the way to the ballpark and getting ready for the greatest game of his career. He had been able to do it countless times in his career on smaller stages, but he would never get the chance to find out what he could do when all the chips were in the center of the table and he was staring down the opposition. The next day, Holtzman tired in the fifth inning and gave up four runs, three of them earned. Paul Lindblad pitched the final four innings, but Boston starter Rick Wise walked off with the win as Oakland was swept from the playoffs ignominiously.

By the next spring, the Oakland Athletics bore little resemblance to the team from the year before. Chuck Tanner replaced Alvin Dark as manager, and Charlie Finley hired a general manager, Syd Thrift, after years of conducting every transaction himself. He had built the team that way, one clever trade at a time. Bringing in Thrift was an admission that times were changing and he was going to need help.

On April 2, 1976, Finley and Thrift traded Reggie Jackson, Ken Holtzman, and a minor-league player to the Baltimore Orioles for Don Baylor, Mike Torrez, and Paul Mitchell. Bosman remembers coming into the clubhouse after Reggie got the news. It was a trade intended to address the impending free agency of Jackson. Finley could not compete with the richer owners, who not only had deeper pockets, but also greater attendance at the park. Dick recalled seeing the famous outfielder sitting in stunned silence in front of his locker like his best friend had just died.

Even without Reggie and Holtzman, the 1976 Oakland Athletics were a good team. Torrez was an able replacement for Holtzman and slotted into a rotation dominated by two starters, much as it had been in 1975. Blue and Torrez would log 298 and 266 innings, respectively, the same heavy use as the prior year. Paul Mitchell took Dick's place as the third starter, and Bosman became a swingman once again. It was almost a certainty that any new manager would place him in the bullpen and make him pitch his way back into the rotation, wondering how he got guys out with his stuff. But this time it was going to be different.

Dick was healthy and had been since the 1973 season. But his slider had lost some of its sharpness, and his command of the sinker was not quite what it had been. He started 15 games and threw 112 innings, down from 151 innings the year before between Cleveland and Oakland. Part of it was the uncertainty that plagued the team from the beginning with the trade of Jackson. Later in the season, Finley sold Vida Blue, Joe Rudi, and Rollie Fingers to the Yankees and Red Sox for $3.5 million. The wily owner was only trying to recoup the value he knew he would lose in the offseason when they went to new teams via free agency. But Commissioner Bowie Kuhn invoked his privilege to act "in the best interest of baseball" and voided the deals.

The constant turmoil seemed to undermine the consistency and cohesion of the team. The players could no longer unite against Finley, because the owner had taken his game outside their realm of understanding. It was no longer about baseball. It was about the money and the control that it bought. Charlie Finley had lost control.

Bosman enjoyed the camaraderie of the Athletics in 1976. It was still a team lead by Sal Bando and Gene Tenace. He had the same fine catcher in Larry Haney. But the 21-year-old Claudell Washington, who replaced Reggie Jackson, was a tremendous drop-off. Don Baylor had a fine season, but he did more to replace the aging Billy Williams than filling the shoes of Reggie Jackson. Phil Garner installed himself as a full-time second baseman, roomed with Bosman, and became a close friend.

Overall, however, the team sagged. The loss of so many of the fine players that had comprised the championship teams could not be overcome. Oakland played its best baseball in the second half and settled into second place, on the heels of the Kansas City Royals. Dick had several starts that reminded fans of the pitcher he had once been, but he was ineffective out of the bullpen. With the team only a few games behind the Royals in September, Bosman was relegated to the pen exclusively.

The demotion from starting had as much to do with the ineffectiveness of the bullpen as anything else. Neither Paul Lindblad nor Jim Todd were as good as they had been in previous years, but Dick's work in the late innings was not appreciably better than anyone else's. The final standings showed the A's two and one-half games back. There would be no postseason, no chance to make up for being passed over in game three the prior October. Dick believed he had pitched well for most of the year, but the numbers suggested the 32-year-old was losing something off the sinker. He went into the offseason believing he had pitched well enough to have a secure spot with the team for the next year and quickly signed the contract that Charlie Finley sent him in the offseason and concentrated on learning the car business.

He reported the next spring to camp without anything amiss and pitched much as he always had in exhibition games. It was the same slider without quite as much spin, but when he was locating both the sinker and the slider, he still got a lot of people out.

"I remember it exactly. It was March 31. There were only six days until Opening Day. I was the player rep, and there was a meeting of all the reps in Arizona that afternoon," Bosman recalled. Jack McKeon was the new Oakland manager, and late that morning he stuck his head out of his office to say that Charlie was on the phone for Dick. It was unusual for Finley to call, but Dick had no idea what was coming. He went into McKeon's office and took the phone from him.

Said Bosman, "He [Finley] asked me whether I was going to the player rep meeting that afternoon. I said, yeah, I was. He said, 'Well you better get them to elect a new Oakland rep because I'm releasing you.'" Dick was incredulous. He asked Finley how it made sense to release a perfectly healthy pitcher who had logged two good seasons for Oakland, but there was no remorse from the owner, nothing but the harsh bottom line. He asked Finley why he had not traded him, and Finley responded only that "he did not have time." Dick continued to argue with Finley, but the best he got from the owner was a terse, "Good luck."

Bosman could not believe the timing, which was the absolute worst it could be. There was almost no time to hook up with another team. Everyone was making their final roster cuts and getting ready for the season. But Dick knew that Cleveland had several pitchers on the disabled list and needed a starter, so he called Indians manager Frank Robinson and asked whether there was any reason to come down for a tryout. Robinson was quite enthusiastic to have a professional with Dick's reputation available at that point in the year. Dick drove to the Cleveland spring camp in Arizona and pitched a few innings in one of the last exhibition games. He pitched well enough to earn a roster spot, but at the end of the day Phil Seghi, the GM, said they could not sign Bosman because of waiver rules.

At this point Dick knew there was something other than his stuff and his record the previous year at play. Waiver rules were a smoke screen, and Seghi was hiding something. Dick believes to this day that his status as a union rep resulted in him being cut at the last minute. Finley was angry at the new labor arrangements, which gave his players bargaining power they had never had when he built the team. He had been forced to let Catfish Hunter go by the union. The union had beaten the reserve clause and initiated free agency, unshackling the players from years of servitude. Charlie Finley had watched his championship team disintegrate, and the union was the culprit, stealing that talent. He had lost control of the situation, and there was Dick Bosman, union rep, as a momentary stand-in for all that undermined and offended him.

Bosman made one more attempt to catch on with a team. The Chicago Cubs needed a pitcher and offered Dick $25,000 to begin the season with their Wichita affiliate. He had their promise to bring him up in May, when they needed an additional starter. Dick had signed a contract with Oakland in the offseason for $55,000. The cut in pay would be difficult to take both financially and emotionally. It was a slap in the face, and the Cubs could make no guarantee he would be brought up to the big club in May. They needed him, but it was no sure thing. He could spend the entire season pitching in Triple-A. Dick was at the end of his rope and knew it.

He called Frank Howard and spoke to his best friend, who counseled him that a minor-league deal was beneath him. Finally, he spoke to his wife Pam, and she said, "You've got your pride. Come on home." He got in the new Ford he had bought off the lot at Koons Ford of Manassas, Virginia, before going to spring training and hitched a trailer to carry his belongings on the long ride home. It was time for one last cross-country journey.

For this trip, he was all alone with his thoughts. He thought about the other long drives he had made throughout the years, about the all-night drive with Jim French to meet Ted Williams, the trek across the Gulf states to Dallas with Paul Lindblad at the height of the 1972 strike. Finally, he thought about that first drive with his dad when they went to Kingsport, Tennessee, for his first camp. At the end of the afternoon, he was heading across Tennessee and saw Kingsport on the map he had stretched out on the front seat beside him. That little Appalachian city was where it had all started 15 years earlier with the Pirates.

He got off the interstate and found the old ball field. There was no one there, and Bosman parked outside in the lonely parking lot before walking into the stadium complex. He went onto the field and thought about the years that had passed since he had been a kid playing his first spring with nothing but hope and optimism. Little had changed. Dick still believed in his talent, but he said good-bye to baseball right where it had all started and drove back to Virginia and his family.

"It was hard," he admitted, remembering how painful it was. Forty years later, there is still a deep reservoir of emotion in his voice when he speaks about the end of his career. He had been working in the parts department of Koons Ford during the offseason before reporting to camp in February. Now he was going to be working at Koons as a full-time employee. He enjoyed the work, but there had always been baseball to give him a lift above the workaday world, something in the back of his mind that took him out of the eight-hour work day. When he drove in for his first day as a full-time guy at Koons, it was a tough trip. The baseball season would no longer be there to sweeten the pot.

Bosman started in inventory and learned how to track every car on the lot. He worked in parts. He sold used cars; he sold new cars. He did it all. He came to work early and left late because he still had the fever, still had something he wanted to forget.

"It took me two years to get over it," Dick claimed, but the emotion in his voice says that part of him will never be able to understand why baseball left him, or maybe he understands why but cannot reconcile that the sport treated him as shabbily as it did. It was a marriage, and he gave everything he had to it and still she left him, without even leaving a note.

In the first few days back on the job at Koons, Bosman was angry enough to call the local sportswriters, offering them a scoop. "Angry Bosman Quits Baseball," was the headline of Tom Boswell's column after a long conversation with Dick.[4] "I'm tired of it and fed up," Bosman told Boswell, adding, "I've lost my heart for the game, so I quit." It was a startling revelation for a man who had loved the game so patiently and with such devotion. He recounted to Boswell the furious attempts to catch on with other teams, the long phone calls to every team with any hope of needing a 33-year-old pitcher.

In his column, Boswell framed the dilemma as that of the typical ballplayer in the late 1970s, when the economic squeeze was catching players like Bosman, whose salary demands had been crafted during a long career but who could be replaced by younger players who would work for less. It was a problem facing more than baseball workers. Boswell articulated the idea that Bosman had been targeted by Finley because he was the player rep. But Boswell could not substantiate the claim and gave it mere polite mention. It did not get the play Dick wanted.

Bosman spoke to Boswell and other sportswriters about the long years of sacrifice for the game, of the 10 cortisone shots he had taken in 1973, just so he could go back out on the mound and keep his career going. He talked about the hardships he and his family had endured for the game, how his wife had given birth while he was on the road playing in Kansas City. Dick was called off the field that day and told that his second daughter, Dina (Nadine) had been born earlier in the day. Then he told Boswell how Pam had surgery just a few weeks earlier without telling Dick because she "wanted me to have a good spring training."

> Dick has confidence that his extensive experience in the game is what allows him to take a young pitcher and make the mechanical adjustments to improve his delivery until it hums with something nearing perfection. Dick can give a young pitcher the necessary pitches to address the daunting demands of the modern game.

Dick ended the interview, explaining to Boswell that he had to take his oldest daughter Michelle to kindergarten. He was a family man now. Sure, he had been a major-league pitcher for 11 seasons, giving everything he had to offer to the game and then some. Now he was moving on, putting it in the past. He said he would not dwell on how badly the game had treated him, how she had walked into the night with hardly a word of explanation. Dick Bosman knew he deserved better, even from Charlie Finley.

II

TEACHING THE
ART OF PITCHING

7

Learning to Teach

Dick was not expecting a phone call from anyone asking him to pitch in the majors. He knew those days were done. But it was a difficult transition. Every day of his life, from the moment he had walked off that high school stage in Kenosha with his diploma in hand until he got the phone call from Charlie Finley, had been about baseball. Even during the winters when he was driving a dragster or a snowmobile, baseball was still what it was all about. Now there was just the long commute from his home in Woodbridge to Tysons Corner. There was nothing except fighting the dog-eat-dog traffic of Northern Virginia.

He had a wife and two daughters, who consumed much of his time. His wife's understanding of how difficult the change was for him was essential in allowing him to find himself in this new phase of his life. The other influence that eased Bosman into his new life was John Koons, his new boss. He was actually John Koons Jr., the second in what would become a long family tradition of automobile dealers in the Washington metropolitan area. Koons's father had begun the business, but the son had expanded it into the megadealership it was when they welcomed Dick Bosman aboard in 1977.

John Koons Jr. was a good athlete, and he loved sports. The Washington Redskins were the major professional sports presence in the area, and the teams of the 1970s were involved with the Koons dealerships. Quarterback Billy Kilmer and safety Jake Scott were at different dealerships. Coach Joe

Gibbs would join this group later, but they were all part of the corporate presence that the Koons family created in an area that spanned from Annapolis,
Maryland, to Manassas, Virginia.

Passing the business from generation to generation was only part of being
a member of the Koons family. It was also the sports. John Koons's son was
a 10-year-old just starting Little League when Dick Bosman began reporting
to the Leasing Division of JKJ Chevrolet. Dick was selling fleets of cars and
trucks to such federal agencies as the Forestry Service. His clients included the
Virginia State Highway Patrol and huge private development firms that bull-
dozed land and needed trucks of all sizes to accomplish that task. The men he
worked alongside worked long hours selling and working on cars.

"With all respect," Dick recalled. "Those guys did not understand the life
of baseball. They could not relate to my life in the game, so I had to adapt to
them. It took a couple of years to totally leave being a player behind."[1] But not
long after starting with Koons, a door opened that would provide an important early outlet for Bosman, one that did much to help with his conversion
from baseball professional to automobile leasing agent.

John Koons ran the Chevrolet dealership and the larger operation, which
was centered in Tysons Corner, Virginia. He asked Dick if he might help out
with the Little League team Koons managed and for which his son played. It
was a moment much like when Dick asked his father if he could try out for
Little League in Kenosha. The answer was already known, but it had to be
asked. It was as much the asking as the answer that set Dick Bosman back on
the road to the majors.

Dick agreed and went to see the young Koons play ball. Johnny Koons was
a good athlete, and there were other fine-looking young ballplayers on the
field as well. Bosman was hooked the
moment he set foot back on a playing field and began to take a growing
interest not only in the boy and his
potential, but also the other kids.
As important as organized sports
can be for the maturation of young
boys, there was another transformation taking place during that Little
League season in Northern Virginia, one in which Dick Bosman the major-
league ballplayer grew into a teacher and coach.

> Dick learned early in his teaching
> career that the "lessons that
> stick are the ones learned when
> something doesn't work, when
> the right pitch in the wrong
> situation leaves the park in a
> hurry."

There was no lack of talent in the affluent suburbs south of the Potomac River in Virginia, and the Koons family was used to being the best at everything they did. There were plenty of kids dreaming that old dream of pitching in the big leagues, and the ability to work with a former major leaguer drew the best talent to the team. As in Kenosha, the talent fed upward in a steady stream from Little League to Babe Ruth League to high school. John Koons Jr.'s teams and players became consistent winners in the Northern Virginia region, first in Little League, and then, as they grew older and progressed, they were the best talent in the Babe Ruth League and then in high school.

For Bosman, it was a chance to add something to his day that went beyond the car business. He was out from behind a desk and on a baseball field again, even if the dimensions of the field were notably smaller and the bleachers less grandly appointed than those to which he had become accustomed. But it was more than that. Bosman enjoyed working with the young guys and saw in them the boys with whom he once had shared a similar experience. They wanted to play the game, and Dick empathized with them on that level whether they had a lot of talent or just a little. He got to know them whether or not they had the talent to make the next jump. He got to know the parents, and he had Paul Tretiak to thank for showing him how important it was to reach out to the entire family. "I saw that I could have an impact on their lives on and off the field," Dick said looking back on that time fondly.

But ultimately it came back to a small group of guys with whom he shared much of the experience. "His kid [Koons]—John the third—and the other kids that survived, played with us for nine years," Bosman said. "That's a long time. They went with us from Little League all the way through high school and American Legion ball." There were some pretty talented players in the mix, some of whom went on to play Division I college baseball and a few that even signed professional contracts.

There was John Morabito, an infielder, who went on to play in college and briefly as a professional. "John was as good a natural athlete as you want to come across," according to Dick. After a college career at Wake Forest, he signed with the White Sox. Chris Shebby was a pitcher with whom Dick worked during those years who went on to pitch at Georgetown University. He signed with the Orioles after college. Dick remains in contact with Shebby, Morabito, and John Koons III to this day.

Shebby remembers the first day he met Dick Bosman vividly. It was June 1978, and Shebby was 12 years old. His McLean, Virginia, Little League season was over, and the league All-Stars—an aggregation of the best players from Little League—had gathered for instruction from the coaching staff, which included Dick Bosman. Said Shebby, "He was pitching batting practice to us. I remember thinking, I am going to have to go up and hit against a big-league pitcher. I still remember that feeling, sitting on the bench waiting for my turn at bat, thinking, gosh, I hope I do okay."[2] Shebby was one of a group of boys who lived in proximity to Johnny Koons III and marched up the ladder from Little League to high school baseball. Dick was involved with them all.

But there was one experience that formed Shebby more than any other. The American Legion experience was the first where he began to get some idea of what a professional baseball career might feel like. Shebby related,

> You played four times a week, which at the time was a lot for amateur ball. And the way the rotation was crafted, each pitcher took his turn on the fifth day. It was as close to a professional simulation as you could get. When I was 16 years old, I remember totaling up all the innings I had thrown in high school and in American Legion Baseball, and I had thrown about 140 innings. It was 60 to 70 games. The same as you might play in short-season A-ball. I remember Dick saying, "That's a pretty decent minor-league season."[3]

The kids were experiencing their baseball season much as they would professional baseball, and Bosman was beginning to see it in much the same way. "It isn't any different than what I am doing today," Bosman said, comparing his status with the Tampa Bay Rays as minor-league roving pitching instructor to coaching guys who were playing baseball in high school almost as much as those he teaches today. The job is much the same. "I know that because I have pitched in the majors, I have a foot in the door. But you had to make that connection. You had to sell them on what you were doing, and then you had an audience." Bosman was taking his first steps as a pitching coach. It was the

> Dick teaches much the same today in the Tampa Bay Rays organization as he did with high school players in Northern Virginia. It is about gaining the confidence of young pitchers so they hear his advice and want to use it in their approach to throwing.

beginning of an extended apprenticeship in teaching how to throw a baseball successfully.

Many coaches, successful or otherwise, did not put in the years learning to teach as Dick did, with young guys from every age group. Yet, Bosman believes it made him a better teacher, one who would later stand out from other former players trying to impart their knowledge of the game to others.

"They were gifted athletes who wanted to play," Dick remembered of the athletes he first began to coach in Northern Virginia, continuing,

> When I say that, I mean they put in the work. And we won plenty of regional championships with those guys. John Koons Jr. gained a reputation as the George Steinbrenner of Northern Virginia. Working in leasing gave me flexible hours so that there were some days when I did not even go to work. I just spent the day at the ballpark, and I was fine with that.

Dick remembers the first February reporting date for spring training, when he was sitting in traffic instead of jumping into a car to drive to Florida. His family and the increasing time he was spending with them—those from Virginia and those who came from Wisconsin—made a huge difference for him. Pam Bosman's parents were an important source of support as well. They had a home with a view of the Chesapeake Bay in Mill Creek, Maryland.

Dick's parents came from Wisconsin and sometimes his sisters. Dick and his father spent months putting in a swimming pool in the Bosman's back-yard for his children. There was never an idle minute, whether it was his new career or life with the family. His life engulfed him, and slowly he quit thinking about what was happening in the major leagues.

As the young players with whom he was working neared high school graduation, Dick began to make contacts with collegiate baseball coaches who were interested in his best talent. Ken Kelly, coach of the Georgetown University baseball program, asked Dick to help him coach the pitching staff at Georgetown. It was not only the players who were moving on to new levels of play, but also Dick was taking his coaching game to the next level, seeing exactly what the young guys he was tutoring could do with his approach to the game.

After several years of coaching, Bosman was working with a wide variety of young prospects from O'Connell High School to local colleges. In the midst of it, in 1984, Tom Seaver and Lee Lowenfish published the book *The Art of Pitching*. Said Bosman,

> I am an amateur coach, wondering how to do this. . . . I've put together a lot of ideas on what's right and what's wrong about how you teach mechanics and how you teach different pitches. I used to cut out pictures of pitchers and the different parts of their delivery from *Sports Illustrated* and various publications. I would paste them onto pages that I kept in a three-ring binder, different poses in the windup, different phases of delivery.

He supplemented the photographs with notes about where pitchers needed to be at different points in their delivery.

With this approach, Bosman was able to tell the young guys with whom he worked, "Look at Nolan Ryan; look at Tom Seaver; look at Jim Palmer; look at his delivery right here. In other words, I did not just dream this stuff up. I told the fellows, this is what the good guys do," and he backed it up with illustrations from his book showing pitching sequences with photographs of many of the great arms of his day. "That's how he taught mechanics," remembered Chris Shebby of the notebook. "I looked through that book many times. He used the notebook for his winter pitching clinics at George Mason University, as well as at other locations around Northern Virginia."[4]

Dick does not remember how he first heard about the Seaver book, just his excitement when he took it home and began reading it for the first time. "I'm reading, and I'm reading, and the birds are singing," Dick recalled. He read it long into the night and said to his wife beside him, "I am right. What I have been teaching is correct." He was elated to learn he had been on the right track all along. The notebook of photographs and instructional remarks was not vastly different than the much more polished and elaborate book by Seaver. The first thing that the Seaver book provided Bosman was corroboration that what he had been telling his pupils was in line with the best ideas in the business. His methods were being employed

> Bosman urged his young charges to learn from the best: "Look at Nolan Ryan; look at Tom Seaver; look at Jim Palmer. Look at his delivery right here." Bosman used a notebook filled with photographs of the best pitchers of the day to illustrate the best in pitching mechanics.

by Seaver and Lowenfish. "Did I learn things from it? Absolutely, but it reinforced a lot of what I had been doing already," he said.

There was one point in the Seaver book that did not translate. Seaver was a "drop and drive" pitcher whose motion was low to the ground, as he used his lower body and legs to generate as much thrust toward the plate as possible. All pitchers push off the pitching rubber with their lower body, but Seaver's approach was an extreme example, one where the pitcher kept his lower half close to the ground. It generated more push off from the pitching rubber but was a difficult motion to master.

"There are not too many guys walking around today that can do that correctly," according to Bosman. Seaver used a knee pad to cushion his back leg, which often scraped along the front side of the pitcher's mound as he completed his delivery. It is not until late in *The Art of Pitching* that Seaver provides a sequence of photos to capture his delivery. He does use Mario Soto, who has a delivery similar to his own, but from the beginning he provides examples of clearly different approaches to his own, for example, those of Steve Carlton and Steve Rogers, who are much more over the top in their delivery.

This other delivery is far more common in the game today. Bosman describes the Carlton and Rogers approach as "tall and fall." It was the method Bosman taught most effectively. "The difficulty with Seaver's motion is the inability to get back on top of the ball as the pitcher finishes his motion. Most guys have a tendency to get under the ball because they drop too far on that back leg and they can never get over the top of the ball."

Dick's three-ring binder did not have the level of sophistication that Seaver's book provided. He keeps a copy of *The Art of Pitching* to this day to help him with young pitchers in the Tampa Bay Rays organization. For Bosman, Seaver's book was "huge." He had been an apprentice pitching coach working with young players in Northern Virginia, but now he knew he had been providing sound teaching fundamentals to his players all along. But there was more to come in the Seaver story.

"Little did I know that less than two years later I would be standing in the dugout in Chicago with that man on the mound and I'm his pitching coach," Bosman remembered. When Dick finally worked his way back to the majors as a pitching coach in the White Sox organization, Tom Seaver was in his final year as a big-league pitcher. It was at the Chicago White Sox spring training camp in 1986 when Dick was officially made the Triple-A pitching

coach for their Buffalo affiliate. He watched everything Seaver did that spring
to prepare. "He had won 300 games at that point, and now I am his pitching
coach," Bosman stated. "All you can do is show him the respect of asking,
'What can I do for *you?*' Are there certain things that happen as a game goes
on that I need to be mindful of? If something goes awry, what is it and how
do I relate that to you?"

Before Bosman joined Seaver and the White Sox, there was one last gambit
left in Northern Virginia. The huge success Bosman had seen in developing
talent attracted the attention of one of the premier high school programs in
Northern Virginia. Flint Hill Academy was one of the best private schools in
the area. They were building a new school on a handsome tract of land front-
ing on Courthouse Road near an interchange with Interstate 66. The address
was significantly closer to Woodbridge than Tysons Corner and the Koons
dealership, which was appealing to Bosman.

Flint Hill Academy intended to build a sparkling new athletic complex as
part of their new school building. Like new, modern athletic complexes at the
collegiate level, it was designed with the hope that it would attract the best
talent in the area and regionally. They already had one of the best basketball
programs in the country, led by legendary coach Stu Vetter, and they wanted
Dick to build a similar program focusing on high school baseball. Dick provided comments on the drawings for the new baseball field and surroundings,
and after the administrators at Flint Hill agreed that he could use the field to
run baseball camps during the summer, much as Vetter did with basketball,
Dick signed a contract with them.

Ironically, just days after signing on with Flint Hill Academy and starting on a career path that was a natural extension of what he had been doing,
Dick read in the press that Ken "Hawk" Harrelson had been named the new
general manager of the Chicago White Sox, replacing Roland Hemond. Hemond's White Sox had won the Western Division of the American League
in 1983, but slipped badly in the two subsequent seasons, leading to his
dismissal. Bosman knew Harrelson from their years together playing for the
Senators. The article stated that Harrelson was hiring Alvin Dark to run the
White Sox minor-league organization.

"Al was like a father to Harrelson," Dick remembered of the skipper who
oversaw Bosman's best season with the Oakland Athletics. The next day,

Bosman was cutting the grass in Woodbridge, thinking only of the Flint Hill position and what he would do there to carve out a reputation to rival Stu Vetter's. He went into the house and called the office to see if there were any messages and found one from Alvin Dark. Dick knew immediately what Dark wanted. He assumed it would be an offer of a position at some low-level farm club as pitching coach making less money than he would make at Flint Hill. "So I called him," Dick recalled. "He said 'Bozie, Syd Thrift has recommended you to be one of our pitching coaches.'" Next, he heard from Thrift himself.

Dick had become close friends with Thrift, who had been the director of scouting for the Pittsburgh Pirates when Bosman signed his first contract. Thrift was originally from the Northern Virginia area and returned there after ending his relationship with Charlie Finley. After the Pirates, Thrift had gone on to work with the Kansas City Royals when that franchise was founded and came to the Oakland Athletics in 1975, as a fledgling general manager at the same time Bosman came over from Cleveland. Thrift was fired by Finley in the spring of 1977, at much the same time as Bosman. It was with Thrift that Dick negotiated his first contract with the Athletics.

When Thrift returned to the Northern Virginia area, he began a real estate business with his wife Dolly. Bosman and Thrift's paths had crossed with some frequency, but perhaps the most important facet of their relationship began when Bosman began to work with Thrift's son Jim, who was playing on the same teams in Northern Virginia with Johnny Koons III. Said Bosman, "He [Thrift] was a pretty darn good high school player. I threw him countless hours of batting practice." From Dick's relationship with his son, Thrift learned how well Bosman connected with young guys learning the game. Thrift and Bosman also spent countless hours talking baseball during their years together in Northern Virginia.

Thrift even sold the Bosman's house in Woodbridge when Dick briefly explored a return to Wisconsin. More than any other connection, it was the relationship with Thrift that got Bosman back into baseball. When Dark was named to oversee the White Sox farm system, Thrift called his old friend to congratulate him on his new post. Dark asked Thrift if he had any suggestions on how to staff the White Sox minor-league system. He brought up their mutual friend Dick Bosman. When Bosman spoke to Dark about the possibilities with Chicago, Dark told him it was Thrift's recommendation that had won him and Harrelson over.

"We want you to come over and help us rebuild this organization," Bosman remembered Dark saying, but there was no specific offer made, only a promise that Harrelson would call with the numbers. The idea of working with Dark again was appealing, but when Harrelson called and offered $45,000 and all expenses paid, suddenly there was real momentum behind the offer to return to professional baseball.

Despite the size and appeal of the offer, Dick was not convinced it was the right move. He had signed a contract with Flint Hill Academy to be their head baseball coach, and Dick liked the idea of continuing to work at that level close to home. That job had all of the appeal that the Yellow Transit Freight Lines had once posed for his father. There was considerable security attached to it, and Dick liked watching his children grow. His daughter Michelle was 13, and her younger sister Nadine (Dina) was nine. They would be grown in a few years, and the idea of missing any of those final years was troubling.

As he weighed the offer, he spoke to Eddie Brinkman, who was with the White Sox as their major-league infield coach. Brinkman told his old teammate, "The one thing you can be certain of in coaching at the professional level is that you will be fired." It was not exactly a convincing recommendation.

Part of Harrelson's rationale for hiring Dick was his belief that former major-league players, or more accurately those who had succeeded at the highest levels, were better teachers than those that the White Sox employed at the time. The current staff had many lifelong employees whose careers consisted of more time on the minor-league side than successful runs in the majors. Hired along with Dick were Dick Allen, Jose Cardenal, and Rico Petrocelli, guys who, as Harrelson said, "could go into our minor-league system and teach these guys how to win."

But it was more than that. Harrelson said of Bosman years later, "Bozie impressed me when we played together, and he impressed me when we played against one another."[5] What caught Harrelson's eye was Bosman's ability to get the "Hawk" out. Harrelson had a .120 batting average when he faced Bosman in the late 1960s and early 1970s. Harrelson managed one home run off Bosman but struck out four times. Just as important, Hawk believed Dick had been a good teammate, one who protected his hitters by pitching inside against the opposition when needed. Harrelson said, "I knew what kind of guy he [Bosman] was and that he had the ingredients to be a good pitching coach."[6]

Initially, Dick only promised to consider the offer. He informed Harrelson that he was coming to Kenosha for a wedding and that he would drive to Chicago to meet with him at Comiskey Park to give him an answer. Harrelson was fine with that arrangement. As Bosman talked about their future with his wife Pam, she was the surprising advocate for him taking the position with the White Sox. "I don't think I am going to do this," he told her at one point. Her response was telling: "Well, you signed a major-league contract and ended up playing 11 years. . . . Now you have somebody that wants you to come back and coach, and you know that you're really a better coach than you ever were a player."[7]

Bosman's wife knew she was arguing against her own self-interest. Their two girls were nearing adolescence, which would only increase their demands on her time and emotions. Life without Dick close at hand could only be more difficult. She knew, however, that she had an extended circle of support from the many friends she and Dick had generated during their time in the Northern Virginia suburbs. She also knew how much her husband missed baseball at the highest levels and how much the game meant to him.

"It was hard," Dick said of the decision. There were many former big-league pitchers for whom coaching was not appealing. Hall of Famer Robin Roberts said when he was offered a job as the pitching coach for the Chicago Cubs in 1966, "I could stand the travel and being away from my family, but not to coach."[8] The words were hardly an endorsement of coaching. Roberts had an obvious change of heart in later years, as he coached the University of South Florida baseball team for nine seasons. For Bosman, the idea of teaching his craft to others, and doing so at the major-league level, justified the hardship of traveling with a team and spending weeks away from his family. Pam Bosman's read of her husband was an accurate one: Dick Bosman wanted back in, and he was fortunate enough to have a wife who supported the idea.

Dick had formed an almost-filial bond with young players like John Morabito and Chris Shebby, many of whom took Dick out for dinner in Georgetown after he announced his decision to join the White Sox. The connections he had made with such fine young men made him believe he could relate in a similar way to young professional pitchers, much the way Sid Hudson had formed a bond with Dick. The job with the White Sox gave Bosman a chance to mentor young pitchers, to help those who had the talent and desire to make the jump to the big leagues. Moreover, it was a chance for Dick to pay it forward, to pass his knowledge of the game to a new generation. The Chicago White Sox gained a new minor-league pitching instructor, and Dick Bosman was back in professional baseball to stay.

Ken Harrelson's position with the White Sox was a curious one at the time. He had been the television announcer for the White Sox since 1981, coming over from the Red Sox, who made him their announcer in 1975, when his brief dalliance with a career on the Professional Golfers' Association (PGA) tour fizzled famously. The biography of Harrelson for the Society for American Baseball Research by Alexander Edelman notes that Hawk was a "shrewd businessman and colorful hustler."[9] It is the latter part of that description that expresses more of how Harrelson talked his way into becoming GM in Chicago.

"Hawk" had been hustling his entire life. He was raised by a single mom who earned only $65 per week, so he knew the value of a dollar. But how he was able to convince Chicago White Sox owner Jerry Reinsdorf to fire a solid baseball man in Roland Hemond and hire the announcer to run the show remains a mystery. Bosman speculates that the conversations between Reinsdorf and Harrelson, "had to be over a heck of a lot of drinks up in the Bard's Room," which was where the baseball men in the front office went after the game. Whatever magic Harrelson worked, it was a brief fling that lasted only a year but had enormous consequence for Dick Bosman.

The first move that Harrelson tried after being hired by Reinsdorf was the firing of pitching coach Dave Duncan. "But [Tony] La Russa would not hear of it," according to Dick. Whatever Harrelson's reasons for wanting Duncan gone, Dick considered Dave a friend and thought it sensible to call him to ask about the environment in Chicago. Bosman did not know that Harrelson had tried to fire Duncan. Dick was puzzled when he got an icy reception, but it was a natural response from a man who had heard Bosman was gunning for his job. There was a war brewing in the Chicago clubhouse, and Dick had stepped into the middle of it.

Bosman did not learn much from Duncan, but as he headed out into his newest career with a major-league organization, his old teammate Eddie

Brinkman's words proved invaluable as he prepared to step into the fray. The words were from the inside, from someone who had been a coach after his big-league career ended and a friend of Bosman's from their many years together in Washington. Brinkman's words guided Dick's actions from day one and are essential to his work.

"You gotta remember how damn tough it was when *you* were in the minor leagues trying to get to the big leagues," he remembers Brinkman saying. "And if you remember how tough it was, then you will have empathy for those young men that you are going to work with," Brinkman said. "And I have lived by that," Dick asserted.

Dick reported to the Chicago spring training camp that season to find that there were two factions aligned like a rugby scrum, each group eyeing the other angrily and warily, waiting for someone to make a move. There was Tony La Russa, Dave Duncan, Deron Johnson, Doug Rader, Artie Kusnyer, and Eddie Brinkman—Roland Hemond's guys—on the one side, and Dick Bosman, Rico Petrocelli, Dick Allen, and Jose Cardenal—the Harrelson guys—on the other. "It wasn't a very comfortable spring training," Dick recalled. The other faction was working at the major-league level, and the new guys were assigned to the minor leaguers. But La Russa and his cohorts believed that was intended to be a temporary solution, or at least one that would last only as long as the White Sox were winning games in the upcoming season.

Bosman needed the help of many of the long-standing members of the Chicago organization to learn the minor-league talent with whom he would be working. Who were they? Where were they headed? How much did the team believe in them, and what did he need to do with them to help them succeed? It was basic information, and he needed to hear from those who had been working in the organization far longer than he had. More importantly, he needed the help of men over whom he had leapfrogged in the hierarchy.

His manager at Buffalo was going to be Jim Marshall, who had played five years in the majors with five teams. "He helped me tremendously," Bosman remembered of those days when he reported to Ed Smith Stadium, where the minor-league players practiced that spring. The major league players remained at Payne Park in downtown Sarasota. "I was blessed with an ability to teach, but my organizational skills were pretty rough. I did not know how to set up a minor-league pitching rotation. I had never put together a workout schedule. I had never done that," Dick admitted. Two long-serving members of the Chicago minor-league staff, Chuck Hartenstein and Buzz Capra, stepped forward to help.

"These guys could have ostracized me," Dick said, thinking back on a pivotal point in his nascent coaching career. "Those guys were pitching coaches in the lower levels, and here I am, the guy going to Buffalo, and they have to be thinking 'why don't we get a chance at that?'" Instead, they both helped Dick learn how to do what needed to be done to get the minor-league rosters set and the young guys ready for the upcoming season. "I am really indebted to those two guys for helping me get on the way," Bosman added.

One thing that helped was Bosman's unpretentious approach to teaching. From day one when he stepped in for the first bullpen session, he put on the catcher's gear and began catching his young pitchers. Some of the pitching coaches were taken aback by this method, but for Bosman it was a key part of getting an up-close look at what the guys were throwing. "What better way is there to create a relationship; what better way is there to evaluate; what better way is there to teach?" Dick related. It was the method Sid Hudson had used with Bosman from the very first day when he wanted to know how and what Bosman threw. Wes Stock had done it as well in Oakland. It was effective, and it worked. That was all that mattered to Bosman.

Dick left Sarasota firmly entrenched as the Buffalo pitching coach, and along with Jim Marshall and the Triple-A roster they departed the warmth of Florida for upstate New York. Dick had never been fond of Buffalo from his time doing a rehab assignment there in his early days with the Senators. But the first day after arriving in the city, he awoke in his hotel room next to the Peace Bridge to see icebergs floating down the Niagara River toward the falls. War Memorial Stadium in Buffalo was known as the "Rock Pile." On Opening Day, there were 30,000 fans, but it was cold—ice cold. "You put on every bit of clothes you could find to stay warm out there." But the Rich family, which owned the team, was as warm as anyone could

One of the trademarks of Dick Bosman's coaching techniques was putting on the catcher's gear and watching what young hurlers threw into the mitt. There is no better way to get a close-up look at what a pitcher is throwing, and it is a positive way to build a relationship with young pitchers.

have been to Bosman, and they eased the time Bosman spent in Buffalo, as did everyone involved with the team.

The best pitcher Bosman may have worked with during this first stint as a pitching coach with the organization was Joe Cowley. He got sent down after being hit hard in his only April start with the White Sox. He was a tall, right-handed pitcher with "great stuff, but he was all over the place," according to Dick. Cowley was already trying to catch on with his third major-league club at age 27. After five starts with Buffalo, he was back in Chicago, where he would log 162 innings and pitch to a 3.88 ERA.

"We had some other guys that went up and did some good things," Bosman recalled, but the White Sox were struggling overall. In early June, Harrelson came to Buffalo, ostensibly to evaluate the team's number-one draft choice, Joel McKeon. During the new GM's visit, he told Bosman that the real reason he was there was to tell Dick, "I'm getting ready to make a move." Harrelson asked Dick the key question: "Are you ready to come to the big leagues?"

Despite the drama of spring training, Dick was still surprised that he was being summoned to become a major-league pitching coach so quickly. But he told Harrelson, "Wherever you want me to go, I will go." Harrelson told Dick, "Don't send out your laundry."

In Chicago, things were not going well. The team was a dozen games under .500, and a week after Harrelson left Buffalo he fired La Russa, who took his pitching coach, Dave Duncan, with him. The night before the firings were announced in the press, Bosman had been drinking beer with Jim Fregosi in the War Memorial Stadium lounge. Fregosi's Louisville club was in Buffalo for a series, and it was 2:00 a.m. the next morning when Harrelson called to tell Dick he had fired La Russa and Duncan. Doug Rader was named the interim manager, but Harrelson wanted Dick in Chicago for the game the next night. Jim Marshall drove Bosman to the airport, and his parting words were, "Keep doing it the way you're doing it."

He walked into the Chicago clubhouse on the afternoon of June 20, and was greeted by the remainder of the contingent that had aligned against him in Sarasota. Doug Rader, Artie Kusnyer, Deron Johnson, and his old friend Eddie Brinkman were still there. There wasn't room for any recrimination, although Dick was certain that if they knew how few real credentials he had for the position he was taking, they might have been a little more hostile. But everyone was civil, and the only question Bosman asked Rader was, "Who's pitching tonight." Rader's response was, "Tom Seaver."

Jim Fregosi was named the new manager two nights later, and Bosman was comfortable with that since the two men had been talking about the situation only a few nights earlier. Yet, as important as those kinds of friendships and relationships were, as key as the connections he had made with Syd Thrift proved to be, something else was more essential to Bosman's success as a coach. It was putting on the catcher's gear and working with kids for nine years that made Dick Bosman a good teacher of the game. Jim Marshall in Buffalo and the others who watched Bosman in the spring of 1986 could see that he built constructive bridges with young pitchers on the Chicago staff.

Bosman incorporated Seaver's methods with his own, and the result was better than what a book could teach. Dick wove "empathy" and thoughtful analysis into teaching the art of pitching. He understood the desire of the young pitchers in a most visceral way, but he also knew the long days of hard work, the endless repetition that it took to get where they wanted to be. He knew he could work with young pitchers, that he could help them take the next step if they were willing to put in the long hours of hard work.

But standing in the dugout at Comiskey Park on a Friday night in June, watching one of the greatest hurlers of his generation finishing out his career, Dick believed he could add value to the efforts of even the best that had ever climbed a pitching mound. It was a long way between Northern Virginia and Comiskey Park, but Dick Bosman was back, and it was like this was where he had belonged from the start.

8

Slide Step

Ken Harrelson, the new vice president of baseball operations for the White Sox, was impressed with Jim Fregosi's record in the minors and told *Sporting News* after he announced Fregosi's hiring, "He's one of those diamonds in the rough."[1] The newly hired Fregosi told the press he would evaluate the team as quickly as possible and emphasize whatever strength he found, whether it was speed or power. There was, in fact, little of either commodity, as the White Sox were the worst offensive club in the American League in 1986, scoring fewer runs than any other team.

Dick Bosman's plan with the Chicago pitching staff was to do what he and Jim Marshall—his manager in Buffalo—agreed was the best approach. "I decided I had to be myself," Dick said in looking back at his first coaching job in the major leagues. He intended to continue catching the bullpen sessions of his pitchers, putting on the gear so he could "see how the ball was spinning." He continued, "I think I can develop a close relationship with my pitchers if I do this."[2] In a sense, Bosman was getting down on their level, but he did not believe that the job of a pitching coach was to become friends with his pitchers, "to take them golfing or go out drinking with them."[3] Bosman wanted a certain distance that he hoped would build respect.

"There are guys that do that," Bosman said of pitching coaches who develop a closer relationship with their pitching staff. "Maybe it works for them, but I think there is a certain distance you have to maintain with guys on a professional level." The concern for Bosman was the potential for disciplinary issues, which he was hoping would not spring up. But if they did, a professional basis for a relationship with the pitchers on his staff would make discipline easier to maintain.

There was an additional problem with the White Sox, and that was the deep respect the team felt for Dave Duncan. Dick understood the regard that his players had for Duncan. He and Duncan had been teammates in Cleveland, and Dick described the well-regarded pitching coach as a friend before he replaced him in Chicago. Dick wanted to build on what Duncan was doing, and the first step in that process was to establish a personal connection with each player. He began his tenure as pitching coach by talking to each pitcher individually, asking them what they wanted to do on the mound and what they needed him to talk to them about when they were having trouble. Only when Bosman understood the mechanical or other failings that plagued a pitcher in his worst moments in a game could he begin to suggest improvements.

"I did not want to come in there like a hurricane," Dick remembered. He knew he could not recommend wholesale changes. "I've seen guys do that, and it never works. It never, ever works," he declared.

Rich Dotson was ostensibly the ace of the starting rotation, having won 22 games in 1984. He had also led the American League in walks that season, a statistic that would have been anathema to Ted Williams and probably most managers.

> Dick believes in the process of assessing the mechanics of each pitcher and working with the individual based on his unique approach rather than asking pitchers to conform to one overarching ideal of how to pitch.

Dotson had encountered unique pitching difficulties when his right pectoral muscle had become enlarged to the point that it shut off the blood flow to his arm. Dotson lost feeling in his arm the further he went into a ballgame. Surgery had been required to correct the condition, serious surgery with no guarantees as to how it might affect his pitching. There was some loss of velocity on his fastball after the procedure, but he was able to return to the mound and regain effectiveness.

Knowing that Dotson had lost something off his fastball, "I wanted to teach him a slider," Dick recounted from his early days with the moundsman. "He was a curveball, changeup, fastball guy who threw straight over the top. He had a pretty good changeup." Dotson is currently a pitching coach with the Charlotte Knights, the Triple-A affiliate of the White Sox. He incorporated Bosman's approach to throwing a slider not only as a pitcher with Chicago that season, but also as part of his coaching repertoire. In 1986, the slider provided Dotson with another breaking ball to throw. "His curveball had lost some of the bite it once had," Bosman said in considering the pitcher's existing arsenal of pitches. With a slider, Dotson showed some improvement in the second half of the 1986 season.

Floyd Bannister was the 31-year-old veteran presence on the staff, although he had walked 100 batters in 1985 as well. "He would strike out 200 guys every year, but he couldn't work deep into ballgames," Dick recounted. Bannister's pitch count elevated throughout the course of five or six innings because he could not consistently throw strikes. He was striking batters out but too often walking the more patient hitters. "He was tapped out by the seventh inning, sometimes the fifth or sixth." Bullpens then seldom had the depth they have developed during past few decades, and in 1986, the White Sox had particular problems in that area, so Fregosi and Bosman needed Bannister to work deeper into the ballgame.

"He was a four-seam fastball, curveball pitcher," according to Bosman. He had learned to throw a two-seam fastball that was more of a sinker, and both Fregosi and Bosman urged Bannister to use the pitch more often to induce contact rather than looking for the strikeout. It was a basic lesson that Sid Hudson had taught Bosman in the minor leagues, but here he was teaching the "worm-burner" philosophy in the majors. Bannister embraced the idea, which was not a foregone conclusion for a veteran who was used to missing bats. But he had success with the new approach. In 1987, Bannister's strikeout-to-walk ratio returned to that of his All-Star season as a 27-year-old, when he led the American League with 207 punch-outs.

Ken Harrelson attempted to improve the pitching staff by trading young White Sox prospect Bobby Bonilla for Jose DeLeon, a 25-year-old pitcher who had shown considerable inconsistency with the Pittsburgh Pirates. DeLeon was a perfect project for Dick Bosman. "He threw a forkball that danced all over the place," according to Bosman. He wasn't a hard thrower, but he "tried to pitch with his fastball to get to his forkball." The good result was that he got a strikeout or ground ball on the forkball, but "sometimes he never got

Dick Bosman demonstrates the grip for the four-seam fastball. It is the control fastball and the foundation on which your pitching is built. It is the pitch you throw the hardest.

to it [the forkball]," because the fastball wasn't good enough to fool hitters consistently.

Bosman asked DeLeon to turn his approach on its head and use the forkball early in the count to establish the pitch in the batter's mind. The forkball broke away from the right-handed batter, and once he was thinking about the outside part of the plate, Bosman suggested that DeLeon work the fastball in on the batter after using the forkball early. "I don't care how good a hitter you are, if you are looking for something soft away, you are not going to get to a fastball in," Dick opines. "He [DeLeon] was bright enough to grasp that, and he had a measure of success that way." DeLeon put together a successful 13 starts with the White Sox in the second half of 1986, pitching to a 2.96 ERA.

The head game is not just the drama that occurs between pitcher and batter during the game. It is the preparation that a pitcher does mentally before a game.

Dick's other project, one that started in the spring, was working with young pitcher Joe Cowley. Cowley would go on to pitch one of the most confounding no-hitters in the game in September of the 1986 season. Bosman had helped Cowley iron out a few mechanical issues in Buffalo after he was demoted to the minors in April. When he returned to the big-league staff in May, he began to pitch far better than previously. "He called me after a good outing and told me he was going to tell the press, 'You're the reason I'm pitching good,'" Dick recalled of Cowley after a few good starts in May and June 1986. "Don't say anything. What you do and what I do should stand for themselves," was Dick's response.

When he pitched in the majors, Cowley was "all over the place," said Dick, "trying to overdo things." When Cowley took the mound, Bosman was constantly talking to his young pitcher between innings or making trips to the mound to focus him. Cowley was able to log 27 starts that year, and the culmination of the hard work came on September 19, when Cowley took the mound in Los Angeles against the Angels. Few no-hitters can rival the one Cowley crafted that day. "Fregosi almost took him out of the game twice," Dick said wistfully. "He was walking guys all over the place." Cowley walked seven batters in the nine innings, but he did not allow a single hit. "How he got out of it with a win, much less a no-hitter, is one of those marvels of the game."

While the White Sox pitching staff improved only marginally that season, they were receptive to one of Bosman's signature innovations, which began early in his tenure with the White Sox. It is important to remember that in 1986, the best teams in both leagues were deploying the running game to great effect. The 1985 World Series had pitted the St. Louis Cardinals, managed by Whitey Herzog, against the Kansas City Royals, which featured Lonnie Smith and Willie Wilson, each of whom stole more than 40 bases that season. "Whitey ball" was the term of art to describe Herzog's offensive tactics, which relied heavily on the stolen base as its weapon of choice.

Herzog's lineup was led by Vince Coleman, who stole 107 bases in 1986, to lead both leagues. The Cardinals had five other players in their starting lineup with the ability to steal 20 to 30 bases in a given season. They could run down balls in the outfield and had Ozzie Smith, one of the best shortstops ever to lace up a pair of baseball cleats. He ran the bases as well as anyone.

The American League was led by Rickey Henderson, who would go on to be inducted into the Baseball Hall of Fame in 2009, with 1,406 stolen bases in his career, a mark that exceeds the closest rival by more than 400 steals.

Against this kind of sprinter speed on the basepaths, Bosman had a pitching staff that featured high leg kicks and slow times to the plate. The popular move for a right-handed pitcher during that era was to raise the left leg almost to the chest and hide the ball in the glove behind the raised knee. Getting the leg lifted to that somewhat extreme position may have added deception to the delivery, but it extended the time it took the pitcher to deliver the pitch to the plate.

Carlton Fisk, who was behind the plate for the White Sox, had been as good a catcher as anyone during his career, but in 1986 he was 38 years old and no longer able to gun down the opposing runners as he once had. "He was having to call pitchouts because he could no longer throw guys out," Bosman remembered. He concluded that his pitchers were a big part of the problem and the only piece he could change for the better.

Dick had begun to think about how to control the running game while working with high school and American Legion pitchers in Northern Virginia. He built on that analysis in approaching his first major-league staff. He started to explore the options with the White Sox staff and found them "remarkably receptive" to ideas that had worked with young pitchers in McLean, Virginia. Said Bosman, "So many times you have guys in the big leagues that are set in their ways, and they don't want to hear anything about changing stuff. But to their credit, Dotson, Bannister, and DeLeon all tried to come up with a way to get the ball to the plate quicker."

The pitching motion has been broken down into distinct components. It begins once the pitcher brings his hands together while standing on the pitching rubber. From there he must either begin his motion to the plate, throw to an occupied base to pick off a runner, or disengage from the rubber. The pitcher commits to throwing to the plate when he lifts his leg off the rubber and breaks his hands to begin his motion. The time from that point until the ball reaches the catcher's glove is called the "release time." For the White Sox pitchers in 1986, their release times ranged from 1.7 to 1.9 seconds. Bosman realized that these times were far too slow.

The rest of the equation relates to the baserunner and the catcher. In discussions with Syd Thrift in Northern Virginia, Dick had timed the best baserunners and analyzed their leads from first base. The leads by aggressive baserunners varied, with the more uncompromising runners extending their leads to the edge of the infield cutout around the first-base bag. A runner that was not likely to steal took a lead well short of the cutout. If the runner was fast and had his right foot just outside of the first-base cutout, it was going to take him 3.3 to 3.5 seconds to reach second base. If he extended that lead to standing with his left foot near the first-base cutout, which was the point where the best basestealers tried to stretch it, the times to second base by the fastest runners could be reduced to almost 3 seconds flat.

Lou Brock acknowledged these times as far back as the late 1960s. "It takes me . . . 3.2 seconds to run from first to second when I get a good lead and a swift jump, when I move well and slide at the right instant," he said.[4] Brock believed that the pitcher and catcher should be able to beat that time and that the advantage lay with the batterymates, but the results showed otherwise, especially in the first half of the 1980s.

For catchers, the time it takes from the point the pitched ball strikes the mitt until their throw to second base reaches the fielder's glove is called their "pop time." It is the time it takes them to pop up from the crouch and get the ball to the base. A good catcher will have pop times at or less than 2.0 seconds. While Dick was the pitching coach with the Texas Rangers, Pudge Rodriguez was behind the plate, and he had a pop time of 1.8 seconds or less, which is about as good as it gets. The White Sox did not have that asset, and their pitchers were taking almost two seconds to deliver the ball to the plate, which made it almost impossible for Fisk to throw out runners.

Bosman realized after some deliberation that the only part of the pitcher's delivery that could be changed was the leg lift. From the set position—with his hands together at his stomach—one of the first components of the delivery occurs as the pitcher raises both his hands and begins to lift his leg. Almost every pitcher did some kind of leg lift, whether pitching from the windup or the stretch position, which is employed when runners are on base. The leg lift accentuates the pitcher's weight shift to their back leg. If they twist their body and knee further behind—as many do— it can hide the ball behind the raised knee, which adds deception, but also a crucial few moments to the overall delivery.

More importantly, the higher the pitcher lifts the front leg, the greater the extension the pitcher can attain when he shifts his weight forward and begins to stretch his front leg out across the downslope of the mound. The high leg lift allows the pitcher to drive forward and push off the pitching rubber with the greatest force. When pitching from the windup, the delivery is the signature move of every pitcher, although it contains the same basic elements. When runners are on base, the pitcher reduces his windup motion and pitches from the stretch position. The leg lift was always thought to be even more important when a hurler pitched out of the stretch position because it was a compensation for not having a full windup. Dick's theory would test that notion.

Bosman reasoned that if the pitcher could reduce his leg lift with runners on base and somehow continue to get adequate extension and maintain his drive forward, he might be able to reduce his time to the plate, or "release time." Bosman's attempts to create a faster "release time" by tweaking the pitching motion came to be known as the "slide step." Dick prefers to call it the "quick step."⁵ Many pitchers vary the basic concept, but most of what is practiced within the game today to lower the release time is called a "slide step," whether or not it comports with Bosman's original approach.

> Bosman's "slide step" is about reducing a pitcher's time to the plate—the release time—by lowering the leg lift significantly, while maintaining full extension and driving forward in the delivery to the plate.

The slide step as an innovation was introduced to baseball by Dick Bosman, according to an article by Pete Williams in *Street and Smith's Baseball Yearbook* in 2002.⁶ Others began to deploy it during the late 1980s and the years going forward. Whether or not teams use the methods that Dick believes work best or some variation, the slide step provided a key defensive tool to cope with the running game that was at its peak in the mid-1980s. It was a major advance in maintaining the pitcher's control of the game as it unfolded and preventing the basestealer from gaining undue influence or disrupting the pitcher's concentration on the batter, where the ultimate danger lies.

With a receptive pitching staff that began to incorporate the basic idea of eliminating or reducing the leg lift, the White Sox staff was able to reduce their times to the plate from 1.7 or 1.8 seconds to 1.3 seconds consistently. "It [the pitcher's release time] has to be 1.3 seconds if you are going to control the running game."

Dick Bosman demonstrates the slide step to young Tampa Bay Rays minor-league pitchers. Dick is emphasizing the need to keep the hands low. The stretch position should begin with the hands near the belly button, and they should come straight back as the front leg begins to come back, as seen in this photo. From this point in the delivery it should be a quick step forward that extends toward the plate as far as the normal motion of the pitcher.

The altered mechanics of the slide step begin with the pitcher holding his hands lower than usual. Dick prefers the pitcher to position his glove, with the ball resting inside, at or slightly above the belly button. The idea is to alter the pitcher's tendency to lift the hands to get the ball into throwing position behind his head. Instead of raising the hands to start the motion, Bosman asks that they draw their hands back instead of lifting them. Conventional mechanics from the windup often involve having the hands in a raised position at the top of the chest or near the face. Moving them to a similar position—raising the hands—from the stretch adds critical milliseconds.

Dick's lower hand position and direct draw back of the hand with the ball happens in concert with a reduced leg lift where the front leg is only a few inches—no more than two to four inches—off the ground. Ideally, it entails moving the leg backward horizontally and torqueing it slightly to the side rather than upward. "The guy in the on-deck circle should be able to see the bottom of the pitcher's shoe," Dick claims, as a way of indicating how the motion should work. The key to the slide step according to Bosman is to place the weight on the pivot with as little leg lift as possible. With the front leg horizontal to the ground at only a few inches off the ground, the pitcher can close his hips and create his normal torque and intensity as he thrusts the front leg forward and down the slope of the mound.

In spring training, when Bosman is introducing the slide step to a group of young pitchers, they stand in rows doing the first part of the slide step in unison. They repeat it until they can rotate the pitching hand directly backward as they simultaneously draw the leg back. Dick is not satisfied until they look remarkably similar in this first release from the initial stretch position. The purpose of the repetition is to make the slide step a "quick twitch" move when they are on the mound, something they can do without thinking about it. They have enough to consider without having to think about their slide step. It should be something that is a rote part of their game.

Dick remembers his first instructional league sessions where he was teaching the slide step in the Orioles organization. "There were 16, 18 guys standing in two rows. Arthur Rhodes was one of them," he remembered. "Young pitchers like that, that are just beginning their careers, are open to change," according to Dick. "Once they get to the majors they are not as willing to listen to ideas that might change their basic mechanics."

Many who believe they are teaching an acceptable variation of the slide step allow the pitcher to continue the leg lift but diminish the height of it. Although a reduced leg lift can lower the release time and maybe even produce one at or near 1.3 seconds, Bosman does not believe it works as well as his strategy. "If the pitcher tries to reduce his leg lift, then in the heat of battle, when he is trying to get something extra on the ball, the leg lift is going to be back to where it started," he contended. The crucial point in a ballgame generally entails having a runner on base, so if the pitcher returns to something approaching conventional mechanics, he is going to be more vulnerable to the stolen base at pivotal points in the game.

The most common concern with the slide step is that it reduces velocity. There are those in baseball who believe many pitchers lose a bit off their velocity pitching from the stretch position to begin with. Further diminishing the stretch motion by reducing the leg lift can only aggravate the loss of velocity, according to one school of thought. Bosman does not buy into this notion and maintains that when properly done, pitchers can actually increase their velocity while pitching from the stretch and using the slide step.

"I have had guys increase their velocity with it," Bosman asserted. "It is all about shifting the weight backward quickly and getting on with it. The difference is at least two- to three-tenths of a second less" in the overall release time, and it can be done with no reduction in velocity as Bosman teaches it.

Moving from the ready position with the hands held near the midsection, the pitcher can draw as far back as he would achieve in his normal delivery. In doing so, however, he has not brought the ball up and around to get there before thrusting the ball toward the plate. A big part of the problem in teaching pitchers how to control the running game is that they have concentrated during their early years of development on mechanics that involve a full windup. For young pitchers who have practiced pitching from the windup almost exclusively, a reduced motion seems counterintuitive.

The full windup is what most fans and many players envision when they picture a pitcher delivering the ball to the plate. It allows the maximum leg lift, a turn away from home plate to hide the ball, and any other personal peculiarities that a pitcher may develop as his own signature pitching motion; however, many of the complex machinations that pitchers employ to

This sequence of photos illustrates Tampa Bay Rays minor-league pitching prospect Brent Honeywell as he demonstrates the slide step on a practice field at spring training. The move forward occurs without lifting the front leg more than a few inches off the mound.

maximize speed and otherwise win the battle with the batter are at odds with the goal of controlling the running game.

"It's simple math actually." Adding the "release time" to the "pop time" has to equal something in the neighborhood of 3.3 seconds for the batterymates to have any chance of controlling the running game. With a pop time that averages 2.0 seconds for a catcher, coupled with a release time of 1.3 seconds, only the fastest runners, getting expansive leads, can consistently avoid being thrown out at second base.

The runner's lead away from the base is, of course, crucial as well, and has become more important as pitchers and catchers have developed more effective strategies to control the running game. It is incumbent on the pitcher to identify the runner's lead effectively. "That's the first part of preventing stolen bases," Dick asserted. The pitcher should be able to mentally mark the point from first base, where the runner is clearly pushing to gain the advantage. The first thing the pitcher must do is make direct eye contact with the runner when he is taking his primary lead away from the bag. It is good for the pitcher to maintain visual contact until the runner has settled on a lead, even if it takes a few seconds.

"A pitcher watching the runner only out of the corner of his eye cannot gauge the runner's lead effectively," Dick maintained. "He has to know exactly where the runner is and how big his lead is." The idea is not to look the runner back to first base, but to look at the runner until he has taken his primary lead. If the runner is trying to position himself to steal second, he will generally establish a primary lead with at least one foot on the other side of the first-base cutout. If that is the case, the pitcher can return his attention to the catcher and get the sign. Out of the corner of his eye, the only thing the pitcher can do is see motion. But once the runner has his primary lead, the pitcher will see any further movement as the runner widens his lead. If the runner makes further moves toward second base, it is time for the pitcher to try to pick the runner off.

This does not happen in many repeated throws to the bag by the pitcher. According to Bosman, there should only be one throw to first, and that should be the pitcher's best pickoff move, employed only when the pitcher sees the runner continue to edge away from first base after achieving an aggressive primary lead.

Some of Dick's best pupils have come up with some kind of exaggerated motion before coming to a set position that allows them to assess a runner's lead. Mike Mussina of the Orioles was a good example of a pitcher who adopted a stylized approach that gave him ample opportunity to gauge the runner's lead from first base. His slow dip toward the mound before raising to the set position was done with his eyes directly on the runner. Pitcher James Shields does this also, and it allows him to maintain eye contact with the runner for an extended period of time while the runner takes his lead.

> With a runner on base, the first thing the pitcher must do is gauge the runner's primary lead. The only way to do that is to make direct eye contact until the runner has settled on a lead, even if it takes a few seconds.

Dick is adamant about not having his pitchers throw to first base numerous times to force the runner to reduce his lead. "The only time the pitcher should throw over to first base is if his manager has ordered him to do so to see if the batter is going to bunt or if the runner gives away the fact that he may run." *The pitcher should only throw to pick the runner off.* Throwing otherwise only gives the runner a better chance to assess the pitcher's motion to the plate. Repeated throws to first base "slow the game down," according to Bosman. "And I hate that," he said. "Your infielders are losing their edge.

Your catcher is up in a stance getting ready and you throw to first, and he has to get back down and repeat his stance all over again. It is just counterproductive."

The other element is the umpire, who is watching the entire affair with disinterest, and it is keeping the crew from getting "to the tavern on time. If a guy throws over to first base five or six times, he has no fricking clue," Bosman asserted pointedly. The game of cat and mouse between baserunner and pitcher, which was commonplace during the era of such basestealers as Maury Wills, Lou Brock, and those that followed in the 1970s and 1980s, is not nearly as common today because many pitchers have concluded that it accomplishes little or nothing.

There is a final question that begs asking concerning the changes in the running game since 1986. Did the phenomenon of the slide step, as initiated by Bosman and others in the second half of the 1980s, diminish the running game to the secondary status it has in baseball today? Or does the explanation lie with some other variable? In the modern era, the zenith of the stolen base was, oddly enough, in 1987, Bosman's first full year as a pitching coach. That apogee is derived only by examining the total number of stolen bases per season and does not account for the effects of expansion and other valid concerns. But in the modern era of baseball, no individual has stolen more than 100 bases in a single season since Vince Coleman in 1987.

There is another variable of possible concern. The predominance of African American speedsters has diminished directly proportional to their declining participation in the game of baseball overall. Thus, has the decline of the stolen base as a weapon been the result of fewer speedsters or better defensive deployments against it? The easy and perhaps reliable answer is all of the above.

In Tampa Bay, Bosman found their best speedster was Carl Crawford. Crawford was a fine outfielder and offensive threat of considerable proportion who spent nine seasons with the Rays and led the American League in steals four times. Bosman knew that Crawford's time to second base was 3.0 seconds, even with a relatively modest lead, which probably had only his front foot at or near the cutout at the first-base bag. In that situation, where even the best release time and pop time have limited ability to catch the runner, "you have to disrupt his timing," Bosman stated emphatically. "Even if your pitcher is 1.3 and your catcher is 2.0, you're still too late.

"The reason that you see less stolen bases today is twofold," according to Dick. "There aren't as many guys who have a really, really good feel for stealing bases, because there is a technique and knack to that, of course. And then, like I say, there are the efforts that a lot of pitchers have put into getting the ball to their catcher with a better time." That is the other half of the equation.

"Now I have had pitchers who could get down to 1.1, but you're losing efficiency when you do that. You don't have as much on the ball," Dick continued. The idea that the pitcher can overcompensate in trying to control the running game is a popular vein of discussion in baseball today. If the pitcher's conventional delivery achieves a 99-mile-per-hour fastball and pinpoint control of that pitch—as only a few of the elite arms in the game can accomplish—what sense does it make to employ a stretch position that could reduce his velocity by several miles per hour and diminish his control? That is the most frequently heard counterargument to the slide step.

Even today, where the deployment of the slide step is widespread, it is not taught uniformly or practiced in the same manner. "There are organizations around that will make a halfhearted attempt to speed up their guys, but there is an art to teaching a guy a decent slide step so that it is mechanically correct to the point that you can still pitch effectively with it. Of course, there are those pitching coaches who will say, 'Well don't let the batter get on first base.'" That is the approach that most infuriates Bosman.

Regardless of how the slide step is taught or how uniformly it is adopted by teams, it is a big part of pitching today. It likely will remain an essential tool in controlling the running game for the foreseeable future. As such, it will remain an important innovation introduced by Dick Bosman, and for the 30 years he has been teaching baseball in the major and minor leagues, few have taught it more consistently or made it a bigger part of their bag of tricks. It is a significant part of Dick's reputation and contribution to the game.

Joe Maddon saw the results of Bosman's efforts when he was manager of the Tampa Bay Rays from 2006 to 2014. The pitchers in the Rays minor-league organization came to the majors knowing how to control the running game because of working with Bosman extensively on the slide step. Said Joe Maddon, "Boz really teaches the holding of the runner, the pickoff, extremely well. He presents it in a way I have never really heard of before, and I think it's a way they can really grasp onto and build off of it."[7] Bosman can tighten a young pitcher's slider, evaluate his arsenal of pitches, and sharpen all of them. But his signature contribution to coaching may be his impact on how pitchers control the running game, and his innovations have had a measurable effect on the game since he began teaching the slide step in 1986.

Dick Bosman demonstrates the form that made him the best pitcher to put on the expansion Washington Senators uniform. He won 16 games in 1970—the high-water mark for the team. *From the personal collection of Dick Bosman.*

Paul Casanova, Dick Bosman, Toby Harrah, and Tom Raglin celebrate the Washington Senators' 1971 Opening Day victory. *Reprinted with permission of the DC Public Library, Star Collection © Washington Post.*

Dick Bosman and his good friend Frank Howard pose on "Arctic Cat" motorcycles, which were sold by Dick in the offseason in Kenosha, Wisconsin. Howard and Bosman were not only the best players for the Washington Senators from 1969 to 1971, but also in Texas they led the first strike by the players against ownership the spring after the move from DC. *Reprinted with permission of the DC Public Library, Star Collection © Washington Post.*

A day of significant notoriety in Washington baseball history occurred on September 30, 1971, when Dick Bosman took the mound to start the last game in the brief history of the Washington Senators expansion team. "Short Stinks" refers to owner Bob Short, who moved the team to Arlington, Texas, where they became the Texas Rangers. *Bettman/Getty Images, used with permission.*

Dick Bosman hands the ball to Washington Nationals pitcher Livan Hernandez on April 14, 2005, when Major League Baseball was played again at RFK Stadium for the first time after an absence of more than three decades. *Courtesy of George R. Clark, Esq.*

When working with pitchers, Dick frequently put on catcher's gear and watched what the pitcher was throwing all the way into the mitt. Here he is working with Chris Shebby, with whom Bosman worked from Little League until Chris signed with the Orioles. *Courtesy of Mike Harris.*

Bosman was asked to evaluate the Orioles minor-league pitching ranks in 1989. Here Dick is working with a group of minor-league prospects in the spring of that year. *From the personal collection of Dick Bosman.*

Dick served as the Baltimore Orioles major-league pitching coach from 1992 to 1994, working with Pete Harnisch, Curt Schilling, Ben McDonald, and Mike Mussina during his years with the minor-league and major-league team. *From the personal collection of Dick Bosman.*

Like many presidents, George H. W. Bush was an avid baseball fan. He is shown here in the Orioles clubhouse with Dick Bosman in 1992. *White House by David Valdez.*

Dick Bosman has never lost his love for cars and working with old friend Dan McKown of Sanders Paint and Body Shop. He tears down old cars and rebuilds them, sometimes selling them to major-league ballplayers, including David Wells, Bobby Witt, and Alan Mills. *Courtesy of Dick Bosman.*

9

Baltimore Pitching Coach

One of the great joys of Dick's brief tenure with the Chicago White Sox was the few weeks in which he worked with Tom Seaver at the major-league level after first being introduced to him during spring training. Bosman's first night in the dugout—after his call-up from the minors—was June 20, and by June 30, Seaver had been traded to the Boston Red Sox for utility infielder/outfielder Steve Lyons. Although the two pitchers had only a few months of work on the same team, Bosman pointedly tried to establish a relationship with the future Hall of Famer. As the pitching coach, establishing a connection with every pitcher on the staff was part of the job.

But it was different with Seaver. "After all, it's Tom Seaver," Bosman recalled of his desire to create a bond with the famous pitcher who had come to the majors in 1967, roughly the same time Dick was breaking in.[1] "We knew he wanted to get back to Boston. He had a home in Connecticut." It was when the White Sox were playing in Oakland that the trade was announced, and Seaver called Bosman to tell him that he was leaving. "I've got a case of Heineken on ice, come on over. We need to talk a while," Bosman remembered Seaver saying

> Dick gives his pitching students a candid appraisal of their talents, their mechanics, and the situation. From there his students must do the hard work, have the grit and commitment to put into practice the ideas that evolve as they work together. There must be something burning within.

to him at 3:00 a.m. in the morning after the trade was announced. "A lot of baseball was talked about, and quite a few Heinekens were consumed that night," Dick revealed.

Talking shop with the author of *The Art of Pitching* was a highlight of Dick's tenure with the White Sox, but the time was short overall. The 1987 season was Dick's first full season as pitching coach, but it was one of turmoil after owner Jerry Reinsdorf replaced Ken Harrelson as general manager with Larry Himes. Harrelson returned to the broadcast booth at the end of the 1986 season, and Dick was in the familiar position of working with someone new on a team that was going nowhere. Whether it was Whitey Herzog in his first year in Texas or Frank Robinson in Cleveland, new management had always meant that change was in the air for Bosman.

Larry Himes had ambitious plans for the White Sox and big plans for the pitching staff to become "pitchers they were not," according to Dick. "It was also pretty apparent from the get-go that he wanted his own people in there." Jim Fregosi, who remained the manager for the White Sox until the end of the 1988 season, told Bosman that if he knew people in baseball, it might be good to talk to them, meaning that his days with the Chicago organization were probably numbered. Dick knew all too well that part of the game was moving on, whether as a player or coach. "If you wanted to stay in the game, you better have someone to call," Dick asserted, speaking from experience.

"We were playing the Orioles in Baltimore, and I was talking to Phil Wood," Dick recalled. Wood was a radio personality with deep ties to both the Washington Senators and the Orioles as an announcer. Dick knew him well from his years in Washington and mentioned his precarious position with the White Sox. Wood offered to put him in contact with Doug Melvin, who was working in the Orioles farm system at the time. There was nothing explicit ventured by anyone, just a placeholder for the future. "Phil had always wanted me in his heart of heart's to be a Baltimore Oriole," Dick admitted. "Actually, he wanted me to be a Washington National, but that wasn't in the cards."

As the 1987 baseball season in Chicago progressed further toward its end, there was little advancement toward the lofty goals that new GM Larry Himes had set for himself. The team was mired in last place in the American League West until embarking on a remarkable run beginning in early September. It was reminiscent of the 1969 Washington Senators. The White Sox won 20 games and lost only seven after September 6, winning nine of their last 10 games to close out the season in fifth place.

The White Sox called up first-round draft pick Jack McDowell—taken fifth overall in the 1987 Amateur Draft—on September 15, and he won two games down the stretch. Dave LaPoint came over in a trade from the St. Louis Cardinals in July and thrived under Dick's tutelage, registering a 2.94 ERA and winning six games for Chicago in the second half. The White Sox had gone from being one of the worst pitching staffs in the American League in 1986 to the fourth best in the league in 1987, but it was not enough to convince Himes that these results were a portent of better things to come. Himes would remain in Chicago for another three years, but the White Sox pitchers would regress after Dick left, until 1990, when McDowell and other young White Sox pitchers finally began to come into their own.

Dick Bosman was fired at the end of the season in a process that was less than optimal from his perspective. But the initial contacts he had made with Doug Melvin, via Phil Wood, proved both wise and fruitful. Shortly after the conclusion of the 1987 World Series, Dick was hired by Melvin to be the minor-league pitching coordinator for the Baltimore Orioles. In the beginning, his explicit role was to evaluate talent in the minors and decide which pitchers should be assigned to the various levels of the organization. For a coach that was new to the organization and the talent in it, the task was daunting.

But in 1988, the issue for the Orioles was a dearth of legitimate major-league prospects in their minor-league affiliates. The team sank to a historic low point in 1988, losing 21 straight games to begin the season, and when the final pitch was thrown, the team had lost more games than the first Orioles team in 1954, when the St. Louis Browns had relocated to the Charm City. Bosman's first look at the system revealed the minor-league organization could offer little help in the short term.

"Doug wanted to know why the minor leagues were barren. What were the problems and how were we going to address them?" said Bosman. Melvin had been in player development for the Orioles several years before Bosman took his new job with the club. Together they were tasked with not only nurturing talent for the big-league club, but also finding out why the pipeline had dried up.

Dick was not impressed with the performance of the coaching staff in several minor-league locations. The money being spent to build from within was being wasted, as the team often failed to develop its higher-level draft picks each year. Bosman made his final report at the end of the year, but knew he badly missed teaching and working with young pitchers. He asked Melvin whether he would be considered if an opening in the upper levels of the Orioles organization appeared. At the end of the season, Dom Chiti—the pitching coach at Rochester—left with Orioles third-base coach John Hart to go to Cleveland.

During the 1989 season, Baltimore rebranded the organization with the "Why Not" campaign to instill a more competitive fire throughout. Replacing Chiti in Rochester, Bosman came in on the ground floor of that movement as the Triple-A pitching coach for the Red Wings in 1989. Dick spent the next three seasons developing the talent that would lead the Orioles back to respectability. He brought his approach to controlling the running game to Rochester and once again began to put on the catcher's gear to watch bullpen sessions and appraise the offerings of his pitchers.

In 1989, the Rochester Red Wings had a rotation that featured some of the fine arms that would go on to pitch in the majors with the Orioles and other teams. Pete Harnisch and Curt Schilling were roommates when the season began and were the "odd couple that were always at one another, always funny." Bosman had been tasked with teaching Schilling the slider. "He was a fastball, forkball guy, and it took me three months to teach him to throw a slider," Dick related. Harnisch gave Bosman similar credit for diversifying his arsenal of pitches. "When I came out of college, I was fastball, fastball, fastball," he said.[2] Bosman worked with Harnisch to develop a slider and a changeup.

Schilling asked his agent to tell the Orioles that he could pitch in the majors with just the fastball and forkball, but Bosman knew he needed another pitch to succeed at the next level. He convinced Schilling that if he went to the big leagues with his two pitches, he would be back in the minors all too soon.

"Schilling was a joy to work with. He was young and dumb and full of energy," Dick remembered fondly. "I had a lot of fun with those guys because they were willing workers, they would listen to what I had to say and would try to incorporate it into what they were doing." Schilling went on to have a wonderful career that included two world championships, the most famous in Boston in 2004, behind the much-televised bloody sock.

There were many other talents on that Rochester team who would become household names in Baltimore. Steve Finley and Brady Anderson were the stalwarts of the outfield, and Chris Hoiles was the catcher. Greg Biagini was the manager at Rochester, and he began to have success working with the improved level of talent. In 1990, the Rochester Red Wings won the International League championship, 33 games over .500. Future Orioles third baseman Leo Gomez joined Rochester as a 24-year-old in 1990, and much of the success came from the offense. But it was also the addition of Ben McDonald, the first overall pick in the 1989 draft out of Louisiana State University, who turned the tide for the Orioles organization.

Mike Mussina came as a first-round draft pick in the 1990 draft—taken 20th overall—and suddenly the team was finding the right formula in its selections, as Mussina and McDonald gave the Orioles two success stories that would reverberate for many years. McDonald reached Rochester in 1989, and was in Baltimore by 1990. Mussina had a similarly rapid rise to the majors. Mussina, more so than McDonald, had a full assortment of pitches from day one, which would carry him to the show in short order.

Dick had no input into the decision-making behind the draft picks that began to pump new energy into the structure from top to bottom. He was in player development. It was his job to work with the talent as it came aboard. The one consistent issue Bosman worked on was the running game, from spring training until the last pitch was thrown and they were headed to Baltimore. Some of the new pitchers came with more tools than others, not only in how they pitched, but also how they controlled the running game. Mussina and McDonald came from two of the best collegiate baseball programs in the country. Mussina had developed a more personalized method for pitching out of the stretch and ensuring that runners did not run freely on the bases behind him.

> To be successful against big-league hitters you have to be able to throw secondary pitches in fastball counts.

The most important project Dick undertook was McDonald. McDonald was an inordinately tall pitcher, standing 6-foot-7. "He was not some tall gangly kid," Dick recalled of the Louisiana State product. "People forget his height because he was such a marvelous athlete." McDonald had the body of a football player, perhaps a tight end, or a strong forward on the basketball court. "He could hold six or seven baseballs in one hand," according to Bosman. And he had sound mechanics despite his height. "He wasn't 95 miles per hour plus, but he was 90 to 95 miles per hour with a lot of life. He could spin the ball. He had a lot of things going for him coming in of a very positive nature."

Mussina came out of Stanford with a wider array of secondary pitches than McDonald from the start. "Moose had secondary stuff going in," whereas McDonald had to work to refine his secondary offerings. Part of the problem with McDonald was getting him to develop confidence in his secondary pitches and throw them more often. "As big as his fingers were, he could slide the ball back in his fingers to throw a forkball," remembered Bosman. But he did not throw it as often as might have been optimal. "To be successful against big-league hitters you have to be able to throw secondary pitches in fastball counts and get those guys out," asserted Bosman emphatically. McDonald had a big overhanded curve, but it never had the bite it needed to be a plus-pitch, and so he relied too much on his fastball location.

Mussina came out of college with a formidable changeup and curveball. His fastball sat at 94 miles per hour consistently, and he could locate it effectively. Bosman taught Mussina a second curve. "He could make it into a slider. He could make it into a bigger breaking ball when he wanted to." It was called a knuckle curve quite often by the press, but the traditional knuckle curve that Mussina threw originally was very different, with a more common placement of his two fingernails on top of the ball. The pitch Bosman taught Mussina had a tendency to act more like a traditional curve because it came out of the hand with the knuckle on the side of the ball—something that caused a natural tumbling spin. Dick does not see that pitch as the typical knuckle curve. Mussina used a different grip, and the placement of his fingers allowed him greater flexibility to adapt the pitch to fit different game situations.

Bosman did not throw a curve himself, but he was savvy enough about the pitch to help Mussina refine his already-advanced curve and provide an additional pitch that expanded the assortment of what he threw. "The last curveball I tried to throw," Bosman asserted whimsically, "went over the bullpen in Memorial Stadium" for a home run. Senators manager Gil Hodges told Dick after the pitch that "he need not throw another one."[3] Dick continues to regret that so much innovation in pitching has occurred in the years since he quit the mound.

Dick Bosman demonstrates Mike Mussina's knuckle curve grip. The ball shoots out of the fingers, although Mussina had the ability to vary his motion slightly to get a broader variety of movement on the pitch.

Ben McDonald and Mike Mussina became a formidable duo atop the Baltimore rotation, and the Orioles began to bring in additional hurlers to fill out behind them. Gregg Olson had been chosen as a first-round pick out of Auburn University in the 1988 Amateur Draft. He became the everyday closer almost immediately and, in 1989, recorded 26 saves. Olson won Rookie of the Year honors in 1989 and was an All-Star the following season. Dick only had Olson in instructional league.

"Olie had an outstanding curveball. It was his out pitch. He was a max effort kind of guy," Bosman remembered. "His mechanics were not pretty, but he got it done. He was an outstanding competitor. The curveball was his go-to

Dick Bosman demonstrates Mike Mussina's spike curve. Mussina had one of the most varied repertoires of any pitcher in the majors and could vary the motion of almost all of his pitches to fit the situation.

pitch, and in the end the curveball really took its toll on his forearm. He ended up having trouble with that at the end."

One of the more unfortunate occurrences during this period of player development for the Orioles was the Glenn Davis trade. In 1991, the Orioles infield consisted of the Ripken brothers up the middle and newly promoted Leo Gomez at third base. Randy Milligan was at first base, and while he had hit 20 home runs in 1990, he was much better against left-handed pitching and did not produce enough power as a right-handed first baseman to justify his spot as a corner infielder. In January 1991, the Orioles traded Steve Finley, Curt Schilling, and Pete Harnisch to the Houston Astros for Davis, a 30-year-old first baseman who had hit 20 or more home runs for Houston in the prior six seasons, topping out at 34 home runs in 1989.

Davis's numbers had dropped noticeably in 1990, however, and the Astros were willing to trade him for three players with significant upside. Neither Bosman nor anyone else knew for certain that Harnisch or Schilling would develop into stars, but Dick was sorry to see them depart after working with them closely during their minor-league careers. Schilling's slow rise did not reach its climax until he was in his mid-30s. Harnisch would have a successful big-league career. But it was Finley who provided immediate return to the Astros, as he began a long career as a speedy center fielder with power. He would hit 304 home runs and steal 320 bases in a 19-year career.

Baltimore was hoping it had a productive center fielder already in the fold in the person of Brady Anderson. Roland Hemond did not guess wrong on Anderson, but Davis had a congenital spinal defect that surfaced in his first spring training in Baltimore. The curious malady diminished his offensive production, and early in his third season with the Orioles he was released when he could not return to action after being hit by a foul ball while sitting in the dugout. The net effect for Dick Bosman was the loss of two of his better arms, but he was nearing the end of his time in Rochester when the Davis trade went down.

In mid-May, with the Orioles again beginning the season poorly, manager Frank Robinson was replaced in the dugout by Johnny Oates. Robinson took a position in the front office as an assistant general manager. Bosman and Rochester manager Greg Biagini remained in the minor leagues but in September were told they would be replacing the existing pitching and hitting coaches, respectively. The two men arrived in Baltimore in time to watch the final game be played at Memorial Stadium. The ceremony for retiring the old field was a special one.

"To me that was one of the most emotional, well-orchestrated ceremonies that I have ever been part of," Dick recalled of the final game at Memorial Stadium, where the legendary players who had spent their careers there were called out one by one. "The way they did it. I mean, I am a pretty emotional guy, and it got to me several times during that whole thing." Bosman had pitched in Memorial Stadium many times and played against Orioles for 11 seasons. He had been a teammate with some of those being honored, one of whom was Boog Powell.

The Memorial Stadium festivities underscored an important tradition that was almost 40 years old for the Baltimore franchise. The well-conceived and executed gala send-off was indicative of the team's commitment to excellence according to the banner of the "Oriole Way." Rick Vaughn was the front-office person in charge of promotions and public relations. He pulled the event together, and Dick enjoyed working with him in Baltimore and would encounter him again when Vaughn went to work for the Tampa Bay Rays. As good as the closing of Memorial Stadium had been, the festivities surrounding the opening of the new park were even better. "They were like a Broadway production," Dick declared.

Both Vaughn and now Bosman were part of that proud tradition, one that had developed players from within, using excellent scouting and player development personnel to keep the roster filled with top-tier talent. Bosman was leaving the player development system and moving to the next level. In the spring of 1992, Dick came into his second camp as the pitching coach in charge of a staff of big-league hurlers.

McDonald and Mussina were the established core of the Baltimore staff, although they were only 24 and 23 years old, respectively. The Orioles had also signed Rick Sutcliffe as a free agent in the offseason. Sutcliffe was 36 in 1992, and was coming off eight successful years with the Chicago Cubs. He had thrown 242 innings for the Los Angeles Dodgers as a 23-year-old. He knew exactly what was being asked of the two young Baltimore pitchers and lent an important veteran presence that could provide stability.

The other members of the starting rotation were, at various times, Bob Milacki, Jose Mesa, and Arthur Rhodes. Bosman had worked extensively with Mesa at Rochester and was a believer in the young pitcher, although not as a starter. He knew that the hard-throwing Mesa was better suited for the bullpen. It was the top of the rotation, however, that would carry the team. The difference in the overall success of the Orioles pitching was the first round of the Amateur Draft: Mussina, McDonald and Olson. Teaching those three talents how to refine their repertoires was easier and more rewarding than working with some prior players Bosman had encountered. "They were young; they wanted to get better; and they had the tools to do it."

There were high expectations going into the Orioles' 1992 season, and Dick was upbeat about the situation as well. Rick Sutcliffe pitched a complete-game shutout for Opening Day at the new stadium before a sellout crowd of 44,568. Camden Yards drew rave reviews from everyone in attendance and the press. The design for the stadium would become the model for new stadiums throughout the country in every venue. Bosman was proud to be part of the event, and the excitement of the initial success bred its own ongoing momentum.

The 1991 team had been plagued by the worst pitching record in the American League, with a 4.59 ERA. These frustrations had been mitigated by Cal Ripken's MVP year, when his batting average was a lusty .323 and he slugged 34 home runs, mostly over the short porch in left field. In some way, the expectations for the 1992 season were lowered by the prior year's finish near the bottom of the American League Eastern Division, but the addition of a quality starter in Sutcliffe created optimism.

Dick's approach to Sutcliffe was much as it had been with Seaver in Chicago. Successful pitchers with that much experience knew how they did it. Bosman's job was to learn their mechanics, especially how their motion worked when they were pitching at their best. When things started to go wrong, it was Bosman's job to see the flaws as quickly as possible and report them to Sutcliffe so he could get back on track with minimal damage. "He was a professional," Bosman recalled. "I treated him no different than Seaver or Carlton."

Like McDonald, Sutcliffe was 6-foot-7 and had a complicated delivery. "But he knew how to manage it," Dick related, "so that he could stay on top of that rubber long enough to give his arm a chance to do all the kinks and bends and twists that it did to get into the throwing position and go downhill." One thing Bosman remembers from the first moment that Sutcliffe reported to spring training in 1992 was how much he stood out from the rest of the crowd with his full beard and mustache. "The Orioles over the years were a very straightlaced organization," Dick opined. "You wore a coat and tie on the plane; you were clean shaven, and your mustache was to the corners of your mouth. You had a decent haircut."

The facial hair policy changed when Sutcliffe joined the team that spring, and the team learned to adjust because Sutcliffe was, as Bosman remembered it, "on the list of the five fiercest competitors I was ever around." Johnny Oates and the Orioles had brought him in to teach that fire to the younger guys, not how to shave.

There was enthusiasm in the Baltimore region about the changes in the team. In particular, the *Washington Post* gave a passionate endorsement to Bosman in his new job. Tom Boswell wrote of Bosman that he had brought to his new job with the Orioles "his reputation as a fierce competitor and his innovative baseball intelligence."[4] Boswell complimented Bosman as "the quality pitching coach who can make a major impact," one that was sorely needed in Baltimore. Boswell discussed the many failures that preceded Dick, "how much quality pitching has escaped Baltimore . . . how many good arms have regressed once they reached the Majors." The optimism about Bosman poured forth from Boswell, who knew Dick's body of work from his years with the Senators. He no doubt remembered the exit interview Dick had done with him in the spring after being let go by Charlie Finley. There was none of that bitterness on the part of Bosman now, just a focus on the here and now. Bosman wore a t-shirt that spring that said, "Get Ahead, Stay Ahead, Use Your Head."[5] Nothing could have summed up the basics of Bosman's pitching philosophy better.

By the end of the year, the early endorsements had been born out. By October 1992, the Orioles pitching staff was statistically ranked fifth best in the American League, after finishing dead last in 1991. Bosman gave the credit to the pitchers themselves, and they deserved it. The most notable change came from the first full season of Mike Mussina as a starter. After his call-up in 1991, he had logged 12 starts and posted a 2.87 ERA. In 1992, he proved to be the workhorse of the staff, throwing 241 innings. He won 18 games and lost only five. His ERA of 2.52 was one of the best in the American League and in the top 10 in the major leagues.

Sutcliffe and McDonald each pitched more than 200 innings as well, and the threesome gave Baltimore a formidable rotation. Gregg Olson saved 36 games, and the team climbed to third place in the American League East, winning 89 games. There was one source of frustration, however. Bosman believed in Jose Mesa from their time at Rochester, and he knew the young flamethrower's potential as well as anyone. Dick's concern was that Mesa was being miscast as a starting pitcher.

Bosman recognized the need to try talented pitchers out as starters in the minors. It was a chance to develop their repertoire of pitches and see how well they did with them. But when there were consistent indications that a pitcher was ill-suited for the rotation, it behooved the front office to figure that out. Dick did not fault Mesa so much as the situation that forced him to fit into a role for which he was not intended.

"He [Mesa] was a lot like a pitcher I have now, Alex Colome. They are one-speed guys. They are wide open without a lot of finesse. They are going to go at you as hard as they can," Dick opined of both Mesa and Colome. Bosman had Mesa through two Tommy John surgeries and another minor surgery to remove bone chips from his elbow. "Through it all he threw the ball 97 miles per hour." Bosman's baseball intellect was pushed to its limits with Mesa, but they were ultimately successful, although not in Baltimore and not with Mesa starting.

The Orioles had a talented bullpen in 1992, and Bob Milacki could not get anyone out, so the audition for that slot fell to Mesa, regardless of how well-suited he may have been for the job. In the offseason, Baltimore traded Mesa to Cleveland for an insignificant minor-league pitcher. For the Indians, Mesa would become the highly successful closer that Bosman had foreseen, leading the American League in 1995, with 46 saves, and helping the Tribe win 100 games and ultimately an appearance in the World Series, where they lost to the Atlanta Braves.

Arthur Rhodes was another talented young arm who struggled to find his way in the early going at the major-league level. He had been drafted in the second round of the 1988 Amateur Draft, just behind Gregg Olson. Rhodes threw from the left side and had an electric arm. His fastball sat in the mid-90s with a seemingly effortless delivery. But there were serious mechanical flaws with his secondary pitches and Bosman worked with him until Rhodes developed a slurve—part slider, part curve—which the young pitcher managed to control consistently. He began to throw his changeup more often at Bosman's urging. Arthur Rhodes was a group project, however, and Johnny Oates suggested changes in the pitcher's footwork. The end result was a promising 15 starts in 1992 with the big-league club.

Dick attended Rhodes's wedding after the 1992 season and was as supportive of the young man as he could be. There were high hopes for Rhodes heading into the 1993 season. Bosman said of Rhodes's new changeup, "He may throw it 15 times a game this year. Three pitches are enough for him now. We don't want to muddy the water. He doesn't even throw a two-seam [sinking] fastball yet."[6] Rhodes would regress during the 1993 season and, like Jose Mesa, ultimately find his best role in pitching out of the bullpen.

For those that struggled, the antidote was Mike Mussina, who had established himself as the unquestioned ace of the Orioles pitching staff. He had the good looks of Jim Palmer and an intelligence all his own. He managed to graduate from Stanford in less than the full four-year term with a degree in economics. He was "chilly, precise, focused," according to one reporter, who went on to say that manager Johnny Oates did not "want to insult him with my stupid questions." Dick Bosman was not intimidated by his brainy hurler, but he was impressed nonetheless. "He throws all out, every pitch," Bosman observed during Mussina's breakout 1992 season.[7]

As much as Mussina was a polished product when he arrived from Stanford, he credited Bosman for working with him to control the running game. Mussina already had an acceptable release time, according to Bosman's initial assessment. But the moundsman was willing to learn from the best and incorporated Dick's suggestions into his signature stretch motion. With a runner on first base, Mussina was inordinately deliberate and developed what one writer called a "spy-on-the-guy" look over his left shoulder.[8] Bosman said it was all about gauging the baserunner's primary lead, and Mussina attributed the look to his time working with Bosman at Triple-A Rochester. The look was a few parts Bosman and a few parts Mussina, but it was effective and both men were happy with the final result.

The success of the 1992 season—when Baltimore climbed to third place in the American League East and had a winning record—bred higher expectations for the following year. The reviews on Bosman and his new pitching staff had been glowing, and the improvements were generally across the board. Dick was called on by the writers to compare Mike Mussina and Tom Seaver, both for their makeup and consistency. There was disappointment in Ben McDonald's 1992 season, but the big guy had learned to throw a slider and was no longer a shell-shocked, gopher-ball king.[9]

Bosman believed that the new pitch cut McDonald's ERA in half during the second half of the 1992 season. He also believed that for McDonald, it was just a matter of timing, that the pitcher had taken a few years to "unlearn what he was taught in college."[10] The comparisons to Mussina started at the beginning, as the two young pitchers launched their careers alongside one another. Bosman did all he could to deflect the head-to-head evaluations, saying, "He [McDonald] is on the right track. He's not on the fast track like Mussina. . . . Ben's going to make improvements in smaller increments."[11] He noted the huge expectations McDonald had labored under and expressed his belief that his young protégé would get there in the end.

As important as the relationships Bosman formed with his staff in 1992 were, the most important may have been the new relationship with manager Johnny Oates. Oates had been impressed with Bosman's record at Rochester, and as soon as Oates was named the replacement for Frank Robinson early in the 1991 season, he began to call Dick about the young pitchers on the farm. Oates wanted to know about Mussina and Rhodes, and when they would be able to help the major-league club.

Dick was not named the pitching coach until well into the offseason, but once his position with the team was set, he and Oates began to talk more frequently. "'The pitching staff is yours,' Oates told me. 'You do what you see fit, but if there is something I need to know, then I expect you to tell me, otherwise it is yours,'" Dick remembered from one of his earliest conversations with Oates. "He never second-guessed pitch selection or any of that." The relationship worked and survived through several iterations. Roland Hemond, Johnny Oates, and Dick Bosman became a management team that was able to accomplish good things with major-league clubs.

With the new season waiting around the corner, Hemond brought in a new and colorful personality to supplement the pitching staff. The Orioles were looking more and more to the free-agent market for talent and signed Fernando Valenzuela, whose luster had faded after several remarkable seasons for the Los Angeles Dodgers. Jamie Moyer was the second free agent brought aboard to bolster the staff after the departure of Jose Mesa.

Valenzuela was seven years away from his last All-Star appearance and the 21-win season in 1986. From that pinnacle, El Toro had seen his stuff fade and the numbers run downhill until he had been released in 1991, and had been out of the American game completely in 1992, pitching only in Mexico. But his appetite for major-league competition remained strong, and the Orioles gave him one last chance at age 32. The Orioles needed something behind Mussina, McDonald, and Sutcliffe. Rhodes was still unproven, so Valenzuela, Moyer, and Rhodes were in the mix for the final two slots in the rotation.

Bosman was quite impressed with Valenzuela almost immediately. "His skills had diminished and his arm strength had diminished, but he was trying to resurrect the screwball. It no longer had the sharp break that it once had," Dick reflected. Despite the concerns, Bosman found the veteran pitcher a "joy to be around," adding, "We just had a great time together." Bosman broke his own rules and took some of his pitching staff golfing during his seasons with the Orioles, and Valenzuela was almost always along on those outings in 1993. Dick remembered a specific day in New York, north of the city, on a resort golf course, when the foursome included Valenzuela and Olson. Hispanics who worked in the clubhouse and throughout the resort heard that Valenzuela was playing on the course that day and began to show up to watch. Said Bosman, "When we made the turn at the ninth hole, there were people hanging out the windows of the hotel and the clubhouse yelling, 'Viva Mexico!'"

Valenzuela and Moyer gave the Orioles a new look in 1993, but only Moyer succeeded in adding any appreciable number of quality innings. Valenzuela had a better season than the ones he had spent in Mexican exile, but in many ways he was just another veteran arm to serve as a bookend to Rick Sutcliffe. The biggest problem may have been the unexpected injury to Mike Mussina, who was hurt for several months in the middle of the season and finally went on the disabled list in late July. He was only 24 and too young to have a significant injury, but a variety of shoulder and back problems kept him at less than full strength or out of action completely for five months. He lost velocity on his fastball, which at 86 miles per hour was more hittable than at 94.

The injury was aggravated during a brawl between the Seattle Mariners and the Orioles, and even after taking several weeks off in August, when he came back he was not the same pitcher as in 1992. He did not fault Dick Bosman for asking him to keep pitching through the injury. "It was my decision to keep pitching," Mussina admitted. "Athletes are stubborn. Most of the time they learn the hard way," said the Stanford graduate.

The best arm other than Moyer was Ben McDonald, and it was as if the need to replace Mussina as the ace of the staff brought out the best in him. His 34 starts led the club, along with 224 innings with a 3.34 ERA, but he won only 13 games. Somehow, even with a bum shoulder and a 4.46 ERA, Mussina still managed to win more games than McDonald, with a 14–6 record for the 1993 campaign.

Baltimore's pitching finished the season in the middle of the pack, and the team failed to improve from the prior season. Yet, there was much going right with the team despite the lack of visible progress. There was a new stadium, which had brought out fans in record numbers. Most games were sellouts, and the sweet smell of success brought the financial dogs running. Camden Yards and the entirety of the Orioles franchise may have been the most lucrative property left to Eli Jacobs, who, in August 1993, was forced to sell the team in an auction conducted by Judge Cornelius Blackshear in the U.S. Court of Bankruptcy in Manhattan.[12]

The auction was well-attended, and the price for the Orioles was bid up by Jeffrey Loria and a group of investors from Ohio, headed by William O. DeWitt Jr. from Cincinnati. DeWitt was close to finalizing a deal at more than $143 million when wealthy Baltimore attorney Peter Angelos said, "The ownership of this team is not going to Ohio. It's coming back to Maryland. We are going to bid whatever it takes."[13] Angelos had an expanded group of investors that included such Baltimore notables as Pam Shriver, the professional tennis player, and Tom Clancy, the successful novelist. Together they submitted a successful final bid of $173 million. It was $100 million more than Jacobs had paid four years earlier.

Angelos was the majority owner. As a hard-charging personal injury lawyer and with his iconoclastic view of the baseball world, he would come front and center all too soon. After the successful bid for the team, he quickly made his presence felt. Free agency had become what one writer called a "feeding frenzy that saw a combined $280 million spent to sign players at the 1992 winter meetings."[14] Angelos found the waters to his liking, and even before the winter meetings in December 1993, he signed Sid Fernandez, the longtime New York Mets pitcher who had helped take the team to the 1986 World Series. That November deal was succeeded by the inking of Rafael Palmeiro in December, followed by the additions of Chris Sabo and Lee Smith in January 1994. Lee Smith had led the National League in saves in 1991–1992, and replaced Gregg Olson, who had signed with the Atlanta Braves.

It was an impressive haul, but Palmeiro would prove to be the most significant upgrade. Taking over for Randy Milligan at first base, he brought with him a slugging reputation from the Texas Rangers, where he had hit 37 home runs in 1993, batting .295. Taken as a whole, the signings signaled the willingness of the new owner to spend money to put a winner on the field at Camden Yards. The Baltimore payroll went from $27 million in 1993—17th among the 28 major-league teams, to $38 million—10th overall.

The big spending by the new owner pointed the team in new directions. There was no doubt he wanted a quick return on his investment. Marginal improvement did not appear to be enough to keep the new owner content, as he ramped up the pressure for a winner in Baltimore. Those expectations created a building pressure on Johnny Oates and Dick Bosman as they began the 1994 season, their third together in the Charm City. But a larger pressure point was crowning within the business of baseball, one that would have historic implications for the game.

10

Money and Baseball

The free-agent signings of new owner Peter Angelos were more fuel on an already-raging fire. The explosion of free-agent salaries could not be capped, and the economy of baseball was in an inflationary spiral that seemed out of control to many of the owners. They were looking for some way to rein in their own worst impulses to overspend. In 1990, they had locked the players out, only to settle before the beginning of the season. But most of the issues that had forced action then remained on the back burner, simmering slowly.

In 1992, the baseball owners voted by a margin of 15–13 to reopen the collective bargaining agreement (CBA). After the first strike in 1972, in which Dick Bosman had played a substantial role, there had been three more in 1980, 1981, and 1985, as well as three lockouts by ownership—in 1973, 1976, and 1990. The 1980s saw a steady escalation in television revenues for baseball. The money fueled an escalation in free-agent salaries such that the owners and others in baseball believed a counterbalance was needed to their own worst impulse spending.

Collusion had worked in the 1980s to keep the top player salary at $2 million annually.[1] But the dike broke in 1989, and new owners like Angelos fed the blaze, as salaries roared higher. Baseball had been divided into three warring parties: the rich owners, the less rich owners, and the players' union. Angelos had aligned himself with the wealthy owners.

As a more or less united front, ownership had been mulling a variety of proposals to address their concerns. One popular notion was revenue sharing between the rich and poor teams. But such ideas were not widely supported by the wealthy in the larger society, and enough of the owners were skeptical whether such ideas made sense for them. They could not reach agreement about revenue sharing, and the issue of player salaries was at a similar impasse.

Players were afraid of any governor placed on salary arbitration and even surlier at the mention of a salary cap, which they knew would be the beginning of a steady reduction in salaries. Without an updated CBA, the 1994 season began with only the promise from both sides that they would continue to work toward solutions for issues that appeared intractable.

Against this backdrop, Dick Bosman and Johnny Oates began the spring of 1994 with high hopes, created by Angelos's offseason acquisitions. And the new owner believed he had something to say about the team as well, sparking a level of owner involvement Bosman had seen only once before. Bob Short had served as his own general manager, and his presence had defined the direction of the team through player acquisitions that were often ill-considered. Peter Angelos appeared to be cut from similar cloth.

"It became apparent very quickly that he and his sons [fantasy baseball aficionados] were going to be a part of things. Ill-advised as it was, you were going to have things that would happen upstairs that baseball people did not quite agree with," Bosman opined with considerable diplomacy about the new ownership group.[2]

In the clubhouse and on the field, Johnny Oates, Dick Bosman, and Greg Biagini were more focused on winning games. The labor drama of the day was an off-stage riot, and the new owners were involved in that, as well as consulting the fantasy directives of the day. Their interaction was mostly confined to working with the front-office staff, which included Roland Hemond as general manager, along with Doug Melvin and Frank Robinson as assistant GMs. Bosman attended to the issues in front of him. How could he make the pitching staff he was given into a winner? How could they improve on the results from the prior season?

"When we showed up for the game in the early afternoon, the only thing that we paid attention to was the game that night," Bosman related. "We had an advance scout in Deacon Jones, who reported to us on the teams we were playing, and Elrod Hendricks, who had his own scouting knowledge of the other teams." Nothing got in the way of the day-to-day operation of the team, although, of course, there were the Ripkens, who were in the clubhouse and were still a link to the Oriole legacy of the prior three decades. "The Oriole Way was as good a fundamental brand of baseball as you ever will find," Dick attested.

There was more to it than just the sound fundamentals. Dick recalled a day when Greg Biagini was running batting practice for the big-league roster. In much the same way the team in Rochester had worked, he asked Cal Ripken and the other regulars to shag fly balls while another round of their teammates got into the batting cage. "These guys need to go back inside and get ready for the game," said Cal Ripken Sr., explaining to Biagini and the other new guys the special rules of the pecking order. The deference due to established players was another part of the Oriole Way, which was almost as trying as the overzealous owners.

Bosman believes that Biagini was particularly astute in how he handled what could have been a difficult situation. In 1994, there were a lot of moving pieces in the clubhouse and the front office. It was complicated. Dick found that some of the new pitchers who were brought on board did not want to try new things, like the slide step routine. Sid Fernandez was able to incorporate it into his motion and in retrospect, "We had about as much success with it [the slide step] as could be expected. Chris Hoiles at catcher was a converted infielder who threw average at best," said Bosman.

For all of those limitations, the team was able to control the running game relatively well. They were able to limit the damage overall, as the Orioles pitching staff finished the 1994 season with the third-best ERA in the American League. Much of the credit went to Mike Mussina, who

> "Keep it simple." How comfortable is the young pitcher with his mechanics? The delivery has to be an almost unconscious element that the pitcher takes to the mound each time he enters a game. The more natural and calm the mechanics of the delivery, the easier they are to replicate each time he throws the ball.

returned from his injury-plagued season to reestablish his position as undisputed ace. He took the Opening Day start against the Kansas City Royals on April 4. Kevin Appier was the opposing pitcher, and the two hurlers would hook up for some well-pitched games in the coming seasons, but this one belonged to Mussina, who went eight innings and allowed only a single run.

Ben McDonald started the second game and outpitched David Cone to win by a 4–2 margin. The gritty performance of the two hurlers carried the club as the season wore on, but the club could score runs as well. They managed 5.26 runs per game for the strike-shortened season, but that was only good for sixth best in the American League.

Like player salaries, offensive output in baseball was exploding. The average number of runs scored by each team in a game was climbing toward a late 1990s heyday when Mark McGwire and Sammy Sosa would set the stage for Barry Bonds. Against that backdrop, Mike Mussina was able to fashion a 3.06 ERA, which once again was among the best in baseball. He won 16 games against only five losses and would almost certainly have won 20 games had the season lasted the full 162 games. McDonald posted a 14–7 record in one of his best seasons as well.

Behind good pitching and a lusty offense, the Orioles settled into second place in early June behind the New York Yankees. They were on the heels of a Yankees team led by Don Mattingly, Paul O'Neill, and Bernie Williams. The 1994 campaign marked the second year of play for the Colorado Rockies and the Florida Marlins, who were added to the National League, but more important was the boldest new feature added to the game in many years, the wild card as a facet of the postseason. With this new feature, the Orioles, although trailing the Yankees in August, were just a game or two behind the Cleveland Indians and Kansas City Royals for the fourth spot in the new expanded round robin, which would determine the American League championship.

In 1994, there were many in baseball who believed there would be no wild-card games or anything else in the postseason. The labor situation did not improve as the season wore on. If anything, it got worse. With no progress toward a new CBA, many expected a lockout or strike at the end of the spring in 1994. But the games continued under a sword of Damocles hanging by an exceedingly worn thread. As a former player rep, Dick Bosman talked about the situation with Mike Mussina and Jim Poole, the team's two player representatives that year. Information coming from them indicated it was just a matter of time until there was a strike.

Dick was in an awkward situation, part of management but still being paid by the licensing program run by the MLBPA. He did not have the security that the union provided and was more subject to the whims of ownership than the players, but he benefitted from revenue streams past union wins against the owners had gained for the players overall.

Everyone knew that television revenues fueled the abundance teams were spending on free agents, but the owners were aware that the golden goose was not going to be laying for long. The existing national television contract was losing money for ESPN and CBS, and was due to be renegotiated. Additionally, the owners had just paid $280 million in collusion penalties in 1992. At the end of the 1992 season, they fired the commissioner, Fay Vincent, and installed Milwaukee Brewers owner Bud Selig in the position on a temporary basis, although he would later be named the permanent commissioner and serve until 2015.

Selig and Chicago White Sox owner Jerry Reinsdorf were labor hawks who were willing to play high-risk games to rein in the runaway financial structures of the game. Reinsdorf was from the faction of wealthy owners, whereas Selig was a stalwart of the "small-market" teams, some of whom were struggling financially. Small-market teams wanted revenue sharing from the richer franchises. It was the thorniest issue on the table, although it was one that affected only the owners and their ability to govern themselves. But the proposals for revenue sharing were woven into the CBA.

Reinsdorf's pet peeve was salary arbitration, and he hated when negotiators forced him to pay his players higher salaries because of, as he put it, "what my stupid competitors pay."[3] The issue that united the owners—small market and large alike—was their desire to gain salary concessions from the players. The most obvious mechanism for achieving salary concessions was a cap like the ones in place in the National Basketball Association and the National Football League. With so many owner factions to deal with and stiff headwinds on so many issues, the players union could make almost no headway in the negotiations. To bring matters to a head, the MLBPA announced that if no new CBA could be reached, they would strike on August 12.

The union calculated that date to give them maximum leverage because the players would have received most of their pay for the year. They believed such a late date would put maximum pressure on the owners to resolve their issues before the postseason, from which ownership derived much of their money. The owners responded by withholding the August payment into the Players Pension Fund. The MLBPA filed a grievance that would be won later.

But the owners further escalated their demands beyond a salary cap and revenue sharing to include a share of the players' lucrative licensing fees.

Licensing fees were a boon that Bosman knew well. Anything that required the participation of all major-league baseball players, things like baseball cards, most notably, or computer games, which would become increasingly popular, earned the MLBPA and its members licensing fees. Innocuous sounding to the average fan, licensing fees have grown to almost $3 billion in total revenues and in the early 1990s, during the various strikes and lockouts, gave each player as much as $80,000 annually with which to withstand the economic pressures the owners could marshal against them.[4]

When Ben McDonald beat the New York Yankees and Jimmy Key on August 10, no one knew it was the last game of the season. The Orioles had won five of their last six games and were playing their best ball of the season, but it came to end that night at old Yankee Stadium. The players walked off the field on August 12, in lockstep, and no one was particularly happy.

The fans were divided in their loyalties. Some said the players were "overpaid crybabies," while others faulted the greed of the owners, but in unison they groused about the steady rise in ticket prices, which were driving the average family away from the game.[5] Dick Bosman told his wife Pam that the strike would probably be over soon, and he stayed in the Baltimore area playing golf with John Lowenstein and Don Buford. They traveled to Bowie, Maryland, to watch the Double-A Baysox team play minor-league ball for a while. That team had a talented pitching staff, featuring a closer named Armando Benitez. The staff took the team to the Eastern League playoffs in the first part of September.

Within days of watching the Eastern League playoffs in Bowie, it became clear that Dick would not be working with Benitez or any other Baltimore pitchers in the near future. The negotiations between the MLBPA and ownership went nowhere as the two sides dug in their heels. There were alarming indications that the strike could go on indefinitely, and on September 14 the owners met and declared that the season was being called off, along with the postseason and the World Series.

The timing of the MLBPA backfired. They had forced the issue in hopes of bringing the owners to the bargaining table, but the immediate loss of revenues from the postseason was not as daunting as the long-term financial issues confronting ownership. They had failed to reach an agreement on such issues as revenue sharing and found no way forward in general. Their response was to push back against the MLBPA, the devil that united them when all else failed. There were some owners—most notably Marge Schott—who wanted to play the World Series with replacement players.[6] But that would become a story for the following spring.

Realizing that everything was over, Bosman told his wife to come get him and his stuff. Shortly after the season was canceled, Johnny Oates was fired by Angelos.[7] The press reported that only a handful of teams had been as successful as the Orioles under the tutelage of Oates and his staff, but it did not seem to matter. Roland Hemond, the general manager who had brought Oates and Bosman to Baltimore, was retained, along with Frank Robinson, to run the front office. Bosman's future remained undetermined, but Dick knew he was part of the Oates decision as well. He heard as much about it in the press as from ownership. The *Washington Post* carried the news on September 29, amid speculation that former Orioles pitcher Mike Flanagan would replace him.[8]

Dick told the press he was not bitter, even though he would have preferred a phone call from someone rather than hearing the news in the local papers. "Bosman inherited a pitching staff in disarray in 1991, and presided over a dramatic turnaround," opined *Sporting News* in an article after the firing.[9] Ben McDonald, in the same article, was quoted as saying he knew Oates would be fired because the "communication was not there." But he expressed surprise that the front office had followed suit with Bosman. "He [Bosman] was not only a good pitching coach, but a good friend and someone you could talk to about anything," McDonald declared. Ben lauded all Dick had done not only for his career and Mussina's, but also the senior players who were brought in as well, mentioning Rick Sutcliffe and Jamie Moyer, in particular.

It was a sad time for baseball, but there were silver linings almost everywhere. Doug Melvin called Dick once he and Pam were back in Palm Harbor, Florida, where they now made their home in the offseason. Melvin had been hired as GM for the Texas Rangers, and Johnny Oates was going to manage. Melvin had come under fire for hiring Oates so quickly, without interviewing others. He told Dick he would need to interview other candidates for the job as major-league pitching coach but that the post was, in essence, his. Dick was going back to Texas.

There was no Oriole Way in Texas. Baltimore had returned to the major-league fold as the relocated home of the St. Louis Browns in 1954. A dozen years later, they were vying for the American League championship. The Texas Rangers had relocated from Washington in 1972, along with Frank Howard and Dick Bosman, but after 23 years in Arlington, the best they had ever done was finish second in the seven-team American League West. The Rangers had managed that trick six times but had never won it all, never played in a single postseason game.

The Texas Rangers were bought in 1989 by an ownership group fronted by George W. Bush, son of then-president George Herbert Walker Bush. Bush withdrew from his position as managing general partner when he was elected governor in 1994, at a time when the strike was at full fury. Tom Schieffer, a friend of Bush's, took over as team president and, along with co-owner Edward Rose, became the voice of ownership.

Schieffer was no Peter Angelos, and the Texas ownership allowed their front office to run the team without a heavy hand, as had been the case in Baltimore. But the expectations created by the new structure of the two leagues and the wild-card provisions raised the hopes of ownership and fans. With the new divisional structure of the two leagues, the Rangers had a one-in-four chance of making the playoffs every season going forward. For a team that had never seen postseason action, the future had new meaning.

The sense of possibility buoyed Bosman as well. "It was special to be back," Dick remembered, and there was an underlying emotion of returning home. But so much had changed. When he had tried to relocate to Milwaukee after his playing years, he had learned how difficult it was to go home again. Now he was revisiting his baseball roots and wondered whether he would fare any better with this move. He had started his major-league career with the Texas Ranger franchise when it was located in Washington. He and Frank Howard had been the best players on a bad team when it moved to Texas, and then they had led them on strike in their first spring training with the new team.

"We weren't very good," Dick reflected. "We were the Texas Rangers, but we were still the Washington Senators in different uniforms. Actually, they weren't even different. They just took Senators off the front and put Rangers on it."[10] Bosman and the Texas Rangers had history together. He had been the Opening Day starter for the first game ever played by the Rangers, and now there was going to be a new chapter written in a new ballpark, which, for all intents and purposes, looked rather like Camden Yards.

The Rangers played in the old Arlington Stadium for more than 20 years. The original park had held little more than 10,000 fans, but the seating capacity had been augmented with numerous additions to the original facility so that it held 43,000 fans. The new Ballpark in Arlington, which replaced it to begin the 1994 season, was commissioned at much the same time as Camden Yards and built with many of the same design features. Its brick and granite façade was reminiscent of many of the original baseball parks in the first half of the twentieth century, as were its irregular dimensions.

The new stadium and the new circumstances of playing in the diminished American League West promised much to the faithful in the Dallas-Ft. Worth metropolitan region, which was home to the Rangers. The irregular dimensions of the park had been built to order for first baseman Rafael Palmeiro, who was the heart of the Texas batting order when the stadium was commissioned.

"The alley in left-center field where the visitor's bullpen is, the ball did not carry there," recalled Dick. The ball carried "easy" into the right-field bullpen. The left-handed-hitting Palmeiro pulled the ball naturally to the right side of the field and hit many of his home runs into the first two rows of the right-field bleachers. Later, when Juan Gonzalez was the slugger who anchored that lineup, "I saw many of Juan's fly balls die on the warning track in left-center field," Dick stated with certainty. Palmeiro was still earning his free-agent millions in Baltimore in 1995, when Gonzalez had replaced him batting cleanup for the Rangers.

The stadium dimensions may not have been perfect for their best hitter, but in 1995, Texas was counting on new management to turn their fortunes around. They had invested in Johnny Oates and Dick Bosman to help them realize their high hopes in the first year after the strike, the first season when the wild card could conceivably carry them to the playoffs. From the last time that Bosman had pitched for the Rangers in 1973, there had been a constant procession of managers cutting their teeth and trying new things. Whitey Herzog, as a rookie manager, had wanted pitchers who threw harder than Bosman. His vision of a competitive pitching staff had quickly given way to the more pugnacious style of Billy Martin. The merry-go-round of new managers and the increased expectations that came with them had produced only close calls. Now there was an expectation with better odds for success. The Rangers had finished atop the newly configured American League West during the strike-shortened 1994 season in front of crowds that cooed throughout the new stadium all summer long.

The wild card sat on top of this new configuration like fine millinery on a beautiful woman. Three divisions created an odd number of winners at the end of the season, each of whom automatically qualified for postseason play. To those three were added a wild-card team with the best record in the league outside those three winners. The Rangers now had two chances to make the playoffs, as did every other team in both leagues. If Texas failed to win the Western Division, there was always hope they might win the wild-card slot.

The resulting round robin added another layer of competition in determining each league's representative in the World Series. More importantly, it created new interest in the outcome of each summer's pennant races, as there were now four teams with a chance at the postseason in each league rather than only two.

There were flaws in the system, and nothing illustrated those weaknesses better than the Texas Rangers in 1994. The team was 10 games under .500 that year but still led their division when the players walked off the field. Their position atop the Western Division was a precarious one, as both the Seattle Mariners and the Oakland Athletics had been within easy reach when play ended. But the idea that three teams in the American League West were within easy shot of the playoffs—none of which were playing .500 baseball— illustrated the appeal of the new league structures to fans, but also why it was a bugaboo to purists who wanted to see only the best teams in the postseason.

In October 1994, when Doug Melvin, Johnny Oates, and Dick Bosman signed on with the Rangers, there was an assumption that the labor dispute would be resolved well before the beginning of the next season. But as the fall turned into winter, there was no progress with the negotiations. President Bill Clinton got involved, to no avail. The owners attempted to dictate the terms of the subsequent new agreement when they declared in late December that an impasse in negotiations had been reached. They hardwired a salary cap and their latest ideas for revenue sharing into what they considered the ultimate agreement, which would govern baseball moving forward. The MLBPA filed an unfair labor practices claim with the National Labor Relations Board (NLRB), which ultimately ended up in the courts.

To make matters even worse, the owners seized on Marge Schott's notion of replacement players and announced they would begin the season with nonunion players taking the field when the 1995 season began. Spring training began with only replacement players in camp, but the log jam was finally broken when the NLRB ruled by a 3–2 margin that the owners had acted to try to force a settlement on the players illegally. The responsibility for working out a settlement fell to federal judge Sonia Sotomayor, who acted quickly and ruled that the owner's declaration of an impasse in negotiations was illegal and voided their actions.

The union voted to end the strike and announced they would play according to the terms of the prior CBA. It was as if everything from August 1994 to March 1995—232 days of lost time—had been a bad dream, and Judge Sotamayor was the good witch from the *Wizard of Oz* who told Dorothy to click her heels and return everyone to Kansas. The usual weeks devoted to spring training in Port Charlotte, Florida, had been spent by Dick Bosman and Johnny Oates trying to get the replacement players into shape for the season. Bosman was in a difficult position as part of management and took a lot of heat from the MLBPA.

"There were some threats made that we would be removed from the Licensing Program and the Pension Fund," according to Dick. He added,

> Bucky Dent and I drove from Port Charlotte over to Orlando for a meeting of the Players Association, and I addressed that group. There were a lot of guys there, and I said, "Look you guys need to understand where we have been with this thing. We were the first guys who stood up to ownership in 1972, when we went out on strike then. Do you think we *want* to do this?"

Dick's call for understanding was heard, and the threats to managers and coaches largely disappeared.

The Rangers' principal owner, Tom Schieffer, had been determined to go through with the charade of having players who were, at best, minor leaguers taking the field on Opening Day. "They had stuff set up in the clubhouse for these clowns on Opening Day. And the video board was ready to display their faces," Dick recalled. "When that strike broke, Schieffer was not a happy man." Bosman and Oates, who had been working out with the replacement players in Port Charlotte and had flown with them to Dallas for Opening Day, were almost as ecstatic as the players when the strike broke and the Rangers regulars were welcomed back into camp. Everyone—players and management—flew to Florida for an abbreviated seven-day spring training, which was not enough but had to suffice.

"Part of spring training is getting to know your guys, how they tick and what you want to do with them eventually," Dick said of the abbreviated 1995 preseason. "There was a certain amount of chaos that spring and no time to really formulate a plan for the season."

Although they had not owned a winning record in 1994, the Rangers were a far better team than their record indicated. They were anchored by three All-Star players, catcher Ivan Rodriguez, first baseman Will Clark, and outfielder Juan Gonzalez. "Pudge" Rodriguez was one of the best catchers in the history of the game and was voted into the Baseball Hall of Fame in 2017. Clark was coming off a year in which he hit .329 and had been considered for a Gold Glove. Before the strike, Gonzalez had hit more than 40 home runs in 1992 and 1993, to lead the American League. The Rangers could score runs with the best of them. But as with so many teams that had hired Dick Bosman, they could not pitch.

In 1994, the Texas Rangers were saved from the bottom of the barrel by the woeful Minnesota Twins pitching staff. The presence of left-hander Kenny Rogers spared Texas pitching the cellar. He was the staff ace and as dependable a pitcher as the game could offer in his 20-year career in the majors. Overall, the Texas Rangers staff was reminiscent of the 1986 Chicago White Sox for its tendency to issue bases on balls. Like the White Sox, there were few young arms in the Texas Rangers organization on which to pin hopes.

Kenny Rogers was 30, and the rest of the staff included two 34-year-olds, Kevin Gross and Bob Tewksbury. Gross had led the league in walks and hit batsmen in prior years, neither category an indication of tight control of his pitches. The complicating factor was the quickly emerging tendency of the Ballpark in Arlington to give up inordinate quantities of home runs. Long fly balls that would have been caught in many major-league parks were aided by the heat and swirling winds in Arlington, which carried them into the stands as home runs. Giving a free pass to batters too often led to two- and three-run homers by the opposition.

Once again, Dick was the "new guy on the block," as he recalled the feeling of working with a veteran staff, many of whom had been with Texas for several years. More importantly, he was replacing Tom House, who had been the Texas pitching coach for a decade. In those years, House worked with Texas Rangers icon Nolan Ryan, who credited House in his Hall of Fame acceptance speech and called him a "cutting-edge" pitching coach.[11]

Dick was in agreement that House's approach to teaching the art of pitching was unique in the profession, although all pitching coaches have a similar approach to teaching mechanics. "There are certain things in the pitching delivery that are absolutes," Bosman stated. House's methods were generally within the bounds of those concepts, but Dick disagreed with his emphasis on weight training and an overemphasis on "trying to trick the hitter." Texas pitching had quit fooling as many hitters as it needed to, however, and in 1991, the team ERA was the worst in the American League and nearly as bad in 1994.

Dick had few hopes of changing the veterans on the Texas staff, but he knew from prior experience that he could not "come in and barnstorm the whole thing." As in Baltimore, much of Dick's first year was one of evaluation, of figuring out "who I wanted and who I did not want." One hot summer night in Arlington, Dick remembers being on the mound trying to counsel a young pitcher who was struggling mightily. Umpire Daryl Cousins came out to the mound and said, "Come on Boz, let's go." Dick asked for a few more moments to work with the young pitcher. "Dick, you should have thought of that months ago," said Cousins, according to Dick.

Bosman was playing catch-up, but to counter some of the ideas that were ascendant with the Texas staff, he emphasized the need to throw strikes. "When a pitcher gets ahead in the count, it opens a lot of options," Dick explained to a reporter a year later, during the 1996 season. "The reward is that he gets to throw a bigger selection of pitches into a bigger strike zone."[12] It was a simple philosophy, but it required more than just stating the obvious. It was a subtle campaign as Dick tried to tinker around the edges with the established pitchers, while working with others who had a tenuous hold on their big-league status. As writer Mel Antonen observed, "It is a Rangers tradition to be short on pitching."[13] Bosman was determined to turn that tradition around.

Bosman was no longer a minor-league pitching coach trying to help young hurlers make the majors. He had to find ways to help the entire staff become more consistent. There was one relatively young pitcher on the staff who was a possible project for Bosman. The 27-year-old Roger Pavlik had pitched well in 1993, but he suffered a setback in 1994, when he encountered his first of numerous injuries. Pavlik's pitching motion was unorthodox at best. He was an extreme example of throwing across the body. Bosman knew there was only so much change he could bring to some of the Texas pitchers, and "Roger was a perfect example of that."

Dick compared Pavlik's mechanics to other pitchers whose mechanics are idiosyncratic. "Try visualizing Jake Arrieta's delivery, only exaggerate it once more again. It was like he was trying to throw the ball into the third-base dugout." But Bosman tried a patient approach for the most part. He suggested to Pavlik that they try minor improvements in his mechanics, which might help him throw strikes more consistently. It was in the bullpen, and Dick had the catcher's gear on when Pavlik asked for some time to think about the notion. Said Bosman, "He walked over to the water fountain and came back and said, 'I can't do that.'"

"It became pretty clear early on that his approach was pretty well ingrained in him," Dick recalled. He was surprised that the Texas organization had allowed Pavlik to develop at the lower levels of the minors without altering his mechanics, but as it was, the young pitcher had an ability to "repeat an unorthodox delivery so many times that he was able to make it work for the most part." More importantly, Dick knew that butting heads with Pavlik was not worth the risk of losing the confidence of one of his starting pitchers. Dissension could spread, and there were already minor dissatisfactions brewing.

Whether or not the moving parts achieved poetic perfection, the numbers posted by Pavlik in 1995, under the watchful eye of Bosman, were better than they had been in prior years. He posted his best career numbers, winning 10 games and pitching to an ERA of 4.37, significantly better than the league average of 4.71. The rest of the staff found similar success, but it did not come any easier for Bosman than it had with Pavlik.

Left-hander Kenny Rogers was a converted bullpen pitcher; he was just beginning to find his form as a starter. The 1995 campaign would be his best as the anchor of the rotation, and despite the success they achieved together, the relationship between Bosman and Rogers was inconsistent at best. At the end of the season, Rogers signed with the New York Yankees as a free agent, and early in the next season he opined to the press that his former team—the Rangers—"had never been a major-league organization." Laying bare the emotions that existed between player and coach, Bosman responded that he was happy without Rogers in his 1996 rotation because without him, "There won't be any mood swings."[14]

Whether or not there was complete agreement on the approach everyone was taking, the Texas Rangers pitching staff showed marked improvements overall, as it posted an ERA that was in the top half of the American League rather than at the bottom. Every starter improved his ERA for the season with the exception of 34-year-old Kevin Gross, who was nearing the end of his career and had lost much of his effectiveness. The bullpen of Roger McDowell and Jeff Russell was a strong late-inning resource, and the team finished above .500, with a record of 74 wins against 70 defeats for the second consecutive strike-shortened season. That record was good for only third place in the American League West, four and one-half games behind the Seattle Mariners.

In one area that was of particular interest to Bosman, the running game, the Rangers had one of the best weapons Dick would ever have at his disposal: Ivan "Pudge" Rodriguez as catcher. "I never saw Johnny Bench very much, except at spring training," Dick opined as he mused about the catcher he believes had the best defense of any against the running game. "But to watch this kid catch and throw on a daily basis, and he caught a lot, it was a real treat. He did not come out of the lineup much. Could he hit the fastball? You betcha. He was allergic to the breaking ball, which a lot of guys are, but he could hit."

It was a simple equation for Pudge. He did not call the games expertly, and Dick told his pitchers that they needed to "make damn sure that what he is calling for is something that you want to throw." Rodriguez was going to call for a fastball away if there was a runner on first base to give him the best position for throwing the ball to second. But hitters figured that out quickly. It was incumbent on the pitcher to make certain they only threw the fastball away in counts that made sense to them, not every time Rodriguez called for it. Pudge was a great catch-and-throw receiver, but too often his own concerns about the runner on first came at the expense of what the pitcher might throw to the hitter.

The offense could count numerous starters that had been brought up through the Texas organization. Aside from Rodriguez at catcher, there was Juan Gonzalez in right field, who would win two MVP Awards and hit almost 500 home runs for his career. There was Dean Palmer at third base, who was a reliable fielder and could hit the ball out of the Ballpark in Arlington as well as anyone. Moreover, the outfield featured Rusty Greer and the middle infield Jeff Frye and Benji Gil, all of whom had come up with the Rangers. There was little of the same kind of homegrown talent on the pitching side with which Bosman could work.

On the pitching side, Bobby Witt and Roger Pavlik were perfect examples of high-end talent taken by the Rangers in the Amateur Draft. Both men were gifted throwers who might have benefitted from an orchestrated effort to teach them the fundamentals of pitching at the minor-league level. Witt would become a dependable member of the Texas rotation in 1996 and 1997, but Bosman believed he could have been better. There was an important flaw in Witt's approach to the game, one that he shared with many others but that undermined what could have been a special talent.

"He had a big, live fastball and a pretty good slider," Dick said of Witt. "We had a great relationship—I thought we did at least—but when things got tight in the game, he tried to do more, and inevitably doing more became doing less." Bosman believes it is a crucial point that pitchers, especially young ones, fail to understand adequately. When Dick went out to the mound during those high-stress moments in games Bobby Witt pitched,

> Try as I might to talk to him, to reason with him, to get him to back off a little bit. . . . Rotella says it all the time. If you think trying hard is difficult, try trying less. When you are a competitor, to be able to breathe, to relax and rationalize what you are going to do, and trust what you *can* do at a reasonable effort, is a very, very big challenge for a lot of guys.

Bosman continued,

> Edwin Jackson is another perfect example of that. Edwin Jackson has electric stuff, but when the chips are on the line, he wants to throw it 150. He wants to throw the slider from hell, and it never happens to get there. When you are out there, you are your own man. You have to control your emotions and your effort to get the job done. It doesn't work sometimes, and in Bobby Witt's case that was kind of the way it was.

There was one other pitching talent drafted by the Rangers who was showing some semblance of success: a 24-year-old left-hander named Darren Oliver. He was coming off two arm surgeries when he arrived in the majors.

"They had been pitching him out of the bullpen," Dick remembered. Bosman was not convinced it was the proper role for the young hurler.

After outlining the hazards of pitching Oliver out of the bullpen, Dick recommended to Johnny Oates that they convert him to starting. He said, "We'll let him throw only 75 pitches his first few starts, but he will know what day he has to pitch." Bosman thought their best chance to keep Oliver healthy was to provide him a regimented pitching routine, and the best way to do that was by adding him to the rotation. "He was probably one of the best examples of what we [Oates and Bosman] were able to do there," declared Dick, speaking of Darren Oliver as a dependable piece of a starting rotation that took the Rangers to the playoffs three times under their tutelage.

> Not every pitching talent is made for the starting rotation. To make it through a big-league lineup three, four times, the pitcher must master the elements of strategy. He has to know what each batter's strengths and weaknesses are, and have an idea what he will throw them and adjust his knowledge as the game unfolds.

11

Returning to Texas

The 1995 season was a difficult one for Johnny Oates and Dick Bosman. The strike ended suddenly, and the season seemed to start late and end early. Many of the players were just gaining confidence in the new management team when the season came to a conclusion. Those who had not bought into the new scheme, such as Kenny Rogers, moved on to something new. But for the most part, the strategies Bosman and Oates employed in 1995 laid the groundwork for a leap forward in the 1996 season. Such projects as converting Darren Oliver into a starting pitcher were part of using the 1995 campaign to figure out a plan for moving ahead. In the spring of 1995, there had been too little time to assess the talent and devise a plan, so much of the job of strategizing the Rangers had been done on the fly during the season.

Repetition of the delivery is the first test of pitching talent for scouts after they take the first radar gun readings. Once the flamethrowers are drafted, it is left to professionals like Dick Bosman to streamline that initial motion, to work the kinks out so that as a young man progresses through the organization, there is an easy fluidity to his motion.

When the following spring rolled around, there was better knowledge of what worked and what did not. There was a robust offensive attack, that was a certainty, and with improved pitching, the Rangers approached the 1996 slate with new hope. Kenny Rogers was in New York City, but Doug Melvin brought in Ken Hill to replace him. Hill was a right-handed pitcher, but like Rogers he had top-tier talent and desire. He "did not throw particularly hard but had a split-finger fastball that was his out pitch," Dick recalled. "He threw hard enough but had to locate the ball a little bit. He was a competitor, and he went after you."[1]

Part of being a competitor was having the ability and willingness to throw inside to keep the batter honest. In one of Dick's pitching bibles, *The Art of Pitching* by Tom Seaver, there is the following admonition: "Somewhere in the sequence of pitches in each game to every batter, the fastball must be thrown *in*, off the plate, as a message that says, 'Don't forget, I might come back in here at any moment.'"[2] Hill was that kind of competitor.

In Bosman's book, being a competitor had just as much to do with being smart in how you set up a single game plan or a season-long plan for success. Like most pitching coaches, Dick wanted his Texas starters to go as deep into the game as possible. His belief in pitching more to contact provided a realistic strategy to accomplish the goal, and getting his pitchers to throw or add pitches that induced ground balls was an essential mechanism for implementing one of Bosman's best strategic approaches to any game during any season. Introducing new pitchers the likes of Kenny Hill to these concepts became an early part of the program. Pitching to contact and throwing ground balls was Bosman's favorite approach. It led to fewer walks, better defense, and fewer pitches per start. The approach had proven effective in 1995, as the Rangers pitching staff led the majors with 19 complete games that season

Hill pitched 250 innings with a 3.63 ERA in the 1996 season, when the league average was an ERA of 4.99. He averaged more than seven innings per game, which made him the top student in Bosman's pitching class. Roger Pavlik added 201 innings of his own, and the rotation as a whole helped keep the bullpen fresh throughout the season. Bosman knew he could not overwork guys like Mike Henneman, who had been signed as a free agent the previous December. Henneman had been extremely effective as the closer for both Detroit and Houston in 1995, pitching to a 2.15 ERA.

> Pitching to contact and throwing ground balls was Bosman's favorite approach. It led to fewer walks, better defense, and fewer pitches per start.

Henneman moved Jeff Russell from the closer role to that of primary late-inning setup man. "Russell was one of the best right-handed arms I was ever around," Dick remembered. With Henneman they had two quality bullpen arms to complement a much-improved rotation. "Henneman was nervous on the mound," Dick recalled. "My god, he was nervous. But it was a situation where I learned that you can be nervous and still get it done. He was that guy because he could keep those butterflies flying in formation."

The bullpen had become a more important element in winning games for almost every big-league club. The closer was the showcase, and every team wanted a big arm coming into the ninth inning. It had become an essential component of the game, but being able to bring high-quality arms into the game even earlier than the ninth inning gave the 1996 Rangers a weapon many teams did not have.

The rotation was bolstered by the return of Bobby Witt to the Rangers fold in August 1995, from the Florida Marlins. After spending the first six seasons of his major-league career with Texas, Witt had been traded in 1992, along with Ruben Sierra and Jeff Russell, to the Oakland Athletics for Jose Canseco. He spent three seasons in Oakland and the first half of the 1995 season with the Marlins before being traded back to Texas. Witt had been the third overall pick in the Amateur Draft in 1985, from the University of Oklahoma. He had the live fastball that made scouts drool but no idea where the ball was going when it came out of his hand. He was promoted to the majors in his first full season in 1986, when the question of his readiness was underscored when he led the American League in walks, with 143, and wild pitches, with 22. He posted a 5.86 ERA and led the league again in walks in 1987, with 140.

Witt was 32 years old in 1996, and as a seasoned pro, he would have one of his best campaigns using the concepts that he and Bosman agreed on in the spring. Again, it was Bosman's idea of pitching to contact. Witt was able to incorporate a two-seam fastball into his repertoire. "He was able to get more ground balls instead of four-seam fastballs that were fouled off all the time. It allowed him to pitch deeper into ballgames," where he stood to win behind the Texas offense. Implementing Bosman's strategy, Bobby Witt won 16 games in 1996.

He also bought one of the first hot rods that Dick would build and sell. The car was a 1946 Chevrolet, and Bosman put a large new engine into the car and such modern components as power steering, cruise control, power windows,

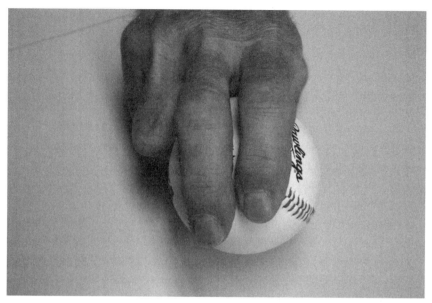

Dick Bosman demonstrates the grip for a two-seam fastball. It's your movement fastball that is thrown at the knees. The arm slot should not be too high to keep the ball low in the zone.

and air conditioning. Bosman considered pitching and automobile mechanics from a similar angle. "I like making them better than they were before," Dick said of the old classic American roadsters he remade into modern driving machines. "It's kind of like teaching pitchers and making them better than they were before."[3]

Darren Oliver established himself as a quality starter in 1996. He managed 30 starts but only 173 innings, as Oates and Bosman tried a slow transition in moving him from a bullpen pitcher to the rotation. Oliver was another of Bosman's projects that paid dividends and helped establish a deep starting rotation that took off from the start of the season. Even Kevin Gross would manage double-digit wins, as did the rest of the Rangers rotation. Both Hill and Witt won 16 games, Pavlik won 15, and Oliver accrued 14, to give Texas as formidable a set of starters as any team in the league. Pavlik was chosen for the American League All-Star Team in 1996, behind his 10–2 record at the end of June, although he faded badly down the stretch.

Juan Gonzalez's MVP season was one of the driving forces behind Texas in 1996. Hitting in a lineup with Dean Palmer, who had 38 home runs, and Rusty Greer, Gonzalez gave the Rangers three players who drove in more than 100 runs during the 1996 season. "It was a great lineup from one to nine," Pudge Rodriguez would say years later. "Up and down the lineup we could hit, and we scored a lot of runs."[4] It was seemingly an embarrassment of riches, at least from the perspective of almost any era in baseball. Winning games was easy when your offense was scoring almost six runs per game.

But the average runs per game for an American League team was 5.39, and Bosman had no illusions about what was behind the power surge. Performance-enhancing drugs (PEDs) were far too prevalent to miss. It was easier to count the players who did not use them, but the statistical profile of baseball makes it clear that they were part of the game as a whole, not just in the Texas clubhouse. How much of a role they played in boosting performance is unclear, but the Rangers scored 5.69 runs per game, which explained much of the overall success of the team.

There was more at play than just Juan Gonzalez and his .643 slugging percentage. The pitching staff allowed only 4.9 runs per game, fourth best in the American League. The run differential of almost .7 runs per game powered Texas to its first-ever American League West title at the end of the 1996 season. One huge factor, according to Bosman, was his infield defense. His strategy of pitching to contact demanded capable gloves on the diamond. Bosman believed in his defense almost as much as his pitching staff.

Kevin Elster, as a 31-year-old, was the anchor of the Rangers infield at shortstop. He had played his early years with the New York Mets, where he had managed no more than 10 home runs in more or less full-time play there. In 1996, his power surged to 25 home runs, and 99 RBIs helped as well. "For his age, he found the fountain of youth somewhere because he played really, really well," Bosman asserted.

"Dean Palmer was a blue-collar infielder at third who could whack it a bit. He's not going to make you forget Brooks Robinson, but he made the average play consistently so that the left side of our infield was very good," Dick stated. Former Baltimore Oriole Mark McLemore was at second base, and "he did everything we asked him to," Bosman continued. First baseman Will Clark had won a Gold Glove while playing for the San Francisco Giants, and his defense was still extremely solid. Sound infield defense was able to turn "pitching to contact" into an effective defensive strategy that gave the explosive Rangers offense an edge throughout the season. In a ballpark that was famous for fly balls that stretched into the first few rows of the bleachers, the Rangers staff gave up only one home run per game in 1996, second only to the Yankees staff. Bosman had them throwing ground balls, not big flies.

For the first time in the history of the Texas franchise, one that stretched back to 1961, when the expansion Washington Senators first took the field, the team won something of note. They were not the best team in the American League. Texas only won 90 games in 1996. The Cleveland Indians won 99 games, and the New York Yankees won 92. But the Rangers won the Western Division with a four-and-a-half-game margin over the Seattle Mariners. The Mariners had an offense led by Ken Griffey, Alex Rodriguez, and Edgar Martinez. Rodriguez was voted Major League Baseball Player of the Year in 1996, by *Sporting News*, but Seattle was without ace Randy Johnson for the season and the staff that Dick Bosman and Johnny Oates cobbled together was significantly better.

The writers took note of the difference in the Texas staff. Mel Antonen of *USA Today* asked Bosman to explain what was new with the Rangers pitching crew. Dick responded, "They are following a simple plan: Throwing strikes."[5] Commenting on the need for pitchers to get ahead in the count, Antonen noted that "coaches are happy when their pitchers get ahead 50 percent of the time. Witt is at 60 percent." Pitching coaches ask their pitchers to throw more strikes, but only the best ones can find effective mechanisms to help their hurlers do so. Texas pitchers were not trying to miss bats; instead they were throwing ground balls.

A crucial trade in early August helped Texas down the stretch. The Rangers sent young prospect Ryan Dempster and unsuccessful right-handed prospect Rick Helling to the Florida Marlins for John Burkett. Burkett was an established pitcher who had won 22 games for the San Francisco Giants in 1993. Before the trade, pitching for the Marlins in 1995, Burkett had won 14 games and posted a 4.30 ERA. "I think I am a consistent pitcher who can give them six, seven, eight innings each time out," Burkett told the press after the trade.[6] It was a made-to-order prescription for the Rangers going into the stretch.

When the trade was consummated, the Rangers maintained a precarious lead in the American League Western Division of only a single game.

Brian Cashman, general manager of the Yankees, had the endless reserves and boundless desire of George Steinbrenner behind him, but Doug Melvin proved as shrewd a GM as anyone else in the late 1990s. The Burkett trade may have been one of his best. Melvin's team had been in command since mid-April and had built their lead to six games over Seattle by late June. But the Mariners whittled away at the margin steadily in July, and Texas was on the verge of losing the advantage completely when Burkett arrived from Florida.

The Rangers pitching was leaking runs and undercutting the still-explosive offense. Roger Pavlik struggled after the All-Star break, winning only three games, and Kenny Hill had a 6.00 ERA for the month of June. Neither Oates nor Bosman wanted to depend on Darren Oliver or Bobby Witt to win the pennant for them, so the addition of Burkett was done based on necessity. When Burkett joined the team, Oates and Bosman pushed Kevin Gross to the bullpen, where he helped shore up that part of the staff.

Burkett gave the Rangers a right-handed ace who could help win the division, but perhaps more important for a team looking at its first chance for postseason play, he provided a second high-quality starter who could be paired alongside Kenny Hill against whomever Texas might face in the play-offs. As important as adding Burkett, Bosman was able to get Hill back on track in July. Dick informed the moundsman that he was rushing his delivery. "He was getting hit because he left his pitches high in the strike zone," Bosman lamented.[7] It is difficult to find ground-ball outs pitching in the hitters' wheelhouse.

After making mechanical adjustments, Hill began to finish his pitches the way he had early in the season, and he went 5–0 in his final seven starts. Burkett won five of the 10 starts he made, and suddenly the team had two successful pitchers as they headed into the final weeks of the season, where the duo's presence would be crucial.

On September 20, the Rangers had eight games left on the schedule. They had just lost four games in Seattle to the Mariners, which shaved the Texas lead to a single game. The Rangers continued the long road trip to Anaheim, California, for a three-game series against the Angels. In the first game, Darren Oliver pitched into the seventh inning, but Texas lost when reliever Mike Stanton allowed two runs in the bottom of the ninth inning. Five losses in a row threatened to starve the Rangers' appetite for the postseason. Badly in need of someone to stop the bleeding, Johnny Oates and Dick Bosman gave the ball to their newest right-handed ace, John Burkett, the next night.

Burkett rose to the occasion, going eight innings and giving up only a single run to win, 7–1. The next day Kenny Hill, pitching against his former club, threw a complete game to win by a 4–1 margin. Those two wins pointed the way for the remainder of the season and made it easier to carry the extra weight Oates and Bosman knew the team had shouldered. "We are not just trying to beat out the Seattle Mariners," Oates told Dick that September. "We are trying to beat 25 years of history as well." Oates was speaking only to the years the team had been in Texas. Dick knew the losing tradition dated back much further than that, to Washington and the hapless Senators. He was gratified the fortified pitching staff played a pivotal role in throwing off the burden of a 35-year losing habit.

On the night the Rangers clinched the pennant, the celebration featured 150 bottles of champagne after the Seattle Mariners lost to Oakland and ended the suspense. "It was extremely special," Dick said of the win. "Having been there to begin the Texas Rangers' history in '72 and get back there as pitching coach. To be the pitching coach to finally win a division title, it was special." Bosman told the press it was better than "working at Sanders Paint and Body Shop in Safety Harbor, Florida, where he said he would be turning wrenches" if the team had not made the playoffs.[8] For Dick Bosman, Octobers had almost always been about going back to working on cars.

Owner Tom Schieffer was particularly magnanimous in crediting the success of the season to Johnny Oates, saying, "There was a great atmosphere here, and it was a reflection of Johnny Oates's character. He's just full of integrity."[9] *Sporting News* chose Johnny Oates as Manager of the Year for the job he had done in guiding the team to its first playoff appearance, and they named Doug Melvin Executive of the Year for putting the team together and the shrewd addition of Burkett at the trade deadline.

The awards and plaudits could not equal a chance to play the New York Yankees in the postseason. "Walking into Yankee Stadium was special too," Dick recalled. Few believed the first-time Rangers would be a match for the New York Yankees, who had won the American League East. But Bosman and Oates believed that in Kenny Hill and John Burkett they had two starters that could compete with anyone. Their faith was not misplaced, as Burkett won the first game of the series against David Cone. Juan Gonzalez and Dean

Palmer each hit home runs, and the same power that had beaten a good Seattle team was on display, as Texas won by a 6–2 margin.

Dick remembers that first game fondly and the sense of possibility that flowed from it. But the next three had some painful moments, as the pitching staff failed to keep the Yankees in check. Kenny Hill started game two, and Dick recalled in the second inning, with the Rangers ahead, Hill "ally-oop[ing] it to second base and pull[ing] Elster off the bag so that Elster [couldn't] get the force at second *or* the guy at first." An ever-fiery competitor, Bosman was deeply disappointed that the many drills done in spring training had not immunized his pitchers against sloppy play. The mental error led to a key run in a game that the Yankees went on to win by a single run, 5–4.

Darren Oliver outpitched Yankees lefty Jimmy Key for eight innings in game three in front of 50,000 fans, but Johnny Oates left him in to finish the game. With a 2–1 lead, Oliver went to the mound in Texas to start the top of the ninth inning against the Yankees. Only three times during the season had Oates and Bosman allowed their newly converted reliever to pitch into the eighth inning, and he had only a single complete game. Oates defended his decision to the press, saying, "In today's game a lot of clubs automatically go to their closer in that situation. We're not one of those clubs."[10]

Between innings, Oliver told Bosman he was not tired, but more important may have been his assertion to his pitching coach that, "It was my game to win or lose."[11] Oliver gave up two singles, to Derek Jeter and Tim Raines, to start the ninth inning. Oates called on his closer, Mike Henneman, to shut off New York without a run or, worst-case scenario, give the Rangers a chance to win a tied game in the bottom of the ninth. But both Jeter and Raines came around to score before Henneman could get the third out. Yankees closer John Wetteland shut down the Texas offense in the bottom of the inning, and the Rangers lost the game, 3–2.

In the deciding game four, Kenny Rogers started for the Yankees against Bobby Witt. Neither pitcher factored in the decision, but once again the New York bullpen outpitched the Rangers and Wetteland closed out the ninth for the second day in a row with the game and the divisional series on the line. He would go on to be named the MVP of the World Series that year.

There were no awards for pitching coaches. But Dick Bosman believed that the 1996 season was proof that he could get as much out of a pitching staff as anyone else. He had been equally effective with the Baltimore Orioles, something Tom Boswell of the *Washington Post* had acknowledged. "It's easy to get carried away . . . with how spectacularly the Orioles pitching has improved," Boswell opined early in 1992, citing the influence of Bosman as key to the turnaround in Baltimore.[12] There was little doubt that Bosman had done even more to get the best performance out of the Texas Rangers staff in 1996.

Oates believed that Bosman's gift was not just his ability to analyze the pitcher's delivery and tweak mechanics, but also his people skills, his ability to form positive relationships with his pitchers. "Dick has earned a lot of respect from these guys," Oates said in 1992, speaking about the Orioles pitching staff. "He's able to get through to them."[13] In Baltimore, Jamie Moyer called him a "genius" after Bosman added the cut fastball to the left-hander's arsenal.[14] Boswell described him as a "Dutch Uncle," for the empathy he had for young pitchers.[15] The Bosman pitching philosophy started with Bosman putting on the catcher's gear for his pitchers' bullpen sessions. It was not about getting down on their level, but about getting the best vantage point to watch how they threw the ball.

"Being able to create a professional relationship with a pitcher is paramount," declared Dick when talking about the intangibles of coaching. "It is an absolute necessity if you are going to get anything done with a guy." Bosman believes to this day that working with the mitt during pitchers' bullpen sessions was an important element that linked him to his staff. It allowed him to become familiar with how the pitcher throws and what the ball looks like coming out of his hand, and how it moves on the way to the plate. It was the best way to spot something different if the pitcher was in a bad stretch. "Being his personal warm-up catcher in the bullpen on side days when you are teaching, when you are working, it allows you to see what he is trying to do, what the ball is doing," Dick added.

"It is not the personal relationship," he said with some emphasis. "Maybe when you are at a crossroads with a guy at a key juncture in the season, maybe then you take him to lunch to talk." For Bosman, it is like parenting. Yes, you can try to become a father figure to young pitchers. His father said as much to him when Dick first became a pitching coach. But the conversation is, "I am your parent, not your pal. I can be your pal when you grow up, but for now I am your parent." Bosman believes that the similarity between parenting and coaching is built on the day-in and day-out work that goes into raising children. With parenting and coaching, it is the persistence of it that counts more than anything else. The relationship depends on the work that is put in each day, and that may be the most important thing, the constancy of it.

One of the few sour notes in 1996 was the death of Dick's father, George Bosman, on June 3. His father's voice was a constant in Dick's life, whether it was leaning over the fender of a car or truck as they worked on an engine or tossing a baseball back and forth. There was a simple credo that Bosman's father lived by, one where your word was your bond. Honesty was what everything was built on. It made everything work at the most basic level, and Dick knew that it was one of the most important assets he had, his word with his pitchers. They knew that whether or not they liked what Dick was telling them, he believed it as an honest assessment of the moment or the longer view of the pitcher's talents and approach.

> Building trust with players is the first and most important facet of Dick Bosman's philosophy of pitching. Everything depends on that starting point. Whether it is a young pitcher or a veteran, they must believe in Bosman's integrity. They must judge his advice to be rooted in not only his knowledge and experience, but also principle.

George Bosman had been an inspiration, a sounding board, and a source of constant advice for Dick, and he was greatly missed by Dick and his mother. Nella Bosman continued to provide support and was the center of the family in Wisconsin, which remained Dick's most fervent fan club. There was a fair fan club in Arlington as well. Bosman had taken a pitching staff that no one believed could succeed and, with the patience of a parent, found a way.

12

Creating a Winning Combination

The sellout crowds were back early in the 1997 season, the fans believing that the success of the prior year was but a stepping-stone to something more. Everything had gone right in 1996, like the extraordinary year Ted Williams had as Washington Senators manager in 1969. But luck would not hold for Texas, as a string of injuries struck the team during the 1997 campaign. There were changes in personnel as well, and the magic of chemistry that had cast a spell on the 1996 team failed to hold the following season.

One of the first changes was the departure of Kevin Elster to free agency. Replacing him was Benji Gil, who had played shortstop for Texas in 1994, but had failed to hit enough to stick. Nothing much changed, as he hit only .224, and his defense was not enough to make anyone forget a light-hitting shortstop in the era of PEDs. Dean Palmer and Will Clark were hurt, as were Kenny Hill and Roger Pavlik. Pavlik pitched well in April and September but was out the rest of the year. Dick Bosman remembers his competitive fire fondly, saying of Pavlik

The pitcher is the one who stands tall on the mound with a unique responsibility for how the game unfolds. Only the pitcher knows whether he is going to try to blow the hitter away with a fastball or something off-speed. Dick stood there for more than a thousand innings but learned far more about his craft during his 30 years of teaching the game at the highest levels.

that he was a "Texas hard-nosed brawler." Bosman added, "He would go out there and fight you at the drop of a hat,"[1] but his across-the-body motion caught up with him, and his career would be over in 1998, after only five appearances.

The Rangers sank to third place in the American League West in 1997, and gave the Seattle Mariners their turn at the postseason, where they did battle with the Baltimore Orioles, losing the American League Division Series after Mike Mussina beat Randy Johnson in game one and the deciding game four. Johnson had returned to the Mariners rotation after injuries limited him in 1996. He won 20 games in 1997, and almost won his second Cy Young Award, coming in second to Roger Clemens, who won 21 games for Toronto. Texas would never have that level of pitching excellence. Ken Hill and John Burkett were both on the back nine of their major-league careers when they led the staff in 1996. Darren Oliver was the only member of the Texas staff younger than 30.

The Rangers tried to turn the page at the end of the 1997 season. During the offseason, in an attempt to change the mix, Texas let Hill leave as a free agent. It was clear that Pavlik's career was likely done. Burkett was back and would be a mainstay in the rotation, but Texas imported two new faces through trade: Rick Helling and Aaron Sele. Helling had been a first-round draft pick by the Rangers in 1992, from Stanford. He rose quickly in the Rangers farm system and was in the majors by the second half of 1994, but he could not stick. It was said of Helling that he was in love with the high fastball and the macho spirit of challenging hitters.[2] Texas traded him to Florida for Burkett in late 1996, reacquiring him in August 1997. He would become a mainstay of the Rangers rotation under the tutelage of Dick Bosman, where he would temper his love for the high heat.

Aaron Sele was acquired from the Red Sox in November after the 1997 season. He was a tall right-hander who had shown early promise and been drafted in the first round from Washington State University. He was quickly promoted to the major-league roster, thriving until 1995. That year, shoulder problems sidelined him for much of the season.[3] Boston gave up on him and traded him even though Sele had found success in the Boston rotation in 1997. There was conflict between he and Boston pitching coach Joe Kerrigan, and the Red Sox shipped him to Texas for Jim Leyritz and Damon Buford. Texas got back quality backup catcher Bill Hasselman in the deal as well.

Texas had made an important addition to the team in 1997, adding closer John Wetteland, who as a New York Yankee had so bedeviled the Rangers in the 1996 playoffs. Wetteland had been a marked contrast in that divisional series, perfectly closing out the Rangers, while Texas closer Mike Henneman could not. Wetteland's addition prior to the 1997 campaign made imminent sense as a necessary improvement if the team wanted to advance further in the playoffs. When the rest of the pitching staff scuffled in 1997, Wetteland had lived up to the hype. He appeared in 61 games and pitched to a 1.94 ERA, outstanding numbers for a season when the average league ERA was 4.56. Bosman was much impressed with his iconoclast closer.

"Did he march to a different drum? You bet he did," Dick remembered of the first time he set eyes on Wetteland as a member of the Texas pitching staff, continuing,

He drove a Harley to the ballpark with leathers on and headband flying back from the bike. The bike had those high chrome handlebars, which Wetteland grasped above his head. Directly beneath his hands was the other dominant feature in the picture: the cowboy boots that poked out near the front wheel. Looking at him you would never guess that he was the Most Valuable Player from the 1996 World Series.

Bosman acknowledged that Wetteland had "looked down the barrel of some of the best hitters in the game with everything on the line on one of the biggest stages there is, in New York City." Dick added, "Does that make you stronger? You bet it does. There is something in the standard major-league contract about riding motorcycles." No major-league club wishes to invest huge sums of money on a closer who puts his health at abnormal risk on a Harley-Davidson. But the risk is acceptable for a guy who did what Wetteland did on a regular basis in the 1990s. Wetteland was not just one closer; he was emblematic of the culture of the bullpen pitcher that had developed through the years.

In finding which pitcher is suitable to close in the ninth inning, Bosman believes the only way to know who has the right mentality is to send them out there in high-pressure situations when the game is on the line.

"Bullpen guys are wired extremely different than the average guy," Bosman admitted. "Wetteland said famously that 'the ninth inning is not for everyone.'" Bosman acknowledged that the only way to find out who has the mentality to pitch in high-pressure situations when the game is on the line with every pitch is to "send them out there to do it."

Equally fascinating is how much the bullpen is an area where the pitching coach has less influence. Said Bosman,

> Wetteland was the guy who ran the bullpen. There was no question that he was the dean of the bullpen. He set the policy. They had rituals, and they did things out there that would boggle the average person's mind. But everything that was done out there was attuned to winning a baseball game that day or that night. They do kooky things out there to put up with the pressure.

Wetteland came into Bosman's office late one night after a ballgame and held forth in his own inimitable fashion for some time. It was maybe two in the morning, and Dick was trapped listening to Wetteland rant because he had the stage. When he was done, he stood and walked out of Dick's office, jumped on his Harley, and drove off. "I just sat there wondering what the hell the man had said," Bosman reflected. Driving home Dick realized that the entire conversation had been an attempt by his closer to tell him that he ran the bullpen and there was no need for Bosman to worry about it.

Similarly, it is a different situation for a pitching coach when he goes out to the mound in the ninth inning. "You can't get into paralysis from analysis. It's got to get done right now. You can't get too deep into deliveries. It's about how to get this guy out right now," Dick asserted. It was more about the situation with the hitter and what pitch would work against the specific batter in question. One of the strategies Bosman employed in the ninth inning was to go out just to break the flow of what was happening. "Sometimes they just need a break and you talk about the big blonde in the first row," Dick revealed.

It was Bosman's job to get his starting rotation to hand off the ball to Wetteland with the lead in the ninth inning as often as possible. Rick Helling and Aaron Sele were the two Texas pitchers who earned Wetteland more saves in 1998 than any others. Dick achieved perhaps more success working with Helling than with any other member of the Texas staff in 1998. The first issue was to convince Helling to keep the ball low in the strike zone regardless of what he was throwing and forego his love for the high heat.[4]

"It was apparent from the beginning that he struggled with his breaking stuff. His slider wasn't much, and his curve did not have much bite to it." To get the batter not to sit on the fastball, "we had to have something that was going to disrupt their timing, and the changeup was really the only viable option that we had," Dick stated. He knew Helling could throw the fastball but told his pitcher, "Speed is a good asset, but changing speeds is better."[5] Helling was a willing pupil, a hard worker, and one who knew his limitations. "He was a bright enough kid to know that he had to go out there and pitch down early and then up in the zone late in the count."[6]

In the spring of 1998, Bosman began working with the 27-year-old Oklahoma right-hander to add a changeup to his repertoire. "It is one of the most difficult lessons for a pitcher," Bosman said of his efforts to teach Helling the pitch. "Hall of Famer Tom Seaver took two years to get confident with it."[7]

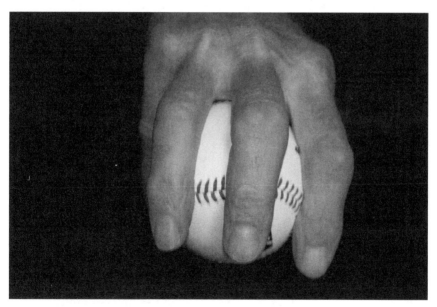

Dick Bosman demonstrates the changeup grip. It is the only pitch that looks like another. The delivery must be exactly the same as the fastball, but the velocity should be eight to 10 miles per hour less, which is done largely by placing the ball farther back in the hand. Tom Seaver noted, "A changeup thrown at the knees in the middle of the plate is 100 percent effective."

Helling admits that his changeup was always a work in progress. "I never quit working on it," he said, and there were certain games when it "clicked." There was one game he remembers in particular where he threw 20 changeups because it was working that day. But for Helling the changeup would always be a pitch that "came and went."[8]

After early success in the 1998 season, Helling told the press, "Greg Maddux shows you that changing speeds is important. . . . I'm still primarily a fastball-curveball pitcher, but a changeup gives me another pitch to fall back [on]." Helling's fastball was an excellent pitch. Although it was only 91 to 92 miles per hour most of the time, "it had a lot of high carry to it," according to Bosman. "Being able to throw the changeup off that fastball really accomplished quite a lot."

Helling was convinced of the efficacy of Bosman's approach after Helling began the season with six straight wins and a 2.93 ERA. The fifth win had been particularly sweet, as it came in Minnesota, in front of a crowd that included family and friends from his hometown of Fargo, North Dakota. There were 300 of them wearing hats that spelled out Helling's name and his uniform number, 32. His father was among the crowd. Rick pitched into the ninth inning that day and fanned 10 Twins batters. "I'd be lying if I said it wasn't special," Helling admitted.[9]

Helling became the ace of the Texas Rangers pitching staff in 1998, based on the excellent results he achieved from the beginning of the season. "He logged innings (216.1 in 1998) and went to the post every time his name was called," Bosman recalled with admiration for what Helling was able to do that season. Helling accomplished a feat that Bosman had sought 30 years earlier, winning 20 games and finishing the 1998 campaign with a 20–7 record. "He was an outstanding competitor."

Helling also attributes Bosman's help with controlling the running game as an important part of the success he and others on the Rangers staff had. "Looking over to first base the way that Bosman taught it. That was the first time I had ever done any of that," Helling said. He acknowledged that with Pudge Rodriguez behind the plate and Bosman's techniques in play, it was especially hard to steal against the Rangers.

In truth, it was tight competition as to who was the best pitcher in the rotation. Aaron Sele began the season equally as well as Helling. On April 21, he tossed a complete-game shutout to win his fourth straight game without a defeat and lowered his ERA to 1.16. By the end of May, he had come back to earth but had an 8–3 record and an ERA of 3.03. Sele had one of the best curveballs in the game. "He's rare in that he has the ability to throw his curve over the plate in today's strike zone," Bosman said. "That takes a lot of skill and ability." Sele credited Bosman and Johnny Oates saying, "I have a good pitching coach and a manager who sticks with me."[10]

Sele's signature pitch, the big breaking curveball, started at 12 o'clock on an imaginary clock face and broke down to six o'clock, diving toward the plate seemingly within the last few feet as it crossed home. Dick Bosman said on reflection that the "strike zone in 1998 was about the size of a 13-inch TV screen." Getting a curve to drop through that frame and have the umpire recognize that it was within the strike zone had grown increasingly difficult through the years. The pitch was high risk, not only because umpires had difficulty knowing whether it had crossed through their smaller strike zone, but also because if the break was not sharp enough—the famous hanging curve—it was likely going to get hit hard.

The top of the strike zone was officially restricted by the baseball rules committee in December 1968, lowering it from the bottom of the shoulders of the crouching batter to the bottom of the armpits, or across the letters. The zone continued to shrink during the ensuing years until the curveball, once legendary, was diminishing in influence directly proportional to the smaller strike zone. The pitch had once been second only to the fastball in baseball, hence its nickname, the "deuce." There were other traditional names for the curve, for example, "Uncle Charlie," the "bender," or the "hook." Call it by whatever name you want, the curveball was losing its place in the game by the 1990s, as the pitch became increasingly less effective for pitchers the more the strike zone diminished.

Dick Bosman knew that the curveball had been replaced with the slider as the most popular breaking pitch in the game. There were only three pitchers on the Texas staff who still threw a traditional curve: Aaron Sele, John Wetteland, and reliever Mike Munoz. According to Dick, "The number of people who throw it is very low, and it is getting less and less."[11] Bosman himself had never mastered the pitch, although his pitching coach, Sid Hudson, had tried to teach him early on when Dick was in the minors. Whether based on his experience as a pitcher or a coach, Bosman believed the pitch was difficult to

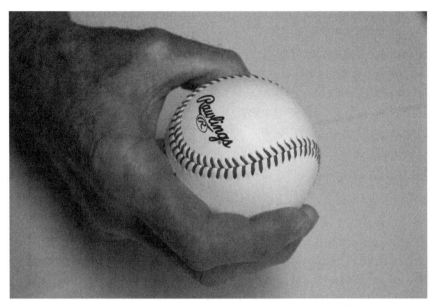

The curveball grip is intended to impart downward spin on the ball. Thrown over the top or from a three-quarters arm slot, the ball should tumble off the first two fingers with no "door-knobbing"—sideways motion of the wrist.

learn. "I don't even teach it unless a guy comes to me first and wants to learn it," Bosman told reporter T. R. Sullivan.[12]

Bosman as a pitcher had always preferred the slider to the curve. It was an easier pitch to learn to throw effectively. The pitch also could accommodate the smaller strike zone. The slider had tighter break, and umpires were more likely to call that pitch a strike than the larger breaking curve. Pitchers also preferred the slider because it was easier to control and easier to learn.

Sele acknowledged to Bosman that his curveball was more difficult to control. "You have to control both the distance and the direction," Dick said, pointing to the need to have the pitch begin its break at exactly the right point. Anything less and the pitch hung in the batter's eyes, to bad effect. Bosman also believed the pitch involved more wear and tear on the pitcher's arm. Gregg Olson, the closer for the Baltimore Orioles from 1989 to 1993, had an excellent curve, but he had "flexor and forearm problems from the way he threw it."

"It also depends on how you impart spin on the ball," Bosman admitted. "Guys that flip the ball out with their thumb tend to over time have those flexor problems. Guys that throw it with a grip that manipulates the ball tend to have fewer problems." The grip that Bosman prefers places the two fingers across the front of the ball and the thumb at the top, and the natural over-the-top motion imparts the spin to the ball rather than requiring more motion with the wrist to impart the spin that defines a sharp breaking curve. For John Wetteland, it was an important pitch, but he acknowledged that it took longer to gain a feel for it in game situations.

Bosman was enthusiastic about Sele's curveball and encouraged him to use a "back-door" curve, although that version of the pitch was more difficult to control. It was the same pitch, but when thrown by a right-handed pitcher to a left-handed batter it could be devastatingly effective. According to Bosman, the best way to set up the backdoor curve was with a fastball on the outside part of the plate. Then with the pitcher ahead in the count, he threw a curve that started out of the strike zone and broke back across the same part of the plate that the fastball had just passed. The batter often watched it for a final strike three, or if he realized too late that it was going to be a strike he was forced to swing off balance.

> The back-door curve is one that breaks late and just across the outside edge of the strike zone before the batter can understand it will be a strike. It is best thrown late in the count for a strikeout or to get the batter swinging off-balance for light contact.

Joe Kerrigan had forbidden Sele from throwing the pitch, and Sele believed it was one reason left-handed hitters torched him for a .325 batting average in 1997. Sele had also given up more walks and home runs against lefties while under Kerrigan's direction. Bosman encouraged Sele to throw the backdoor curve but also urged him to throw more changeups to lefties. In 1998, Sele was a better pitcher to batters on both sides of the plate, but the splits for left-handed hitters were far less pronounced. In 1997, he had allowed 15 home runs to lefties, whereas in 1998 he allowed only six. Lefties hit only .295 against him in 1998, 30 points less than the prior year.

"Right off the bat I had no problem motivating Aaron Sele," Bosman stated emphatically. "He was extremely motivated to prove Kerrigan and the Red Sox wrong. This guy could spin a curveball," Dick said with obvious delight.

"He didn't exactly light up the radar gun, but he had a pretty good idea how to pitch." Sele had a changeup that gave him a third pitch, but it was his curveball that "hitters really had to fear." Stated Bosman, "He was truly a three-pitch pitcher. He won 37 games for me in two years, and when a guy pitches like that, he is a delight to work with."

Sele and Helling were very different pitchers, which made them an excellent tandem at the top of the Texas rotation. They both achieved early success with the Rangers in 1998, but there was a huge gap between the two starters at the top of the rotation and John Wetteland at the back end. John Burkett, at age 33, had lost something. The Darren Oliver experiment failed miserably in 1998, and both Johnny Oates and Dick Bosman had to admit that he was no longer able to pitch out of the rotation. The rest of his career was spent almost exclusively as a reliever. In July, Oliver was traded, along with Fernando Tatis, to the St. Louis Cardinals for Todd Stottlemyre and Royce Clayton. Doug Melvin was like a wily old country doctor with just the right prescription for the ailing patient. Clayton shored up the defense, and Stottlemyre became a third effective rotation piece, one the team desperately needed.

Bobby Witt was 34 years old in 1998, and like Oliver he was ineffective from the beginning of the season. He was traded to St. Louis on June 23 and would be relegated to the bullpen for the remainder of his career as well. Without Witt or Oliver, the Rangers were left to experiment with how best to fill out the final two spots in the rotation behind Helling, Sele, and Stottlemyre. Veteran John Burkett had lost a few feet on his fastball but was still a valuable member of the rotation. In early July, shortly after Witt left for St. Louis, a 26-year-old pitcher named Esteban Loaiza was acquired from the Pittsburgh Pirates. He was a new project for Bosman, one that would have to be addressed on the fly, during the middle of the season. But he made a contribution in the second part of the slate, making 14 starts.

While the pitching was its usual hodgepodge of wonder and worry, the Texas Rangers offense in 1998 was an awesome thing to behold. They scored 5.8 runs per game behind a lineup that still featured Juan Gonzalez at its core. It was the second MVP season for Gonzalez, as he drove in 157 runs, just off the major-league lead of Sammy Sosa, with 158. He hit 45 home runs and had a major-league-best 50 doubles. The Rangers lineup featured Rusty Greer batting third ahead of Gonzalez, with Will Clark and Pudge Rodriguez hitting immediately behind him. Any pitcher had to be intimidated by that foursome at the heart of the Texas offense.

The defense was not the same, however. Kevin Elster was back, but he was 33 years old. His range was diminished, and he was supplanted by Royce Clayton after the July trade. Fernando Tatis stepped into Dean Palmer's place at third base but could not measure up and was replaced in July by Todd Zeile, who came over in a trade with the Florida Marlins.

As good as the offense was, the Rangers were tied for first place with the California Angels on September 21, and Anaheim was hosting a three-game series against Texas. There were only seven games left in the season, and the Rangers remained on the road until the end, playing four in Seattle. The advantage was clearly with the Angels, but Todd Stottlemyre took the mound in the first game. He played the same crucial role that John Burkett had filled in 1996. He proved to be the stopper at exactly the right moment, throwing seven innings of shutout baseball, which gave Texas an essential win to start the series in Anaheim. Dick was impressed with everything he saw from Stottlemyre. "He was a warrior. He really, really, got after it," Bosman declared.

Rick Helling beat Chuck Finley in the second game of the series by an identical 9–1 score, and John Burkett beat Kenny Hill for the sweep. It was the perfect time for Dick Bosman's signature postgame victory cheer. "Whiskey and cigarettes for the boys," Dick always shouted as they came into the clubhouse after a big win. "The players always liked that one," Helling remembered.[13] Dick adopted the cheer from Doug Rader, who said it was originally a pirate cheer after the capture of a prize ship.

Texas split the series in Seattle and won the American League West by three games, with a record of 88 wins against 74 losses. It was again a situation where the Western Division was the weakest in the league, and even Boston, finishing second in the American League East, won 92 games, well ahead of the Rangers. The Rangers were set to face off against the ascendant New York Yankees in the first round of the playoffs.

The Yankees were playing in a league of their own in 1998. They won 114 games and scored 5.96 runs per game. But more impressive than the offense, which from top to bottom featured double-digit home runs, was the best defensive team in the game. They led the American League with the least runs allowed, and their pitching staff was the only one in the league with an ERA below 4.00 (3.82).

Yankees general manager Brian Cashman had seemingly endless financial wellsprings from which to draw. He used that wealth to outbid the competition for 32-year-old Cuban émigré Orlando "El Duque" Hernandez, who signed a contract during the spring of 1998. El Duque had followed his half-brother, Livan Hernandez, across the Straits of Florida to the United States. Together they were two of the most highly touted Cuban talents to leave the island during the last decade of the twentieth century.

Orlando Hernandez did not join the Yankees rotation until the beginning of June, but he became one of New York's most celebrated stars, as he won 12 games against only four defeats and pitched to a 3.13 ERA. The Yankees had another highly touted and well-paid import in Hideki Irabu, who had initially signed with San Diego but came over to New York almost immediately and began his major-league career in pinstripes. He proved not as dominant a talent at Hernandez, but as the back end of the rotation that included Andy Pettite, David Cone, and David Wells, he was more than adequate.

Derek Jeter was at the peak of his career as the New York shortstop, and Mariano Rivera was the closer. They were two future Hall of Fame players among a lineup filled out from top to bottom with as fine a talent as one could find in the majors. The Rangers could match up offensively with anyone, and the addition of Todd Stottlemyre gave them hope that they might fare better in 1998 than they had in 1996. Stottlemyre was scheduled to start the first game in Yankee Stadium on September 29.

Aside from the usual allure of pitching against the Yankees in the most famous baseball venue of them all, Stottlemyre had the extra excitement of going against his father, Mel Stottlemyre, who was the pitching coach for the Yankees. The elder Stottlemyre had been the ace of the Yankees staff in the late 1960s, winning 20 games in back-to-back seasons in 1968 and 1969. Todd was four years old when his father first won 20 games, but the father's career never left New York, so there was considerable emotional import to the son pitching in the stadium that had been home to every baseball memory he had as a young boy.

Mel Stottlemyre had the pleasure of overseeing what could fairly be called the best pitching staff that money could buy in 1998, and against his son he sent out David "Boomer" Wells. Wells was a veteran hurler whose career stretched back 11 seasons for four different clubs before coming to New York.

He was a colorful character who bought one of Bosman's hot rods, but more to the point in 1998, he was coming off the best season of his career, where he had won 18 games and lost only four. Wells had been to the playoffs with four different teams and with the Yankees in 1997, so he had more experience in the high-pressure environment of playoff baseball in Yankee Stadium than Stottlemyre.

Todd Stottlemyre did not back off for a second, however, and allowed only two runs in seven innings, but David Wells was better, going eight innings and blanking the Rangers. Mariano Rivera completed the shutout, with the Yankees winning by a 2–0 margin. The rest of the American League Division Series was much the same. Helling pitched well in the second game but lost to Andy Pettite by a 3–1 score. In the third game, Aaron Sele, playing in Arlington, matched David Cone with five scoreless innings but in the sixth frame gave up two home runs and lost, 4–0. The vaunted Texas attack scored but a scant run in 27 innings of baseball and gave Wetteland no situations to clean up in the ninth inning.

There could be no recriminations for Dick Bosman and his pitching staff. They had pitched well enough to win any of the three games if the Rangers had scored as many runs as they averaged throughout the season. There was some consternation, however, as Texas was bounced from the playoffs in the first round again by the Yankees. This time the problem was the superior pitching of the Yankees, which had completely shut down Juan Gonzalez. He managed one hit in 12 at-bats. Will Clark, Pudge Rodriguez, and Rusty Greer fared no better.

It had been a good year for Texas regardless of the postseason disappointment. For Dick Bosman, it was a good time in many ways. His two girls were finding their way in life. Michelle, born immediately after the first strike by the MLBPA in 1972, had graduated from the University of Florida in Gainesville with a degree in microbiology. She was attending medical school. His youngest daughter Dina was nearing the end of her studies in Gainesville and would get a degree in photography in 1999. Dick was able to attend their graduations, and one day in June shortly thereafter, he awoke at home in Tarpon Springs, Florida, wondering, "Am I really here?"[14] It was rare for Dick to be home during the season for extended periods of time.

There were other notable events after the 1998 season for Dick. His wife Pam was active in a volunteer organization that helped children in abusive situations. She worked with the Guardian ad Litem program in Florida, which allows volunteers to become advocates for children in a variety of situations, representing them where their welfare may be at risk. Volunteers like Pam become a consistent source of listening and caring for kids who are going through difficult circumstances arising from any number of problems.

Dick and Pam's two grown daughters had lives of their own, and with so many children in need of help, it was only a matter of time before they adopted two girls. Beth, age 13, and Amanda, age nine—whose parents' rights were terminated officially—became members of the Bosman family on January 29, 1999. "It was quite a day," Dick remembered of that moment.

In November 1998, there was a reunion of the 1969 Washington Senators team, held in a hotel in the Northern Virginia suburbs, sponsored by the Washington, DC, Baseball Historical Society. There were 23 players and manager Ted Williams in attendance. Williams was in a wheelchair, but he was in good spirits, telling the press that the get-together was "one of the great moments in my life."[15]

Dick remembers seeing Ted there with great fondness. Their paths had crossed when Dick was in Chicago in his first year as a pitching coach. The White Sox were playing in Boston, and Williams was in Fenway Park at a reunion with his old Red Sox teammates. He spied Dick across the field in the opposing dugout and motioned for him to meet on the field. Williams congratulated Bosman on getting back into the game, telling him that he would be "an excellent pitching coach."

It was a sentiment he had communicated earlier in a letter to Bosman, which remains one of the great treasures in Dick's scrapbook of baseball memories. The one-page note was written by Williams shortly after Bosman had started his short coaching tenure at Georgetown University. "I am sure of one thing, you will be a damn good pitching coach," Williams wrote. "I think you were a smart pitcher and made good use of all the talent you had, not to mention some of the specialty items that were used occasionally." Williams had been a catalyst for Dick's career both as a pitcher and a coach, and getting to see his mentor one last time at the reunion was very special. Dick continued to visit occasionally with his old manager in Crystal River, where Ted lived until his death in July 2002.

13

Johnny Oates

When Dick Bosman reported to camp in the spring of 1999, the pitching staff looked much the same as it had the prior year. Rick Helling and Aaron Sele were the reliable one–two punch that led things off. John Burkett was 34 years old and counted on to fill the third spot in the rotation. Doug Melvin signed free agents Mike Morgan, 39, and Mark Clark, 31, to complete the rotation. Not surprisingly, none of the three eldest members of the rotation—Burkett, Clark, and Morgan—was healthy for the entirety of the season. Twenty-seven-year-old Esteban Loaiza—in his second full year with Texas—filled in for them, making 15 starts and pitching well enough to win nine games. But it was the bullpen that became the more formidable part of the Texas pitching staff in 1999.

Led by John Wetteland again, the Rangers boasted as capable a collection of late-inning arms as any team in the majors. Jeff Zimmerman threw 87 innings of 2.36 ERA and won nine games as the offense scored runs late as often as not. Zimmerman was a great story in his own right. He had quit the game in 1996, to focus on his education, doubting he would ever make it to the majors. A Canadian, Zimmerman had taken one more chance in 1997, pitching for Winnipeg in the independent Northern League. There he had found what Bosman called a "93-mile-per-hour fastball and a devastating slider."

Zimmerman was more than happy to have any kind of role on a major-league pitching staff, but he gloried in the underdog status of the bullpen. "We call ourselves the bottom-feeders. The whole world underappreciates middle relievers. Everyone looks at the lineup, the starting pitchers, and maybe the closers. We pride ourselves in being the plankton of baseball," he said.[1] Zimmerman was also happy to have Dick Bosman guiding his path, calling his pitching coach his "guardian angel."[2]

The bullpen was more than just a crowd of nonconformists fronted by the bull moose oddball in the form of John Wetteland. Burkett and Morgan were used out of the pen, along with Loaiza, at times during the season. Helling and Sele were the only dependable starters, and Johnny Oates and Bosman shifted additional workload to the bullpen to compensate for the weakness of their rotation. "The formula for success used to be five starters, a setup man, and a closer," Bosman opined to the press. "Now you hope for five, maybe six or seven innings out of the starter and match up the rest of the way."[3]

A statistical analysis of the Texas pitching staff bears out the contention that the bullpen was far more prominent in 1999 than in prior years. The two most reliable starters, Helling and Sele, started 35 and 33 games, respectively. Both averaged slightly less than six and one-third innings per start. Burkett averaged less than five innings per game with five relief appearances. Morgan averaged slightly more than four innings per game and was used in nine relief appearances. Loaiza was used in a traditional swingman role, appearing in as many games as a starter as a reliever: 15 each way.

Overall, the number of innings thrown by major-league starters in 1999 was 5.9 innings per start.[4] For Texas, that figure was 5.6 innings per game, well below the league average. The shift of innings to the bullpen by Bosman and Oates was based on simple and sound logic. According to Baseball-Reference.com's wins above average by position, the Texas bullpen was the best in the American League. Only the New York Yankees bullpen, led by Mariano Rivera, was even close.[5] Once again, Bosman and Oates crafted a winning defensive strategy from the hand they were dealt, one that made maximum efficient use of previously discarded pieces like Jeff Zimmerman. Molding veteran arms and capable relievers together, they formed a whole that found a way to win ballgames.

As in 1998, the pitching only had to be good enough to give the formidable Texas offense a chance to succeed. Rafael Palmeiro was back in Texas in 1999, after spending five seasons in Baltimore, and he became the most prolific slugger on a team that featured three hitters with more than 30 home runs. Palmeiro hit 47, Juan Gonzalez slugged 39, and Pudge Rodriguez contributed 35. Will Clark had moved on, with Lee Stevens taking over at first base. Stevens and Todd Zeile each slugged 24 home runs to provide even more thunder in the second-best offense in the American League.

For Pudge Rodriguez, the home run total was the most ever by an American League catcher. He drove in 113 runs and scored 116, the first time a catcher had exceeded 100 in both of those categories in the same season. He stole 25 bases and hit .332, and was awarded a Gold Glove for his defense. The overall package was enough to win him the Most Valuable Player Award and proved the pinnacle of what would become a 21-year Hall of Fame career.

To complement their Gold Glove behind the plate the Rangers had a more-than-adequate infield defense that did much to improve the overall profile of the team. The steady play of Zeile at third base, Royce Clayton at shortstop, and Mark McLemore at second base allowed Texas to keep their average runs per game at better than league average, at 5.30 per game. With the Rangers scoring 5.83 runs per game, the run differential helped boost them to 95 wins for the season. They coasted to their third American League West Division title in four years. They landed in first place on April 13, holding there comfortably without pause until season's end.

It almost seemed preordained that Texas would play the New York Yankees in the playoffs in 1999. The playoff losses in 1996 and 1998 were not the sole source of frustration for the Rangers. When the two teams went head-to-head, the Bronx Bombers were winning an inordinate number of the games. In 1998, Texas managed to beat the Yankees only three times in 11 contests. They won only four games of the 12 the two teams played during the 1999 regular season.

It was a tale of two cities. In New York, the Rangers could not buy a run and in six games barely managed to score two runs per contest. In Texas, they were once again themselves, averaging seven runs per game against the Yankees. Manager Johnny Oates expressed the simmering anger felt by everyone in Texas after another loss at Yankee Stadium in June 1999. In the postgame interview, Oates was undone by a reporter's question about Yankee Stadium's effect on his team. He began pounding a baseball on his desk and then suddenly fired it into a locker behind the press corps.

"You get tired of getting beat by the same team," Oates said after he had cooled off. "They are a good team, but they are not that much better than us. I don't get that way over one game or one inning, that was a 21-game frustration."[6] The tirade was successful in lighting a fire under his team. The next night—June 16—they finally won a game at Yankee Stadium. Rick Helling shut out the Yankees for seven innings, and Jeff Zimmerman and John Wetteland completed the game. That win went according to the way Bosman and Oates had drawn it up. But the playoffs were an entirely different animal for the Rangers when in the Big Apple.

"That outburst was extremely rare," Dick said of Oates losing his temper about the Yankees.[7] It took a long time for his irritation to reach the level that he lost his temper. But the Yankees had been rubbing the same nerve for Oates for many seasons. "Let's face it," Dick opined,

> those Yankee clubs were awfully good. They were balanced. They could score runs any number of ways. They got men on base and could hit the occasional home run. They cashed in their opportunities. We did not get blown out by them, but we plain got beat. Good pitching is going to beat good hitting, and it did.

It was the good pitching more than anything that confounded both Bosman and Oates. At the conclusion of the 1998 season, the Yankees had traded David Wells to Toronto for Roger Clemens, and if anything, their rotation in 1999—still the best in the league—was even stronger. Their bullpen was second only to the Rangers, so the divisional matchup again looked to feature New York's superb arms against the long-ball threats of the Texas Rangers. Could New York manhandle Juan Gonzalez and company the same way as in 1998, when Texas had scored only a single run in three games?

There was little appreciation among Texas fans of the irony of the answer. Juan Gonzalez did manage a home run in the course of the three-game series. That lone dinger was the only run scored by Texas against the Yankees pitching staff in the span of the three games. It was an uncanny repeat performance, remarkable for how well it mirrored the prior year for the Texas faithful.

First Orlando Hernandez and then Roger Clemens blanked the Rangers, anchoring shutouts of a team that had averaged almost six runs per contest in 1999. Although Aaron Sele was roughed up in game one, it wasn't the pitching that lost the American League Division Series for Texas. Both Helling in game two and Loaiza in game three pitched well enough to win. Texas lost game two by a 3–1 margin, followed by game three, 3–0. The Yankees just seemed to cast a spell on the Rangers offense as soon as the team walked onto the green carpet of Yankee Stadium. "Our pitching rose to the occasion," Dick asserted proudly. "But our offense just couldn't score any runs."

There was no way to fault the Texas pitching staff for the team's third disappointing playoff performance. But of equal certainty, there was no denying that they could not match up with their high-priced New York counterparts. The Texas Rangers had not been designed around their pitching staff. They were lucky to have Bosman and Oates find ways to make winners of a team with only two sound starters in Helling and Sele, each of whom was pitching at the best of their careers under the influence of Bosman.

The Rangers were the consummate PED-era team where the sweet sound of long balls leaving the park drew 2.7 million fans. The inimitable crack of the bat as its heart greets the ball and the symphony of motion that follows as the heads of 33,000 fans jerk to catch the flight of the tiny white sphere rushing toward the clouds, that singular baseball ecstasy happened early and often at the Ballpark in Arlington in 1999—230 times to be exact. Rangers fans did not pay to watch shutouts, which was a good thing because the Texas staff wasn't likely to throw many.

There were no dominating arms of the type that the Yankees could feature. In Texas, for Dick Bosman and Johnny Oates at least, it was all about the craft of pitching and the finesse. There were no high fastball pitchers like Roger Clemens on the Texas staff. Only Sele and Wetteland managed to come close to a strikeout per inning of work. Once again, the Bosman game plan of pitching to contact with aggressive infield play made it work. The strategy depended on keeping the ball away from those three or four inches that marked the sweet spot on the bat.

The underlying problem for Texas was the lack of adequate player development skills on the pitching side. During the years he was with the team, Bosman credits the Rangers with developing only one pitcher on their roster, Jeff Zimmerman, and even he detoured the long way around, seeing all too much of Canada before finally finding his way home as the late-inning setup man for John Wetteland in 1999.

Rick Helling had been drafted in the first round by Texas in 1992. They took pitchers in the next three rounds that year. In 1995, they repeated this formula, taking four pitchers in the first four rounds. The top pick that year, Jonathan Johnson, had a brief major-league career but never developed into the pitcher he might have been. Ryan Dempster was taken in the third round and was stuck in the lower levels of the Rangers organization, where he succeeded but was not promoted. The Florida Marlins recognized the talent and traded Helling back to Texas for him. Dempster quickly rose through the upper levels of the Marlins organization and had a successful 16-year career in the majors.

In 1996, the Rangers had three first-round picks and took pitchers with them all. R. A. Dickey was the pick of the litter, and subsequent medical examinations revealed that he lacked an ulnar collateral ligament in his pitching elbow. Dick was surprised that the Rangers scouts did not see the weird way his arm hung at his side until after they had selected him. None of these first-round pitchers succeeded at the major-league level with the training they received in the Texas organization. Dickey's success came when he began to explore the knuckleball after failing with the Rangers.

The Texas Rangers were not the only team that failed to develop pitching successfully. They were part of a trend in baseball, and in American business circles generally. The tendency to maximize short-term benefits at the expense of long-term success was commonplace. It required a significant investment of capital to support a capable network of scouts to identify the talent and an even greater outlay of cash to support a minor-league organization to nurture and mold it. Unable or unwilling to make those investments, Texas—and teams like it—shopped for pitching on the open market.

In that market, there was no equal to the wealth and allure of the New York Yankees. They were the sine qua non for the young man who had labored to reach the top, logged the long hours perfecting his craft in the minor leagues, and beat it to razor sharpness in the hot fires of major-league contests. The Rangers could offer nothing of the long tradition of wearing the pinstripes, just a history of futility that stretched back to the last days of the Eisenhower administration in Washington.

For those young men with exceptional athletic skills in the 1990s, signing up to learn to throw a baseball was not nearly as attractive as learning to hit it. The new ballparks, like Camden Yards, were smaller than the old ones they were replacing, and where the old parks persisted, the walls were brought in. At its greatest run, Yankee Stadium's center-field dimension had been 461 feet, but it had been reduced to 410 feet.

The ball was livelier. "You know it's juiced," Leo Mazzone, one of the most successful pitching coaches in the 1990s, insisted. He used an unlikely home run hit by pitcher Greg Maddux as proof of what both men knew: The ball was flying, and anyone could hit the supercharged sphere over the wall.[8] The players were juiced, the ball was juiced, and the ballparks were smaller. The strike zone was tiny, and pitchers were throwing into a powerful headwind in the 1990s.

Some believed that pitching talent was not at its best in the 1990s. What sane athlete, given a choice, wanted to swim against the powerful currents that faced pitchers who could only stand and watch as baseballs continued to jump off bats with unequaled velocity throughout the majors? The home run race between Sammy Sosa and Mark McGwire had electrified baseball fans during the summer of 1998. The balls continued to fly in 1999, as McGwire hit 65 home runs and Sosa 63. Pitchers needed cast-iron psyches to take their place on the mound each day.

"ERA's soar while shutouts and complete games drop sharply," one article opined.[9] Writers questioned the equation settled on by Major League Baseball wherein increasing attendance was defined "as much by the prospect of seeing a home run as a home team victory." The average ERA in the league had been on the rise since the players returned to the field after the 1994 strike. The average major-league ERA was 3.66 between 1901 and 1986. There had been only one other period in baseball history when the average ERA for the league was greater than 4.00 for a prolonged period of time—in the American League from 1923 to 1941, during the era of the New York Yankees' Bronx Bombers. Baseball was re-creating another golden era where the keenest analysts of the game argued, "The level of competitive play is vastly higher."[10] That level of play was asserting itself on the offensive side of the field in the late 1990s, as hitting became the predominant force in the game. "The toughest thing pitchers have to learn today is that they are going to give up a lot of runs," asserted Larry Rothschild, Tampa Bay Rays manager and former pitching coach with several teams.[11]

Bosman believes that the pitching talent remains constant, that there are those whose talent dictates they take the mound rather than grab a piece of lumber and hit. For those so suited, there were more tools in the pitcher's bag of tricks, and they were better conditioned than at any point in baseball history. But at the end of the twentieth century, the field tilted toward the bigger, stronger hitters in ways that were unprecedented. Teams like the Texas Rangers chose to emphasize the offensive side of the game, and that made the job of pitching coaches like Dick Bosman all the more challenging.

Finding solutions for getting batters out was more difficult, and the road to success for pitching talent in the last decade of the twentieth century was more arduous than it had been when Rothschild and Bosman had plied their craft. Pitchers in the PED era were lucky to have coaches like Bosman who had seen the mound at different heights and witnessed the changes in pitch selection. There were more changeup grips, more ways to deceive the hitter and keep the stronger and faster hitters of the PED era off balance.

> Despite the emphasis on bigger, faster sluggers in the game of baseball today, Bosman believes pitchers have a larger bag of tricks and are better conditioned than at any other time in baseball history, which allows them to compete effectively with the modern baseball slugger.

The game as it was played during the PED era was a far cry from the days of Old Hoss Radbourn, who had pitched a complete game every other day and managed 672 innings in 1884. His muscle came not from a prescription bottle, but from honest toil. When asked if his arm tired, he replied, "Tire out tossing a little five-ounce ball for two hours? . . . I used to be a butcher. From four in the morning until eight at night I knocked down steers with a 25-pound sledge."[12]

Radbourn had been the best "twirler" of the nineteenth century. With the clock winding down on the twentieth century, pitchers seemed a vastly more anemic crew. Hoss had tutored a young teenager named Clark Griffith, who would usher in the first full century of baseball history. But it was a different game in 1999 than the one that began the century in 1900. That game had valued craft and guile. There had been no power hitting, only smart baseball of the kind Dick Bosman valued more than any other. He was his own kind of "Old Fox," and he could teach the wily ways of the baseball wars as well as anyone, but the game was moving to a new level.

Bosman was entering a new century of teaching the game of baseball, and if the last century was any indication, there would be many changes to come. There was one footnote to the 1999 season that was completely old school. It was just an anecdote that harkened back to the days when teams would seek any advantage they could find, employing nefarious tactics that were seldom talked about and never admitted. An allegation was made by a source in Baltimore that Texas manager Johnny Oates and pitching coach Dick Bosman were stealing signs. The accusation came from 94-year-old sportswriter Sam Lacy in an article in the *Los Angeles Times* by Ken Rosenthal.[13]

Dick admitted Johnny Oates stole signs when he could, saying, "When he took enough time to watch the third-base coach, he could usually determine what signs were being used." There were plenty of times, according to Bosman, that they knew the other team was stealing, and Dick called a pitchout. But with Pudge Rodriguez behind the plate, it was not a big priority to steal baserunning signs.

Dick had encountered other teams during his career as a coach that stole signs. One team had a system that used a button in the coach's office to light a bulb in center field, which was used to flash what the catcher had called. During the game, someone was stationed in the coach's office, where they watched a screen hooked up to the center-field camera and then used the light to signal what the next pitch would be. Per Bosman, another team used just a man in the center-field stands with binoculars, who then used his bright clothing to flash the pitch selection to the batter.

But the truth of the matter was that in the late 1990s, the Rangers did not need to steal the signs in Baltimore to beat the Orioles. The Texas coaching staff of Dick Bosman, Johnny Oates, and Jerry Narron had coached the Orioles to winning seasons, and Rafael Palmeiro and Mark McLemore had manned the infield in 1994. But Palmeiro had been too expensive for the Orioles at the end of the 1998 season and had signed on with his old manager, Oates. It was the first of several notable departures that spelled the end of a competitive era in Baltimore.

Much the same was on the horizon for the Rangers in 2000. Juan Gonzalez was due to become a free agent at the end of the season, and before that could happen the Rangers traded him to the Detroit Tigers in a massive deal that sent three players to the Motor City, while Texas received five young prospects. Texas GM Doug Melvin admitted his team would not be able to sign Gonzalez the next fall when he achieved free agency. "It is a very difficult deal to do," he agreed, but he admitted the larger financial picture had forced his hand. "We did not feel we could put a competitive team on the field paying that kind of money [$15 to $20 million] to one player."[14]

The reward for Texas was a 23-year-old right fielder named Gabe Kapler, who would replace Gonzalez. Kapler had played his rookie season in Detroit in 1999, and shown promise. He had huge strength and the potential to hit the ball out of the park as often as Gonzalez, but possibly for many more years in a Texas uniform. The Rangers were trading to rebuild their team. The talent they got from Detroit was younger with longer projection under team control. The prime targets of the trade were 25-year-old infielder Frank Catalanotto, promising 24-year-old reliever Francisco Cordero, and two other pitchers, 20-year-old Alan Webb and 26-year-old Justin Thompson, who was trying to come back from arm surgery after pitching two years in the majors.

None of the new pitchers would have an impact at the major-league level, at least not in a Texas uniform. The trade left Texas still fishing for talent in free-agent waters. Aaron Sele departed to Seattle via free agency before the 2000 season, and Doug Melvin signed 35-year-old Kenny Rogers for another tour of duty in Arlington. Rogers had added a curveball to his repertoire, and Bosman was suitably impressed. "What are you going to do with that pitch?" Bosman asked during his early bullpen sessions with the returning Rogers. Rogers said he used it only as a "show" pitch, but Bosman believed there was enough spin on the ball to "take it to the next level and use it as an out-pitch. It is a big-league curveball," Dick opined.[15]

Rogers had success working with Bosman despite their earlier communication problems. But the rest of the staff was less successful. Darren Oliver was back trying to pitch out of the rotation but failed to pitch effectively in any role. Esteban Loaiza continued in a swingman role. The most notable change was the three younger pitchers who auditioned for the rotation. Ryan Glynn, a 25-year-old, and Doug Davis, a 24-year-old, had both been drafted by the Rangers and brought up through the Texas organization.

"After spring training, looking at the prospects for the coming season did not exactly warm the cockles of my heart," Dick remembered of the 2000 season. "I looked at the minor-league development and asked, where are the kids that are supposed to fortify our pitching staff?" The starting rotation was disappointing, and the bullpen was a problem as well. "Wetteland was done," Dick recalled. "Jeff Zimmerman began to have arm problems."

Doug Melvin was using the trades to keep the team competitive while rebuilding, but the results were not encouraging. Rick Helling and Kenny Rogers pitched well, but every other part of the pitching staff fell off noticeably. The bullpen sank to the lower levels of the American League. None of the young pitchers could get batters out consistently, and the blame accrued to Bosman. The team slid from winning American League West pennants in four of five years to finishing dead last in 2000, 20 games below .500. The pitching staff had the worst ERA in the American League, at 5.51, and the worst in franchise history.[16]

At the end of September, with three games still to play, the team was in Oakland for the final series of the season when Oates called Dick into his office to tell him he was not coming back for the 2001 season. It was as artful a way to say, "You're fired," as Oates could manage. Dick had the cushion of a year remaining on his contract, so he would be paid for the upcoming season, but the news still stung. There was no point in asking who or why, and Dick flew back to Arlington on his own to pack his bags.

Johnny Oates was left to read the news to the press. "He is not the reason we have failed to perform up to expectations this season," Oates said when speaking to the media about Bosman's release from the club.[17] Dick knew it was not his manager's decision to fire him. "I had some empathy for him having to be the one to tell me, quite honestly," Bosman declared. When he got back to Texas, he arranged to meet with Doug Melvin, who was closer to the point of decision for his firing.

"I asked him what was behind the decision to let me go," Dick reflected. "I still want to do this, so I need to know what I'm doing wrong." As he remembers it, Melvin's answer was, "Nothing." Dick assumed that what Melvin was saying was that ownership wanted someone new. There had been some communication issues with some of the pitchers during the season. Esteban Loaiza was quoted in the press as saying he had "rancorous exchanges" with Bosman, but the bottom line was that it was not the lack of communication between Bosman and the players.[18] The talent just was not there. It was not there in 2000, and the following year the Rangers pitching staff would be even worse. Bosman and Melvin shook hands at the end of the discussion, and Dick set about packing for the trip home.

Johnny Oates would resign early in the 2001 season. On May 3, with the team on a losing streak and headed toward a repeat of the 2000 campaign, when they had finished last in the American League West, Oates turned over the team to coach Jerry Narron, who had come over from Baltimore with Oates and Bosman. At the end of January, the Texas Rangers had signed Alex Rodriguez to a long-term contract worth $225 million for 10 years. Rodriguez was a unique talent, one to build a franchise around. But the pitching staff had an ERA of 5.71, once again the worst in baseball, and it wasn't even close. Oates said early in his tenure in Texas, "We don't have one guy that is trying to be bigger than the whole ball club."[19] He could not say that in good faith in 2001.

The signing of Alex Rodriguez left many "scratching their heads," Dick asserted. For Oates, it ran against the grain of everything he stood for as a baseball man. He was managing a team that had never been willing to shop for pitching anywhere except in the bargain bins and gloried in such big-name sluggers as Juan Gonzalez and Rafael Palmeiro. For Oates, it was time to leave when his boss was willing to commit so much to a single player on a team that was so far from achieving even a modest degree of competitiveness.

Johnny Oates would be diagnosed with a brain tumor in November 2001. His stepping down as manager had nothing to do with his subsequent illness. He battled the cancer far longer than his doctors had imagined possible but died in 2004. The obituary noted that Oates had always joked that he was the "25th man on every team he played for." But it also noted his belief that it took 25 men to win a pennant. He was a blue-collar member of the baseball fraternity. He grew up in a family where his father was constantly on the move looking for steady work in another town or city. He never lost his appreciation of baseball for lifting him from that precarious lifestyle.

Dick remembers Oates with complete respect and fondness, saying, "In nine years of working for him as pitching coach there was never a harsh word between us. He was a principled man, honest and loyal to a fault. He was a quiet man, always thinking about something relating to the team or the game. He took his job and his profession very seriously."

There was substantial irony in Oates's tenure in Baltimore with Bosman. Oates had played for the Orioles under Earl Weaver and learned his baseball when the team was a consistent winner, famous for the sound fundamentals it employed in every aspect of the game. Oates tried to instill a similar work ethic as manager of the Orioles from 1991 to 1995, and the team had its best winning percentage in a decade during his years as manager.

It was the job of a lifetime for the old Orioles catcher, but he found the job more trying than he could believe possible. Working for Peter Angelos put more pressure on him than Oates was willing to bear at times, and "he came close to resigning," Bosman remembered. He was at a loss for words trying to describe the kind of pressure Oates was under, but he knew that Oates was internalizing the pressures to a point that it affected him physically.

"He was devoured by it," Bosman recalled of the tension that existed between the Baltimore owner and Oates. Doug Melvin described Oates as "hanging off a ledge" during their years in Baltimore.[20] Through it all, from Baltimore to Texas, Dick believed "you couldn't have a better manager to work for than Johnny Oates." One writer described Oates as the antithesis of Billy Martin. Martin was loud, profane, and pugnacious. Oates was quiet and thoughtful, and scarcely said a cross word. Martin drank; Oates got up every morning and read the Bible. During his tenure in Baltimore, Tom Boswell referred to Oates as "smart, honest, compassionate, a nice guy with backbone."[21] Doug Melvin said of Oates that he "has a phenomenal understanding of the game and, more importantly, knows what motivates people."[22] Dick Bosman agreed with all of it and saw it on a day-to-day basis for nine seasons.

Dick Bosman and Johnny Oates were both blue-collar guys. They believed that winning a game took the coordinated effort of every man on the roster. Bosman may have achieved more success than Oates during their big-league careers, but Oates was always happy to point out that he got his first big-league hit off Bosman in 1970. He could remember the day and the pitch perfectly. It was the top of the ninth inning at RFK, and Bosman was at the peak of his game. Dick was working on a 2–0, complete-game shutout. Oates pinch-hit for Mark Belanger and singled to left-center, over the shortstop's head. Oates would claim to Bosman years later that the pitch was "loaded." Either way, Bosman got a double play two batters later to preserve the shutout. Oates got the last laugh to preserve the friendship.

III

A PHILOSOPHY
OF PITCHING

14

Back to Teaching

When Dick Bosman was fired in Texas, he had been a pitching coach at the major-league level for 11 seasons, nine consecutive ones dating to 1992, when he had come up to the big-league club in Baltimore. He had accumulated an extensive collection of baseball "stuff" that needed to be crated and shipped back home. But the heavier burden was what weighed on Dick's mind. He was at a crossroads, and after he put his personal items into his retro-mod 1936 Chevrolet for the drive to Florida, there was plenty of time to reflect on where he wanted to go in the future.

Bosman admitted there was a bit of soul-searching after he was fired by Texas. "I had been fired two times before, so it did not exactly traumatize me," he remembered.[1] As he thought about it, he realized that one of the greatest sources of frustration had been getting so close with the Rangers and not getting to the World Series. He continued to mull the directions in which he might go when he got home and was working with his partner, Dan McKown, at Sanders Paint and Body Shop. Even his friend at turning wrenches could recognize his discomfort with the decisions that needed to be made about his future. "I was just happy messing with cars," Dick recalled. But McKown told Bosman, "You will starve doing that. You need to stick with what you do best."

He finally had to admit he was done with major-league coaching. "I was burnt out," Dick recalled from a conversation with McKown. He called his former roommate with the Senators, Frank Howard, to talk about his situation in the game in general. Howard was working as a scout for the New York Yankees at the time, and they discussed that option for Dick, but it had no real appeal to him. Then there was a chance meeting with former teammate Darold Knowles during a golf tournament in the fall of 2000.

Knowles suggested the Tampa Bay Devil Rays as an organization Dick might hook on with and enjoy. He suggested Dick call Tom Foley, who was the head of minor-league operations for the Rays. "It was just a cold call," Dick remembered of his first conversation with anyone involved with the Tampa Bay team. "I called the minor-league office, and Foley picked up the phone." Foley lived near Bosman's home in Tarpon Springs, and while the Rays were not a hometown team, their location in the area near his home and the fact that their key staff lived in the area made the prospect of working for the Rays more attractive. Foley was heartened by the idea of having a coach with Dick's experience working in their minor-league organization. He asked Bosman if he would be happy with a job as pitching coach for their Rookie League affiliate in Hudson Valley, New York.

Dick thought about it for 24 hours, and while working at the body shop, lying beneath the chassis of a car he was redoing, he began to "visualize himself working with young men and their youthful enthusiasm." He told Foley he would take the job. Dick was confident it was the right move for him going forward. "I enjoy teaching. I believe it is one of my strong points," he related. Talking to Foley, Bosman admitted, "For the first time in a while I got excited about coaching, excited about teaching."[2] Bosman was going to spend his time with the youngest of the Rays' many pitching prospects.

"This is a good time in my career to get back to some grassroots teaching," Bosman told the local press after his hiring was announced.[3] The idea of working with young players just starting their careers was exciting and harkened back to his earliest days in Northern Virginia. He reported to the Rays spring training camp several months later in St. Petersburg, which was a 45-minute drive from Dick's house. He spent the next few months working with young pitchers in extended spring training in St. Petersburg and commuting home at the end of each day, which was a nice perquisite of working for the Rays organization.

It was a time of adjustment for Dick. He was in a new organization and working in a capacity he had not done since his days as a minor-league pitching coach with the Baltimore Orioles. The Orioles had asked Dick to evaluate their organization in hopes of upgrading their ability to develop pitching talent internally. The Rays did not yet have a specific role for Bosman. The role would change and grow with time.

Dick was joining a Tampa Bay Devil Rays franchise that was still young in the firmament of Major League Baseball, having started in 1997, as an expansion team, along with the Arizona Diamondbacks. The story was much the same as that of the expansion Washington Senators, and Dick Bosman was in a role eerily reminiscent of that of Sid Hudson when he had been both the major-league and minor-league pitching coach for the Senators. Hudson had morphed Bosman from a thrower into a pitcher, and Bosman had taken that philosophy to three major-league teams. Tampa Bay would profit from his extensive knowledge and ability to communicate with young men of potential.

The Rays were not supplying Bosman with much more to work with than Hudson had seen in the 1960s. Dick had been one of the prize pupils in the Washington organization, which had few top-tier talents coming up from the minors. Likewise, as an expansion club, the Rays had little luck in translating their top-tier draft picks into major-league pitching success. In 1998, they chose Texas A&M right-hander Ryan Rupe, and he became their first pitcher to start in the majors after being chosen in the draft.

Rupe was rushed to the Rays' big-league club in 2000, when he made 24 starts and acquitted himself well. He was a big right-hander, standing at 6-foot-6, and despite his initial accomplishments, he was learning how to pitch at the highest level with less than 100 innings of minor-league experience. The team needed talent at the big-league level and did not necessarily have the luxury of letting talent mature slowly, and even later, after Bosman had begun to work in higher levels of the organization, there was an impatience with moving talent quickly when they met minimal developmental goals.

Bosman was tasked with the long-term strategy of developing pitchers. He would be working with young players, more likely drafted from high school, as he had been. Dick began his job at Hudson Valley, the Tampa affiliate in the short-season New York–Penn League—largely for rookie talent—and where the season did not start until June. Dave Howard was the manager at Hudson Valley, and he and Dick established a comfortable working relationship from the start. Howard's love of golf became a source of a long-term friendship with Bosman that has lasted to the current day.

In assessing the organization, Dick had spoken to his old teammate, Joe Coleman, who was the pitching coach for the Rays' Triple-A franchise in Durham, North Carolina. In discussing the team's approach to pitching talent, Coleman asserted that Tampa was a "radar gun" organization. By that he meant that the outfit was overseen by scouts, many of whom had not played baseball at high levels. Their assessment of pitching talent was dependent on the "readings from a radar gun and a bunch of charts."[4]

Dick was not from that school of thought. Radar gun technology placed a premium on velocity, and Dick, as an acolyte of Sid Hudson, had a wider horizon when evaluating pitching talent and helping pitchers get to the majors. If there was a technology that could assist Bosman, it was the ability to detect spin rates, which was a breakthrough that came later. Although Bosman spent many days talking about the philosophy of pitching with the Tampa pitching coordinator, Chuck Hernandez, in the beginning Dick concentrated on "grassroots teaching. I needed to be able to do that," Dick recalled.

Rookie ball, which was what the New York–Penn League was called where Hudson Valley competed, was not a place where those initial evaluations were made. It was where teaching was valued, and Dick needed to dust the cobwebs from the skills he had used with younger players in prior years. Getting back in that frame of mind was where he wanted to be anyway. It was almost as if having raised one set of children, he was trying to remember how he had done it so he could start on a new generation.

To begin the next season, Dick was assigned to Tampa's Double-A affiliate in Orlando as the pitching coach. The assignment had the bonus of being a 90-minute commute from his home in Tarpon Springs, but it also gave him an opportunity to work with talent that was closer to the big leagues. Bosman's staff included pitchers who were on the cusp of making it to the majors and players who had already spent time there. He also began to get a chance to work with pitchers who were on rehab assignments from the big-league club and working their way back to Tropicana Field in St. Petersburg. "It was a whole different scenario," more akin to his days with the Orioles, when he had been a minor-league pitching coach at Rochester. The big difference was the lack of talent at the level of a Mike Mussina or a Ben McDonald.

One talent that Bosman helped reach the majors was Brandon Backe. Backe had been drafted in 1998, in the 18th round, and began his career in the minors as a utility player, logging at-bats both in the infield and outfield. He converted to pitching in 2001, as a 23-year-old, and was quickly promoted through the organization to Orlando. In 2001, he threw 71 innings at three levels and finished the season in Orlando. He began the 2002 season there in the charge of Bosman.

"He was a tremendous athlete," Bosman remembered. He pitched in Orlando both as a starter and a reliever. Backe had 14 starts and three complete games for the Orlando Rays but also closed four times in tossing 92 innings. While no one was quite certain where he was best suited—as a starter or reliever—the big-league club needed arms, and so with fewer than 200 total innings of minor-league work in two seasons and after only a few quality outings, he was promoted to the big-league club to stay.

"Players were moved much too quickly in those years," Bosman admitted about an organization that was trying to compete against teams like the Yankees without any of the resources the Bronx Bombers had available. Backe is an example at one end of the spectrum to show how quickly the Rays sometimes moved talent through their system. That philosophy has changed markedly throughout time, as the team has created one of the deepest pools of pitching talent in the majors, which has given Bosman greater riches with which to work.

"Our philosophy now is more about pitching a full season at each level. We are going to get 25 starts at a level to learn the nuances of everything that needs to be learned *at that level*," Dick said with emphasis. Bringing those ideas along for the Rays was an extended siege of ownership by most of those involved in coaching for the team. The Rays franchise was founded through the efforts of Vince Naimoli, who represented the Outback Steakhouse ownership group. His tireless promotion of the idea that baseball could survive in the Tampa Bay area earned him the admiration and loyalty of fans for several years after 1997.

> The philosophy of Dick Bosman and the Tampa Bay Rays organization emphasizes the need for each prospect to pitch a full season at each minor-league level. They feel this is a vital part of a young pitcher's development and helps him learn the nuances of the game.

Most of his co-owners from the Outback Steakhouse chain were busy fran-
chising restaurants and creating new eating concepts, for instance, the chain
of Bonefish Seafood Grilles and Carrabbas Italian Grilles, which spread like
dandelions in the lawn of southern cities. They let Naimoli run the baseball
side of things, and "budgets were tightened and hopes were squeezed" during
his reign.[5] Naimoli "was known for being cheap,"[6] and he had a contentious
relationship with many involved with the team.

General manager Chuck LaMar had the task of translating Naimoli's directives into baseball logic. The team's doormat status in the American League
East was often laid at the feet of Naimoli's idiosyncratic methods. Ultimately,
Naimoli was bought out by Stuart Sternberg, a New York investment banker,
in 2005. In many ways, the history of the franchise can be divided into the
pre-Naimoli and post-Naimoli years.

Bosman is quiet on the subject of ownership. It is not his realm. Player
development is the field in which he toils, and the conditions improved noticeably in the spring of 2006. During the Naimoli era, the Rays were not successful for a variety of reasons, but the one in which Bosman was involved was
pitching development, and he saw the young players being rushed through
the system, "pitching at levels they were not physically nor emotionally
equipped to handle."

Whatever lies at the heart of it, the Tampa organization did not develop a
first-rate starter for their rotation until 2006, when 24-year-old James Shields
finally made it to the big-league club. Shields was a young pitcher from Santa
Clarita, California, whose high school had turned out several major-league
players—most notably Todd Zeile and Bob Walk. Others would follow, but
Shields was a low-level pick, taken in the 16th round in 2000. He would suffer
the same fate as others, being promoted quickly through the system without
proper instruction.

Dick worked with him in 2001, at Hudson Valley, where Shields had half
a dozen quality starts and was promoted to Charleston, South Carolina,
the Low-A affiliate for the Rays. He showed considerable promise but hurt
his arm and missed the next season after surgery. While rehabbing, he began working out with his cousin, Aaron Rowand, and his cousin's physical
therapist, Tim Soder, in Las Vegas.[7] Rowand was a far more driven athlete
who played collegiately at Cal-State Fullerton with Jeremy Giambi and Mark

Kotsay. Taken in the first round of the draft in 1998, by the White Sox, he was playing in Chicago's major-league outfield by 2001.

Shields's cousin began working out at 5:00 a.m. four days a week. But it was clear to Shields that his cousin's regimen achieved results, and he began to toil at the most important aspect of any athletic endeavor: getting into the best possible physical condition. It wasn't an overnight thing. It was a grind. Even in his first season back in the Tampa system, Shields encountered shoulder problems. "We had to send him back to Bakersfield," Dick remembered after Shields had shown up in Montgomery, Alabama, where Bosman was the Double-A pitching coach. "He couldn't get anyone out. I told Charlie Montoyo, our manager, 'We won't see this kid again.'" But Shields continued to work out and strengthen himself, "through sheer determination," according to Bosman. "There were a lot of twists and turns to Shields's journey to the big leagues."

The one thing that helped that tortured road lead to the majors was taking the proper first step. The idea of conditioning and its importance to the successful pitcher is given 35 pages in chapter 2 of Tom Seaver's *The Art of Pitching*. He and Lee Lowenfish make it one of the most important foundational bedrocks of how a young man begins the ascent to the majors. There are 30 photographs of warm-up exercises and another 30 that detail how to build and condition the proper muscles to prevent injury and strengthen the body to achieve maximum effect when throwing a baseball. James Shields discovered this principle and followed it rigorously.

The idea that an athlete has to work hard to make it is a bromide that is seldom explored, but conditioning is the first element. It is the first indication that the athlete has the "grit" to make it. James Shields was a 16th-round selection in a "radar gun" organization. But he succeeded at a level commensurate with any first-round talent. Angela Duckworth calls it "grit" in her book of the same title. "I found the grittier kids at the National Spelling Bee practiced more than their less-grittier competitors. These extra hours of practice, in turn, explained their superior performance in final competition."[8]

For Dick Bosman, the art of scouting talent is about far more than the radar gun potential of a pitcher. The goal is not only to gage the potential to throw the fastball, but also learn what makes a young athlete tick and how much "grit" they have. The work Paul Tretiak put into his scouting of Bosman—sitting around the kitchen table and getting to know his parents—that extra insight, is at least as important as determining how much movement there is on a young player's fastball. Does the young man have the willingness to put in the long hours of work? This is key because the physical potential for playing baseball is only there for a few years. The light cannot go on 10 years later because by then it is too late. Baseball talent has a short shelf life, and the willingness to make the most of it has to be there from the beginning or, as in the case of James Shields, soon thereafter.

> For Dick Bosman, scouting talent is just as much about the character of the pitcher as the radar gun. They need a certain "grit" to help them through the long seasons it takes to learn the game and thrive at every level.

Shields proved willing to work hard, but he also was a capable student of the game. He worked just as diligently with Bosman in learning to control the running game, as he had in pumping iron with Aaron Rowand. After Shields had achieved success at the major-league level, he became a motivational speaker for the young prospects in the Tampa Bay system in the spring. "What Bozie has taught me has shaved a run off my earned run average," Shields told the younger guys, according to Dick. Shields used the same peekaboo move to watch the runner as he came to the stretch position as Mike Mussina, and his time to the plate was quick enough that with gifted defensive catcher Dioner Navarro, they were a tough combination to steal bases against.

But in the coming years, the team would begin to develop more pitchers like Shields in the farm system where Dick Bosman toiled. It happened because the team learned to "take the normal course of time to develop" their pitching. One of the first adjustments may have been made in the scouting department, as better talent began to come out of the Amateur Draft for Tampa. In 2004, the Rays took Jeff Niemann, Wade Davis, and Jake McGee with their first five rounds, and they progressed through the Rays system successfully to pitch at the major-league level. Davis and McGee both became successful bullpen pitchers with the singular mentality for closing out games.

A significant change was the more patient approach Tampa Bay began to take with their prized prospects. "Wade Davis came to me with a fastball and a curve," Dick asserted. "No changeup, no slider. In the middle of that summer I taught him a cutter." But Bosman did not want him to use the pitch yet because Davis had not reached the point in his development to use it. There

Dick Bosman instructs Tampa Bay Rays pitching prospects on how to put their eyes on the runner at first base. There must be direct eye contact, not just sneaking a peek out of the corner of the eye. The goal is to accurately gauge the runner's primary lead off the base before the pitcher comes set.

was no need to rush his new pitch into his game plan. "Put it in your back pocket," Bosman told him about the cutter. "I don't want to see you throwing it until you get to Double-A."

Davis continued to work with the pitch, although he did not use it in game situations. When he arrived in Montgomery, Bosman took another look at the cutter Davis had been working on and told him it was time to add it to his repertoire. "Today, if you see Wade Davis pitching, he has a 92-mile-per-hour cutter and a 95-mile-per-hour fastball." Wade Davis the reliever still uses the curveball, according to Bosman, but "if he is going to put you away, it is going to be with that fastball or that cutter."

Asked why Davis ended up in the bullpen rather than as a starter, Bosman believes it is in the "makeup" of each pitcher. "I think he had the stomach for it," Bosman said on reflection. There are those guys who "come to the park every day and like the excitement of knowing they may pitch that night. It is the adrenaline rush of it."

Dick Bosman demonstrates the grip for a cutter. The ball is held off center with a modified fastball grip, which provides side spin and late breaking action as it approaches the plate.

There are pitchers who see the excitement running in a totally different direction, who not only prefer the routine of every fifth day, but also revel in the nervous tension that goes with a starting assignment. Ron Darling, in his book *The Complete Game*, articulates a perfect corollary to the high experienced by relievers. "Getting the ball on game day has to be the greatest rush in professional sports," Darling states unequivocally.[9] He liked the deference paid to him when he was the starting pitcher for that day's game, the way his teammates did not disturb him in his routine because so much was riding on his shoulders. He said he started to dream about his next start—the next team on the schedule, their lineup, and the situations that would likely evolve in the game—almost as soon as one start was in the record books.

Tampa was developing those who wanted the ball every fifth day just as capably as they did relievers in the years after Bosman began working in their organization. The guys who wanted the ball every fifth day were not the first-round talents more often than not. Jeremy Hellickson was a fourth-round pick in 2005, and with him Dick Bosman would find success. Alex Cobb was a fourth-round pick in 2006. Matt Moore was taken eight rounds after David Price, the first-rounder who became one of the better success stories of any Tampa Bay draft. Price was the lone first-round pitching talent who lived up to his reputation.

Dewon Brazelton, Wade Townsend, and Jeff Niemann were Rays' first-round picks in the Amateur Draft, and all three failed to achieve the success predicted before they turned pro. Niemann is a good example of one of the problems Bosman saw early on with the Rays. Drafted in the last year of the Chuck LaMar regime, Niemann had a fastball clocked as high as 97 miles per hour. He had a pitcher's body at 6-foot-7, although a touch on the tall side for a repeatable delivery. Coming out of Rice University as a 22-year-old, he was immediately assigned to High-A Visalia of the California League and promoted to Double-A after five starts.

The same injury bug that had plagued him in college flared again, and after Stuart Sternberg deployed a new pitching philosophy across the board, Niemann was allowed to progress more slowly when he returned from injury. He spent two years at Durham and finally made his big-league debut in 2008, pitching for three seasons. But he was never the pitcher that he might have been.

Matt Moore is a good example of the new approach Tampa Bay was deploying in its minor-league organization. Drafted out of high school, Moore spent two seasons in the Rookie League. "He repeated it twice," Dick remembered of Moore, as he learned his craft slowly and was not promoted to the next level until he had learned what was there to be taught and demonstrated enough success to move up the ladder. Bosman saw Moore during a bullpen session in Bowling Green, Kentucky, the Low-A affiliate for Tampa, where Moore achieved his first success.

"He could spin a curveball," Dick attested about Moore early on. "That's a big-league pitch right *now*." Controlling the pitch proved elusive, and he worked on the issue long and hard. "He was arm-side wild sometimes and would have a hard time making the adjustments to get back on track." He has battled through those issues throughout the course of his career, and according to Dick, "He is still on the upside of his big-league career."

Hellickson was another pitcher taken out of high school who progressed slowly through the lower levels of the Tampa Bay organization and then put in more than 100 innings in the upper levels until his arm was strong enough and he had achieved prolonged success, demonstrating he was ready to move up. "I remember Helly from Hudson Valley in '06, the last year that I was there," Dick recalled. "He was as laid back as anyone you would ever want to meet." The young man had not learned the basics of conditioning as taught by Seaver and absorbed by Shields.

Instead of working in the offseason, Hellickson waited until spring training, where he was forced to spend extended periods getting into shape, sometimes "breaking down," so that he had to spend months in extended spring training. He did not progress as a pitcher until he learned to throw a changeup in Double-A ball, according to Bosman, and that is the pitcher he remains to this day, a three-pitch pitcher with a fastball, an excellent changeup, and a "nickel-dime curveball."

Dick Bosman works with a young Tampa Bay Rays pitcher on fundamentals on the back lots of the minor-league complex during spring training.

None of that talent seemed to be coming together for the Rays, as they continued to play losing baseball during the 2007 season. In June of that year, Tampa Bay pitching coach Jim Hickey was practicing his golf game and "bladed a wedge off a curb and the ball came back and hit him in the eye." Surgery was required to repair a detached retina, and Hickey could not perform his duties as pitching coach. As the minor-league pitching coordinator, Bosman was the person who plugged holes wherever they occurred in the Rays organization, which meant it fell to Dick to sub as Joe Maddon's pitching coach in the Tampa dugout during the worst months of the 2007 season. It was not an impressive few weeks.

"We lost 12 in a row when I got there," Dick recalled of the three-plus weeks he was with the major-league club. "We were not a good club in any aspect." After losing eight in a row to the White Sox and Cleveland, the team headed to Boston for a series with the Red Sox. The Rays lost the Friday night game and then played in the afternoon on the Fourth of July. Dick remembers walking in from the bullpen before the start of the game with J. P. Howell, who was the starting pitcher that day.

Fenway Park was sold out, and the situation reminded Dick all too much of the "Christians and the lions, and we were not the lions." He continued, "We got beat bad and came back into the clubhouse and Joe Maddon called a team meeting. George Hendrick—the batting coach—and I expected an ass-chewing after the team had lost 10 in a row." Instead, Maddon calmly told the gathered throng that he was going to go see the Boston Pops Orchestra that evening, but later in the night, after the concert, any of the players who wished could meet him in the bar at the ballpark and "drinks would be on him." Bosman told Hendrick, "Billy Martin just rolled over in his grave." Maddon had a style all his own, even in 2007.

Bosman was grateful for a chance to spend time with Maddon. The coaching staff always gathered at the stadium early in the afternoon before a night game. Dick sat with Maddon on the bench in the dugout, staring out at the field as Maddon explained his philosophy for managing a baseball team. Maddon talked at length about the difficulties of managing the twenty-first-century ballplayer. With a singular style that borrowed nothing from Billy Martin, Maddon achieved considerable success in Tampa. "If you're winning, it works good," said Bosman.

The next season was a historic one for the Rays. Tampa turned the corner not only on the strength of the pitching they developed internally, but also with shrewd trades. GM Andrew Friedman used highly touted offensive prospects to bring in high-upside arms like Matt Garza and Edwin Jackson. The Garza trade may have been the best ever made by the Tampa Bay team. For Garza, they traded to the Minnesota Twins highly touted outfield prospect Delmon Young, who had been taken first overall in the 2003 draft. Young had played his first full season in the major leagues as a 21-year-old in 2007, acquitting himself well. The Rays packaged him with Jason Pridie, a second-round talent, and Brendan Harris, a journeyman infielder, for Garza and starting shortstop Jason Bartlett.

Garza joined Shields to provide the Rays with two hurlers who were in the top 15 pitchers in the American League that season. Scott Kazmir was the other important piece of that rotation. He had been acquired by LaMar in 2004, and had been one of the better left-handers in the American League for several seasons. Andy Sonnanstine was a surprise success story in 2008. Like Shields, he had been groomed from a low-level draft choice into a capable member of the rotation. But it was the addition of Garza that elevated Tampa Bay pitching to the next level. He was only 24 years old that season, and Shields, at 26, was the senior member of a staff on which no one else was older than 25.

The offense, led by Carlos Pena and Evan Longoria, was better than league average and scored enough runs for the team to win 97 games and claim the American League East title for the first time in team history. Tampa Bay was the best Cinderella story baseball had seen in many a year. They went from last to first, which was a feat accomplished by other teams in the history of the game, but Tampa Bay had languished in last place in the American League East for every year of their existence, save 2004, when they rose to fourth in the five-team division. Fans were enthralled by their underdog story when the Rays fought their way through the playoffs and into the World Series.

But in some ways the story of Tampa Bay's ascent to the pinnacle of baseball was lost because the franchise has been so marginalized that even the 2008 narrative fell into the cracks of history. Many prize-winning journalists have plied their trade with the *St. Petersburg Times*. It is one of the better newspapers in the country, a little-known secret of journalism. But their readership does not extend to New York City or the other major media markets, and so the story of the "little engine that could," named the Tampa Bay Rays, hardly made a ripple in the national sporting news.

James Shields was, in many ways, the soul of that team. He was at the heart of a fight that broke out in a mid-season game with the Boston Red Sox, who they would beat out for the American League East title. The game got ugly after a hard slide at second base by Red Sox centerfielder Coco Crisp. Shields held up his team's honor with a brushback pitch to Crisp, which ignited an on-field melee between the two teams. It was June, and the acrimony of that fracas lasted for the rest of the season. In October, the two teams fought once more for the American League championship in a seven-game series.

Shields lost the first game against the Red Sox by a 2–0 score, pitching against Daisuke Matsuzaka. Shields gave up only a single run in seven innings, but Dice-K, as Matsuzaka was known, was better. In game six, Shields pitched almost as well but again lost a tight game, 4–2, to Josh Beckett. Matt Garza was the best pitcher for Tampa in the postseason, and he won the decisive game seven against Boston in a tight 3–1 contest against Jon Lester.

The pitching was good, but the Tampa Bay offense was the decisive factor in beating the Red Sox. Tampa scored 38 runs in the other four contests, which were not pitcher's duels, outslugging Boston in three of those four. Tampa Bay went to their only World Series in 2008, against the National League champions, the Philadelphia Phillies. Shields won Game 2 after going five and two-thirds innings without giving up a run. He pitched most of the game with runners on base, and it was the Dick Bosman school of pitching at work as he labored to keep them where they were. It worked too, as he did not allow a single runner to score, "much to the delight of the sellout crowd of 40,843."[10] It is the only World Series win by a Tampa pitcher in the history of the franchise to date, as Tampa Bay lost the series in five games. Shields's nickname was "Big Game James," and during the playoffs in 2008, he lived up to that reputation.

Bosman felt a sense of connection to the American League champions in 2008, because so many had come through the minor-league system. He had worked with James Shields since the first season when he joined the Rays in 2001, as the pitching coach for the Hudson Valley team, where Shields also began. Like Bosman had early in his career, Shields went from a struggling minor leaguer to an Opening Day starter. He had asserted his leadership, again, via rather visible altercations. There was one with Scott Kazmir, with whom he had heated words during the 2007 season. Dick told Shields, "You run this staff." Bosman believed the young pitcher had the requisite leadership traits honed from the long distance he had traveled in his career. "He is a strong-minded man," said Bosman, which is what Dick admires about him to this day.

Shields and Garza remained atop the Tampa Bay rotation after 2008, along with most of the rest of the Rays pitching staff. The offense continued to be centered around Evan Longoria, Carl Crawford, and Ben Zobrist, making the team a power to be reckoned with in the American League East for another five years. They won the division again in 2010, and went to the playoffs three more times, although they did not advance in any of those years. By the 2011 season the starting rotation had been drafted by and developed through the Rays' minor-league system.

"When Andrew Friedman first came aboard, there was no doubt that we were going to be given a chance to do our jobs," Dick remembered of the changes that began in 2006, and continued to transform the organization. They made the most of the competitive balance mechanisms that gave small-market teams like Tampa Bay compensation for their loss of talent to the higher-salaried clubs. The compensation came in the form of top draft picks, which were then assigned to the minor-league player development team.

"There was a greater importance placed on our roles. They valued our opinions, not that they did what we advised every time, but we were asked," Bosman revealed. Dick believes the Tampa Bay front office put more emphasis on the draft and the development of talent in general, from the top picks to those like Shields and Moore who were not chosen in the first five rounds. There was "free rein to do what was right with these guys," he stated. Dick Bosman the teacher had the freedom to use his ability to communicate with young men and bring them along slowly, adding pitches when it was appropriate in their development, using his instincts and experience in the game to make them successful professionals at the highest level.

Bosman prides himself on being able to relate to almost anyone, and his overall approach to communicating with young men has not changed appreciably since he first began teaching the rudiments of pitching to Little Leaguers and high schoolers in Northern Virginia in the 1980s. "You can't reach them all. My dad always said that, and I don't take it personally anymore," he said about the ones with whom he fails. Dick believes that one of the keys to his job is the ability to determine which ones are listening and which ones want to put in the extra effort that it takes to become a successful pitcher at the highest levels, not just sound mechanics.

He has learned a lot about the rest of the job as well. "I have learned more about how to teach the mechanics, about how to teach certain pitches," he said of the knowledge he has built on throughout the years. It is knowledge that has accumulated through the years, talking to pitchers ranging from Gaylord Perry during his playing days to coaches and players he has met since then. "How do you throw that pitch? What does it feel like coming out of your hand?" Those are the questions every pitcher asks of his teammates and anyone knowledgeable about the art of pitching along the way. And, of course, for Bosman, there is always the notion of putting on the catching mitt and seeing what a pitch looks like. He has built his knowledge of cutters, changeups, and the sophisticated repertoire the modern pitcher uses today from the best of all sources—the pitchers who do it.

"We all copy things from each other," Dick admitted of the universal tendency to learn from watching and listening to others. He is one of those guys who listens and learns. Who isn't afraid to ask questions for fear it might expose his ignorance? A skill for listening at the best of times also informs his teaching. Said Bosman,

> If I can use something that someone else is doing, I'm going to do that. It doesn't have to be a pitch or a way to hold the ball, it can be something a guy says, how he conveys a point that gets it across extremely well. I can use that too. It's about the accumulation of all that knowledge from playing and coaching, of filtering things in and filtering things out.

He confessed he is better at identifying what will help a certain pitcher succeed than when he first began as a coach, saying, "Sometimes you have to tell a guy, 'What you're doing now is not going to get it.'" Then there is the approach with younger guys where Dick will often say, "There is a better way to do this." A big part of the job of a pitching coach is knowing what to say to different individuals to bring them along in the process of developing their talents, what to say as they make progress up the ladder of the organization.

It is not unlike using that old notebook with the illustrations of how successful pitchers have done it, the one he used when he first starting teaching kids in Northern Virginia. Dick still tells young pitchers that players whose names they recognize did it a certain way that may have relevance for them. "Sometimes that can open a door."

There is one thing Dick keeps in the back of his mind as a constant mantra. He is not about "reinventing the wheel." Pitching is an art, not a science, and there are plenty of valid ways to pitch, plenty of approaches that work for certain people, and they should be left to do their thing if it works. If "drop and drive" works for Tom Seaver and Robin Roberts, then who is he to tell a young pitcher who wants to do things that way he is wrong. Maybe he is another of *those* guys. He believes that taking more credit for his own importance and his impact on young pitchers, or on entire pitching staffs, is a mistake, and he does not want to sound like that to his young pitchers or anyone else.

The Tampa Bay Rays are a fine organization that has drafted and developed fine pitching talent. They pay attention to the character of the man, as well as the radar gun readings. The Rays take the time to nurture the talent at each level of the minors without rushing them to the big leagues, even when the players grow restless and think they are ready for the big show. There has to be a relationship built on trust so Dick can calm the impatient young man who knows he is going to pitch one day in the major leagues but is not yet ready.

Bosman said, "I have to be able to explain to him why he is not even close to being ready to pitch in the majors." When their agents or others are telling them they are ready, there needs to be a relationship that trumps the other voices so they understand when Bosman says, "Look at the guys who have come through here before. Look at the Matt Moores, the Wade Davises, and Alex Cobbs of the world. This is how we do it. There are no shortcuts." His boss, Mitch Lukevics, the Rays farm director, has to be even more steadfast than Bosman. He hears more of the feedback from the agents and the kid's uncle who pitched in the minors 30 years ago. Mitch makes Dick's job a little easier, but together they have to get young pitchers to slow it down just a notch. The other road leads to spending years bouncing back and forth between Triple-A and the big leagues because the pitcher did not spend enough time getting ready in the minors before that last promotion.

The Rays are like the Oakland Athletics—they have to do it by identifying and developing talent just a little bit better than the teams with the big television contracts and several million more in attendance annually. The Rays have no choice except to do it right. They do not have the margin for error others have. Dick is proud to be part of a good organization that does it the right way, one that is winning ballgames despite being a little short on cash. He loves the challenge of his current position.

Ultimately, he is proud to be part of the long tradition of professional pitchers, one who is getting a chance to pass on his knowledge of the game to the young players who come through the Tampa Bay organization. He tries to pay forward the chance he got to work with such mentors as Sid Hudson and Ted Williams, to pass on some of the knowledge he gained when his father taught him how to spin a baseball so long ago. Maybe it will have that same impact it once had on a young kid from Kenosha.

A Philosophy of Teaching

As Dick began the 2017 season as part of the Tampa Bay Rays organization, he could look back on a career that has spanned 55 years. It had been that long since Dick and his family sat at the old kitchen table in Kenosha and launched his career as a professional baseball player. Baseball and family began to intertwine on the day he signed his first contract, and it has been a good marriage, one that has endured all things. No one at the table those many years ago knew how far the thread would run. Paul Tretiak was living proof that a baseball career could last a lifetime, but had baseball not proven a source of success and had he not carved out an enduring niche in the game he loved, Dick could just as easily have followed his love for cars and his mechanical aptitude into something different.

The competitive spark that burned within the young Bosman fueled 306 appearances in baseball in 11 seasons and another 141 appearances in the minors in six there. His coaching career is now in its 30th season. Throughout his long career in the game, there has been an underlying commitment to the simple principles his father taught him. George Bosman taught Dick to not only understand how much hard work it takes to reach one's loftiest goals, but also to appreciate what others can teach. Dick came to understand one last lesson, this one more personally: In times of adversity there are more important things than how to spin a baseball.

The beginnings of Dick's pitching philosophy go back to a dictum of George Bosman's. George said, "If you're winning races, don't overhaul the motor."[1] That advice had always restrained Dick Bosman the pitching coach from wanting to rebuild the mechanics of any single pitcher from scratch or trying to remake an entire staff based on a vision that was uniquely his own. In a thousand phone calls and hundreds of family visits, George offered his son the insights of a lifetime on raising children and working for a living. That perspective proved relevant to so many of the problems Dick encountered during his career as a baseball player and coach.

Complex relationships can often be reduced to such simple core values as kindness and hard work. Dick Bosman brings to his endeavors a wisdom that treasures the little things—heart and desire, and a more thoughtful, analytic pursuit of excellence rather than just a dogged one. Those small lessons, sometimes hard won, are wrapped together to form the core of what he calls his philosophy of pitching. Extending that knowledge to others relies on building positive, long-term relationships. Perhaps the most notable aspect of Dick Bosman the man is an approach that does not change to fit the man, or woman, for that matter. No matter whether it has been Frank Howard or Ted Williams, or just a kid on the back lots of a baseball training camp, Dick Bosman has devoted that wisdom to the situation at hand. He may call upon a nugget he learned from mentors like Sid Hudson or Ted Williams—men who saw a spark of competitive fire in him and a desire to put it to good use—or it can be just something he has seen many times while sitting in a crouch and catching bullpen sessions.

The aggregate knowledge Dick has to offer young pitchers has accumulated from the many baseball savants he has known and the countless baseball situations he has observed at the most personal level. That knowledge becomes a philosophy of pitching, one that is like a single game on the mound that evolves to meet the moment, one that is fluid and changing. Dick's philosophy of pitching comes from a lifetime of watching great pitchers—and less-than-great ones—throw in the bullpen, from thousands of baseball games he has seen from the dugout and from the mound. It is the small moments of realization that, rolled together, have formed a solid foundation for how Bosman has approached every pitcher with whom he has worked, every minor-league talent he has tried to bring along.

It is a way of seeing born of the "school of hard knocks," as he calls it. Sometimes the lessons that stick are the ones learned when something doesn't work, when the right pitch in the wrong situation leaves the park in a hurry. Spinners, knucklers, spitters, and changeups. They each have a different feel and look when put in the hands of individual pitchers. That is the *art of pitching*, seeing what a pitch looks like when a particular pitcher throws it. The best way to gauge the nuances of each situation is to watch the ball as it spins its way toward the catcher's mitt, and this is Dick's way. The sum of the observations he has made throughout the years inform what he brings to the game today.

One person who has watched Dick evolve as a teacher is Chris Shebby, who first saw the former big-league pitcher as a 12-year-old boy and has been in touch with him throughout every stage of his development. They have grown together despite the decades of difference in their ages. When Chris quit baseball to pursue another profession, he maintained contact with Dick because his old pitching coach had so much more to offer than just baseball acumen. And Shebby remained a constant sounding board for his old mentor.

Said Shebby,

> Dick is a very meticulous and fastidious guy. The little things mean a lot to him. The subtleties, regardless of what it is. Even when he was learning to ski, he studied the hell out of everyone who skied and figured out all the little things you need to do mechanically. Dick's philosophy of pitching is about doing a lot of little things well.

Breaking down pitching into its simplest parts is a starting point, but it ripples out from baseball into his life as a whole.

Dick is a fine golfer who has mastered the game much the same way he approached baseball and pitching. Anything he wants to do well, he breaks it down into its component parts: the backswing, the follow-through, and the pacing of both of those. Whether it is golf or a friendly game of cards, Bosman is looking for an edge. He is too competitive to just play for the fun of it. For Dick, the greatest fun is in the winning.

There is a fineness to pitching at the highest levels that many do not comprehend, but it is essential and a point that Dick did not appreciate until after he reached the majors. "It is the distinction between working hard on the mound and working nice and easy, and letting the batter get himself out," Shebby asserted in trying to summarize Dick's approach.[2] It is doing the little things consistently and the simple parts of the larger effort that are so important. Bosman is proud that his old student understands this most important of points. The effort the pitcher or golfer makes cannot be a matter of brute force. It has to be easy, and for many that is a hard lesson to learn.

"The simpler the mechanics of the delivery, the easier it is for most pitchers to master it,"[3] Dick said in discussing Warren Spahn with Roger Kahn. Dick grew up during a period when ornate pitching deliveries were more common than not. He watched Spahn during his trips to County Stadium in Milwaukee and on television as the great master rocked his arms back and forth to begin his motion and then bent far back, pointing his right foot toward the heavens as he completed his weight shift before the long follow-through stride, which took him down the incline of the mound with such force that he finished with his hand just a few inches from the ground.

Spahn was inimitable, although his elaborate motion was not out of place among the pitchers of his era. He revealed his most stunning attribute one night with Bosman in attendance at County Stadium. With Dick watching his every move throughout the game, the biggest surprise came at the end, when the old veteran tipped his hat to the adoring crowd. Dick related, "It amazed me that a great pitcher was bald-headed."[4] That famously receding hairline proved far easier to understand for Bosman in future years as pitching mechanics and the conventional wisdom of pitching moved in a very different direction than where it stood in 1965, when Spahn ended his career and Bosman was just starting his own.

Roger Kahn, the baseball writer who was profiling Spahn for a book, asked Bosman what he thought of Spahn after the intervening years. Dick was the pitching coach for the Texas Rangers at the time, and Kahn was trying to explain the direction pitching had taken in the years since Spahn.[5] The biggest takeaway was, "Keep it simple." How comfortable is the young pitcher with his mechanics? They have to be an almost unconscious element that the pitcher takes to the mound each time he enters a game. The more natural and calm the mechanics of the delivery, the easier they are to replicate each time he throws a ball.

Replication of his delivery is the first test of pitching talent for scouts after they take that first radar gun reading. But once the flamethrowers are drafted, it is left to the seasoned professionals, like Dick Bosman, to streamline that initial motion, to work the kinks out so that as a young man progresses through the organization, there is an easy fluidity to his motion, one that takes no more than 1.3 seconds to complete from start to finish if there is a runner on base.

Tweaking the mechanics of a talented young pitcher resonates with Bosman like turning wrenches on an old Chevy: Remove this old, worn-out part and replace it with one that fits and is better. Whether it is an old carburetor or an across-the-body motion like Roger Pavlik's, it is about remaking a pitcher or an old car into something as good as it can be as a physical entity. Maybe the results are more reliably predictable when Dick takes a rusting old hulk and tunes it into a smooth-running modern machine. Humans are vastly more complex and more challenging, but Dick has confidence that his extensive experience in the game will allow him to take a young pitcher and make the mechanical adjustments necessary to improve his delivery until it hums with something nearing perfection. Bosman can give a young hurler the necessary pitches to address the daunting demands of the modern game. That is the mechanical part.

Then there is the ghost in the machine, where the art of pitching leaves turning wrenches in the oil-stained dirt. The head game weaves in and out of baseball like a wisp of smoke, a haunting smell that cannot be named. Command of that side of the game is what makes it so magical and appealing to those who master it. Dick knows it well and can remember those great moments on the mound when he was master of it all, when he knew what the hitter was thinking and what he wanted Dick to throw. Bosman knew exactly what to throw in those situations, and even before he did he could see the batter lunging for it, rolling over the top of the ball and hitting a harmless ground ball to Brinkman.

Dick's appreciation for and love of the mental aspect of the game is what Ted Williams loved about him more than anything else. The mystery of the game intrigues Bosman to this day. It is the spark that lights off his imagination like an old V8. That game begins when the pitcher delivers the baseball to the plate and the game begins officially. The crowd watches and waits for him to lift his hands to begin his motion. He is the one in control. He alone possesses a plan for how it might unfold if he has his stuff, if everything breaks his way. If pitching were a card game, the pitcher is the dealer, the one who sets the tune.

Some talent is not suited for that situation, which is why Bosman posits that not every pitching talent is meant for the starting rotation. To make it through a big-league lineup three or four times, a pitcher has to master the elements of strategy. He has to know what each batter's strengths and weaknesses are, have an idea what he will throw to them, and adjust his knowledge as the game unfolds.

Kahn called his book on pitching *The Head Game*, because the mental side of pitching is the heart of the game of baseball. During one season early in his coaching career, Bosman asked his pitchers to wear a t-shirt that said, "Get ahead, stay ahead, use your head."[6] It is as good a summary of his philosophy of pitching as can be put on a t-shirt. But the greatest substance lies in the third of the essential pitching commandments: *Use your head.*

Pitching mechanics need to remain as simple as possible because the rest of it—the mental side of the task—is so complex. The modern pitcher must compose a score for each game and, like the conductor of an orchestra, lead his cohorts in playing out the tune. Sometimes it is more like jazz because in the heat of the moment, the pitcher must be able to improvise and find a groove where his teammates can play along. Then he must be able to repeat that same variation on a theme more than 30 times during the season.

"I might have faced the same batter three or four times in the same game, but each time there was some new element to analyze, some new strategy at play," said Ron Darling, looking back on his career.[7] It does not take an Ivy League education like Darling's, but the pitcher has a more cerebral task than the hitter, although Ted Williams would argue the point. To succeed in the rarified realm of pitching, a hurler must be able to remember situations and think back to prior confrontations with specific hitters. Bosman kept a log of notes he made after every game because remembering it all was too difficult. He could bring out his notes from the last time he faced a team and its lineup. He had to review how he had pitched to that team's best hitters and prepare based on what he had learned the last time out. If he was in the zone, he could see himself pitching to each batter, throwing each pitch in the perfect situation and the batter reacting exactly as he wanted.

Today, pitchers have computer readouts that are far more detailed and give the modern hurler much more substantial information on the swing tendencies of each player, where their strengths lie, and which weaknesses to probe. Every hurler—be they Old Hoss Radbourn, Clark Griffith, Warren Spahn, or any other in the long line of fine twirlers who have taken the mound—has always devised a plan going in and, on the fly, used it to neutralize what the hitters were hoping to do. It is what Ron Darling said he went to sleep at night thinking about, running through the upcoming team's lineup and what the likely game situations would be.[8]

Dick Bosman says that pitching is like playing the game of bridge. The best contract bridge players know the various conventions for bidding; they count trump as it is played and are all about the finesse of various cards in the heat of a game. They map out a strategy for playing the hand and, as the cards are played, must adapt to game situations as they occur. Nothing could better describe the mental side of pitching.

Any pitcher worth his salt knows what his best pitch is against every batter whether it is early in the count or late. He knows how he got them out in games past, and when he is on his game, when the stars have aligned, he can visualize getting them out in the next game and go out and do it almost exactly the way he pictured it beforehand. A pitcher values what bridge players call "finesse"—setting up the hitter early in the count for something off speed late in the count and then sneaking that pitch by the batter, frozen by the crafty hurler's guile.

There is a less thoughtful approach to Bosman's craft, one he calls the radar gun approach to pitching. It is scout-driven and overvalues the fastball. It is the Philadelphia Phillies when they released Curt Simmons in 1960, because his fastball was losing velocity, and they assumed he could no longer pitch. The St. Louis Cardinals picked him up, and in 1964, he won 18 games for the world champions because he knew how to sneak a jack of hearts through the king.

"The pitcher's job is to take the sting off the ball," Simmons said, according to Bosman's old teammate, Dave Baldwin.[9] By that, Simmons means to say the pitcher is best served by having a batter who is uncertain which pitch will be thrown, what it will look like, and how fast it will come toward him. "If the batter overestimates the speed of the pitch, he hits a grounder; if he underestimates it, he pops up." The trick is to finesse the hitter, to keep him off balance at all times. To accomplish that task requires preparation, knowing what each batter can handle and what he cannot. The fastball is only a small part of the game, and radar gun readings will do little to indicate the success a pitcher will have against major-league hitters.

The best hitters will, on occasion, square up the very best of pitches. The best pitchers will lose the strike zone and give up four balls and a free base to the batter. When there are runners on base, the circumstance changes. And that is where one component of Bosman's game plan has its greatest value: His techniques for controlling the running game are without parallel. The pitcher must know how it is done almost instinctively because the focus must always be on the hitter. But he has to know what the runner is doing and assess the lead and react accordingly without losing focus on the next pitch.

For the pitching coach, the nuance plays out with each hurler he sends to the mound during the course of a season. The pitching coach conceives a strategy for the season based on the arms at his disposal, knowing that the season will play out according to its own plan. It is the weaving together of the threads of uncertainty that creates the unique pattern of a team and its season. Indeed, having a pitching staff in your charge is like being dealt a hand of bridge. You may have an ace or two; you may not. From the first week of spring training, a pitching coach is sorting his cards, determining which ones go where and how strong his cards might be. Each bridge hand consists of 13 cards; a pitching staff will generally have 12 hurlers, sometimes 13. It is the pitching coach's job to assemble the strongest collection of arms he has and equip them with the best tools for the coming season.

There is another game that closely mirrors the art of pitching, one close to Dick Bosman's heart: the game of golf. Rick Helling said his best conversations about pitching occurred with Bosman on the golf course. "They say that pitchers love golf because they only pitch one day in five," Helling asserted.[10] "But it is about more than that. It is about the ability of pitchers to create situations in the game, about how to use my pitches to get guys out, developing an approach hitter by hitter." A starting pitcher uses his assortment of pitches much the way a golfer uses his assortment of clubs. Each game situation demands a different club, a different pitch, and the ball comes off the club face almost like it comes out of the pitcher's hand.

Both Helling and Ron Darling put the pitcher in the center of the picture. He is the one in control of the game or at least has more control than any other player on the field. The viability of the pitcher's vision for success and his ability to execute it on a given day has more to do with whether his team wins or loses than any other single player on the field. It is a team game, but the pitcher is the one dealing the cards. Helling embraces the Bob Rotella school of envisioning success as closely as does Bosman. He was visualizing success before Bosman became his pitching coach, but the two talked about the concept considerably, especially on the golf course.

Helling believes it is a natural part of the game for pitchers. He and Bosman talked frequently about having a vision of getting batters out when they were on the golf course. "It is all about having a vision of how I am going to use my pitches to get guys out," he said in a way similar to how Bosman talked about his best games against the Twins or Orioles."[11] The head game is not just the drama that occurs between pitcher and batter during the game. It is the preparation that a pitcher does mentally before a game. Whether it is Ron Darling going to sleep at night before each start visualizing each hitter and how he will pitch him or Dick Bosman seeing each pitch to batters during the drive to the park, there is more mental preparation and mental execution for pitchers than for hitters.

Duke Snider said, "The best way to hit is to swing without thinking. Follow the ball out of the pitcher's hand. See the ball. Hit the ball . . . slider, curve, whatever. Just see it and hit it."[12] Dave Baldwin, the former Washington Senators relief pitcher who left baseball and gained advanced degrees in genetics and biomedical engineering in retirement, agreed but provided academic affirmation of Snider's theory of hitting. Baldwin described the milliseconds of time in which the mind sees the baseball as it leaves the pitcher's hand, makes a mental calculation as to its flight, and then decides whether to swing. Snider is absolutely correct. According to Baldwin, there is no time for thinking, just reacting, and the more the hitter thinks, the more he clutters his mind with thoughts other than the instinctual reaction to the flight of the ball and the less likely he is to make contact with a pitch.[13]

Neither Baldwin's intent nor mine is to diminish the intellect of the hitter. Ted Williams was a brilliant man, but it was his keen vision and reflexes that allowed him to hit .406 in 1941. The hitter can anticipate the pitch that may be thrown and, according to Baldwin, retain an image of the previous pitch in his mind. The notion that a batter who sees more pitches in a given at-bat has a better chance of hitting the ball is accurate because he retains the image of each previous pitch like a camera can place a picture on hold. But that is a moment-to-moment reflex, and the better equipped a hitter is, the less his conscious mind gets in the way. It is the opposite for the pitcher. He has to engage his mind and reflect on prior situations, and do so before and during the game.

In *The Art of Pitching*, Tom Seaver details how he conceived of each situation in a single game against the St. Louis Cardinals at the end of the 1983 season, writing, "I mulled over the data I had been collecting on the Cardinals over the past week."[14] Seaver knew which hitters were hot and which were not. Bob Gibson, in *Pitch by Pitch*, his book about his 17-strikeout performance in Game 1 of the 1968 World Series, shares how he used scouting reports on Willie Horton and his observations of Horton's actions in the batter's box to determine what to throw him.[15] In that memorable game, which Gibson will forever remember, Horton went 0-for-4, with two strikeouts. But Horton proved able to make mental adjustments to Gibson. In the crucial Game 7 of that same World Series, the one Gibson chose not to highlight in book form, Horton went 2-for-4 and played a pivotal role in Detroit's win. Hitters can benefit from thinking about their approach between games as well.

Nonetheless, the idea of the pitcher being the one who deals the cards and acting as the mental master of the game situations is subject to two important caveats. The first was articulated by Bosman, when he discussed the need for the pitcher to have his own Zen-like concentration when it is time to deliver the ball to the batter. Training and trust are the two key elements, according to both Bosman and Rotella, that must precede that point in time. Physical training and the repetition of simple mechanics are necessary preparation, but then the pitcher must trust in first his talent and then the moment.

Just as the batter has a moment in which the noises in his head must fall away, so too does the pitcher, in that instant when he first breaks his hands, pulls the ball out of his mitt, and begins the delivery. From that point onward, it is about the focal point, the dark stain in the center of the catcher's mitt, and the intensity it takes to deliver the pitch—and then seeing it fool the hitter all the way into the glove. Preparation leads to that instant, but the thoughts cease and the most elemental part of the brain takes over when the pitcher is living in the reality of pitching.

The other caveat is something important Johnny Oates communicated: "It takes 25 men to win a pennant."[16] Every player on a team has a role to play if a team is to win. As Dick Bosman well knows, it takes a capable infield defense to win ballgames. And it takes 12 pitchers and then some to get through a season, and winning a pennant requires that every arm on the staff compete successfully, whether it is the bullpen or the starters. Bosman believes the job of the bullpen pitcher has changed markedly through the years. Where starters once coveted the complete-game win as a notch in their belt, they are now content to walk off the mound at the end of seven innings with the lead and hand the ball to the pen.

Those guys are a "world apart," Bosman said. "They do nutty stuff to cope with the late-inning pressures." But their approach to the game is different as well. There is a preponderance of fastball pitchers who thrive in the late innings because it is a simpler way to approach the game. Relievers have to make adjustments and hit their spots. They set up batters just like any other pitcher, but they can throw a small repertoire of pitches. And for some of them there is nothing more subtle or nuanced than good, old-fashioned hardball from start to finish.

They do not need a game plan, and they do not need the complete arsenal of pitches that the starter needs. "They can go full speed all the time." It helps to have a John Wetteland or a Mariano Rivera as much as an ace at the front end of the rotation. But regardless of what the coach has, when the team readies for its trip north and the beginning of the season, the pitching coach must have a plan that will maximize the effectiveness of the cards he has been dealt.

But notwithstanding the role they play, the pitcher is the one in Dick Bosman's mind—and that of every member of his fraternity. He is the one who must stand tall and alone on the mound, with a unique responsibility for how the game will unfold. Only the pitcher knows whether he is going to try to blow the hitter away with a fastball up—the batter swinging lustily but his bat passing below and slightly behind the pitch—or throw something off-speed, hoping to induce uncertain contact, a soft grounder to short or a pop fly to second. Dick stood there for more than 1,000 innings of pitching in the majors but learned far more about his craft during 30 years of teaching the game at the highest levels.

Teaching the mechanics of pitching and the head game rests on a simple foundation. Dick Bosman's father taught it to him as a boy. You must convince your peers and your charges that you are a man of principle and honesty. Dick's father once needed a transmission to complete the rebuilding of an old engine and went to the "boneyard" to buy one out of a junked truck. He and Dick found the right transmission, but the man behind the counter at the junkyard wanted more cash than his father had brought with him. When George Bosman told the man he would pay him the extra money the next day, the man replied, with a nasty, skeptical look, "How do I know I can trust you?"

Dick's father immediately got hot. "He did not raise his voice, but he was indignant that someone would question his honesty and credibility," Dick reflected. Again, the Bosman family lived by the farmer's credo. An honest day's work was the foundation for living, and a heavy emphasis was placed on honesty. Building trust with other players is the first and foremost facet of Dick Bosman's philosophy of pitching. Everything depends on that starting point no matter whether it is a young pitcher or a veteran. They must believe in Bosman's integrity. They must judge that his advice is rooted in not only knowledge and experience, but also principle.

Whether the pitcher is Tom Seaver or Roger Pavlik, Dick believes in approaching them the same way, seeking to win their confidence with nothing more complicated than simple honesty. He gives them a candid appraisal of their talents, their mechanics, and the situation, and offers his knowledge and expertise from that perspective. From there it is the willingness of Dick's students to work with him as they explore the best approach to the game. They have to do the hard work, to have the grit and commitment to put into practice the ideas that evolve as they work together. There must be something burning within.

There has to be that spark, that fire within that can set an old engine running or a fine pitching talent on a path toward the majors. Even after 50-plus years in professional baseball, Dick Bosman is that same competitor with a keen desire to win. He has enough desire to win to go around, as was the case late in the 1970 season, when his teammates were more interested in watching the Redskins play football than performing on the field. "If you don't hustle while I'm pitching, I'll kick your ass,"[17] Dick declared.

That fiery intensity has never diminished, and it is the most essential element to Bosman's philosophy. That will to win keeps his approach to pitching fresh and meaningful. It keeps him always looking for an edge that could prove the difference between winning and losing. His fire never dies out during the long winter months each year. He is ready at the first hint of spring to go at it like it is his first professional camp. Said Bosman,

> I never got, "It's only a ballgame." All the way back to the beginning, back to when it was 2-on-2 with Jim Renick and kids from around the farm in Kenosha, it was always about the competition and a desire to win. It was like that at the very beginning, and it still is.

Teaching that fierce devotion to winning might appear an implausible absolute, a utopian ideal. But it can be done when the conditions are perfect. The student must possess that same burning core of commitment and desire, have an almost intuitive respect for the game. And if the young man is lucky, he will find a teacher like Dick Bosman—a teacher with a singular gift for forging human connections. Working together, they can hope to climb the great peaks of baseball achievement. That is the path on which Dick remains to this day, chin up and searching for the greatest season of them all.

Notes

CHAPTER 1

1. Dick Bosman, telephone interview by author, May 27, 2016. Unless specified otherwise, quotes from Dick Bosman in chapter 1 are drawn from this interview.

2. Bev Darr, "Baseball Was Paul Tretiak's Life," *Hannibal Courier-Post*, March 31, 2010, 1.

3. Jim Hannan, telephone interview by author, May 26, 2016.

4. Peter Schmuck and Buster Oleny, "The Other Shoe," *Sporting News*, October 10, 1994, 40.

5. Merrill Whittlesey, "Ex-Dragster Bosman Hit Top Speed at Races," *Washington Post*, February 28, 1970, 5.

6. Whittlesey, "Ex-Dragster Bosman Hit Top Speed at Races," 5.

7. Hannan, telephone interview by author.

CHAPTER 2

1. Dick Bosman, telephone interview by author, May 27, 2016. Unless specified otherwise, quotes from Dick Bosman in chapter 2 are drawn from this interview.

2. Dave Baldwin, e-mail interview by author, May 14, 2016.

3. Dave Marran, "I Could Do This," *Kenosha News*, June 1, 2016, 2.

CHAPTER 3

1. Ben Bradlee Jr., *The Kid: The Immortal Life of Ted Williams* (New York: Little, Brown and Company, 2013), 537.

2. Dick Bosman, telephone interview by author, June 7, 2016. Unless specified otherwise, quotes from Dick Bosman in chapter 3 are drawn from this interview.

3. Bradlee, *The Kid*, 532, 535.

4. Stephen J. Walker, *A Whole New Ballgame* (Clifton, VA: Pocol Press, 2009), 116.

5. Walker, *A Whole New Ballgame*, 63.

6. Ted Leavengood, *Ted Williams and the 1969 Washington Senators: The Last Winning Season* (Jefferson, NC: McFarland, 2009), 31.

7. Walker, *A Whole New Ballgame*, 63

8. George Minot, "Bosman Hurls One-Hitter at Indians," *Washington Post*, May 3, 1969, C1.

9. Walker, *A Whole New Ballgame*, 117.

10. Leavengood, *Ted Williams and the 1969 Washington Senators*, 106.

11. Leavengood, *Ted Williams and the 1969 Washington Senators*, 107.

12. Walker, *A Whole New Ballgame*, 117.

13. Walker, *A Whole New Ballgame*, 120.

14. Tom Seaver, with Lee Lowenfish, *The Art of Pitching* (New York: Hearst Books, 1984), 23.

15. Leavengood, *Ted Williams and the 1969 Washington Senators*, 155.

CHAPTER 4

1. Tom Seaver, with Lee Lowenfish, *The Art of Pitching* (New York: Hearst Books, 1984), 24.

2. William Gildea, "Bosman Signs for $27,000, Vows He Will Earn Money," *Washington Post*, February 5, 1970, F1.

3. Dick Bosman, telephone interview by author, July 14, 2016. Unless specified otherwise, quotes from Dick Bosman in chapter 4 are drawn from this interview.

4. George Minot, "Bosman Spits in Their Eyes," *Washington Post*, September 6, 1970, D4.

5. George Minot, "Bosman Raps Mates: Laying Down Blast Follows 10th Loss in Row," *Washington Post*, September 7, 1970, D1.

6. Minot, "Bosman Raps Mates," D1.

7. Boog Powell comments are remembered by Bosman and drawn from the author interview on July 14, 2016.

8. Bill James, "The Trading Record," *Baseball Research Journal* 7 (1978): 31.

9. Morton P. Sharnik, "Downfall of a Sports Hero," *Sports Illustrated*, February 23, 1970, 16.

10. Jerome Holtzman, "Players, Umpires, Books, Lawsuits," *Official Baseball Guide 1970* (St. Louis, MO: Sporting News, 1970), 263.

11. George Minot, "Senators, Yanks Split on Misplayed Drives," *Washington Post*, April 12, 1971, D1.

12. Shelby Whitfield, *Kiss It Goodbye* (New York: Abelard-Shuman, 1973), 110.

13. Whitfield, *Kiss It Goodbye*, 114.

14. Kenneth Denlinger, "Bosman Had Feeling It Would Be Like 6–5," *Washington Post*, June 2, 1971, D1.

15. George Minot, "Short Takes Senators to Texas," *Washington Post*, September 22, 1971, A1.

16. George Minot, "Washington Is a Ghost Town," *Washington Post*, September 26, 1971, F4.

17. George Minot, "Howard Hates Leaving, Saddest Senator Player," *Washington Post*, September 23, 1971, H1.

18. George Minot, "Senators Pay Forfeit as Fans Dance at Wake," *Washington Post*, October 1, 1971, D1.

19. Myra McPherson and Tom Huth, "Rowdy Fans Hand Senators Final Loss," *Washington Post*, October 1, 1971, A1.

CHAPTER 5

1. John Helyar, *Lords of the Realm: The Real History of Baseball* (New York: Villard, 1994), 112.

2. Helyar, *Lords of the Realm*, 113.

3. Helyar, *Lords of the Realm*, 116.

4. Dick Bosman, telephone interview by author, August 2, 2016. Unless specified otherwise, Dick Bosman quotes in chapter 5 are drawn from this interview.

5. Russell Schneider, "Indians Counting on Bosman to Fill Key Role as Starter," *Sporting News*, June 2, 1973, 19.

6. Jim Braham, "Here's Beer in Your Eye? Could Be for Texas' Martin," *Cleveland Press*, May 30, 1974, E2.

7. Dave Marran, e-mail interview by author, July 19, 2016.

8. Marran, e-mail interview by author.

CHAPTER 6

1. Russell Schneider, "1, 2, 3, Easy but Then?" *Sporting News*, March 22, 1975, 47.

2. Dick Bosman, telephone interview by author, September, 13, 2016. Unless specified otherwise, Dick Bosman quotes in chapter 6 are drawn from this interview.

3. Ron Bergman, "Seven-Year Loser, Bosman Savors the Good Life," *Sporting News*, August 9, 1975, 3.

4. Tom Boswell, "Angry Bosman Quits Baseball," *Washington Post*, April 9, 1977, C1.

CHAPTER 7

1. Dick Bosman, telephone interview by author, October 4, 2016. Unless specified otherwise, quotes from Dick Bosman in chapter 7 are drawn from this interview.

2. Chris Shebby, telephone interview by author, January 23, 2017.

3. Shebby, telephone interview by author.

4. Shebby, telephone interview by author.

5. Dave Marran, "Bosman: Hawk a Colorful Character," *Kenosha News*, July 22, 2013.

6. Dave Marran, personal interview of Ken Harrelson, April 2006, U.S. Cellular Field, Chicago, Illinois.

7. Stephen J. Walker, *A Whole New Ballgame* (Clifton, VA: Pocol Press, 2009), 123.

8. Robin Roberts, with C. Paul Rogers III, *Throwing Hard and Easy: Reflections on a Life in Baseball* (Lincoln: University of Nebraska Press, 2014), 211.

9. Alexander Edelman, "Ken Harrelson," *Society for American Baseball Research*, Biography Project, https://sabr.org/bioproj/person/442dbc70.

CHAPTER 8

1. "Chisox Find Diamond in the Rough," *Sporting News*, June 30, 1986, 13.

2. Ed Sherman, "Now Bosman's Happy He Accepted the Challenge," *Chicago Tribune*, July 5, 1986, 1.

3. Dick Bosman, telephone interview by author, October 14, 2016. Unless specified otherwise, quotes from Dick Bosman in chapter 8 are drawn from this interview.

4. Lou Brock and Franz Schulze, *Stealing Is My Game* (Englewood Cliffs, NJ: Prentice Hall, 1976), 118.

5. Dave Marran, Dick Bosman nomination for the Wisconsin Sports Hall of Fame, submitted 2009.

6. Marran, Bosman nomination for the Wisconsin Sports Hall of Fame.

7. Marran, Bosman nomination for the Wisconsin Sports Hall of Fame.

CHAPTER 9

1. Dick Bosman, telephone interview by author, October 14, 2016. Unless specified otherwise, quotes from Dick Bosman in chapter 9 are drawn from this interview.

2. Richard Justice, "Young Arms Tickle Orioles: Milacki, Harnisch, Olson Open Your Eyes," *Washington Post*, February 21, 1989, E1.

3. Jon A. Perkins, "Spinning a 1,600-rpm Surprise toward Home: How the Ball Breaks," *Washington Post*, October 18, 1993, A3.

4. Tom Boswell, "Young Arms Require an Old Head," *Washington Post*, April 1, 1992, B1.

5. Boswell, "Young Arms Require an Old Head," B1.

6. Tom Boswell, "Great Expectations," *Washington Post*, April 3, 1993, W12.

7. Tom Boswell, "Mussina: Perfectly Disarming," *Washington Post*, April 26, 1992, D11.

8. David Brown, "Answer Man: Mike Mussina Talks New York, Orioles, Economics," *Yahoo Sports Blog*, "Big League Stew," August 7, 2008, https://sports.yahoo.com/mlb/blog/big_league_stew/post/Answer-Man-Mike-Mussina-talks-New-York-Orioles?urn=mlb,99203.

9. Boswell, "Great Expectations," W12.

10. Bruce Lowitt, "McDonald Out to Capture Hill in '93," *St. Petersburg Times*, March 11, 1993, 1C.

11. Lowitt, "McDonald Out to Capture Hill in '93," 1C.

12. Murray Chass, "Baseball: Going, Going, Sold; Orioles Sold for $173 Million," *New York Times*, August 3, 1993, http://www.nytimes.com/1993/08/03/us/baseball-going-going-sold-orioles-auctioned-for-173-million.html.

13. John Helyar, *Lords of the Realm: The Real History of Baseball* (New York: Villard, 1994), 536.

14. Ross Newhan, "Some Baseball Officials Frown at Owner's Curve at Meetings," *Los Angeles Times*, December 9, 1993, 5.

CHAPTER 10

1. John Helyar, *Lords of the Realm: The Real History of Baseball* (New York: Villard, 1994), 413.

2. Dick Bosman, telephone interview by author, November 3, 2016. Unless specified otherwise, quotes by Dick Bosman in chapter 10 are drawn from this interview.

3. Lee Lowenfish, *The Imperfect Diamond: The History of Baseball's Labor Wars* (Lincoln: University of Nebraska Press, 1980), 289.

4. Helyar, *Lords of the Realm*, 419.

5. Athelia Knight, "No Say in Strike, but Plenty to Say," *Washington Post*, August 13, 1994, F1.

6. Lowenfish, *The Imperfect Diamond*, 292.

7. Mark Maske, "Oates Dismissed as Manager, La Russa, Lopes Possible Replacements," *Washington Post*, September 28, 1994, E1.

8. Mark Maske, "Reds Johnson Wants to Talk; Cincinnati Gives Orioles Permission to Interview Him for Manager's Job," *Washington Post*, September 29, 1994. B1.

9. Peter Schmuck and Buster Olney, "The Other Shoe," *Sporting News*, October 10, 1994, 40.

10. Chuck Johnson, "Bosman Elated after Long Wait," *USA Today*, October 3, 1996, C7.

11. Nolan Ryan, "Hall of Fame Acceptance Speech," Baseball Hall of Fame, Cooperstown, New York, February 12, 2013.

12. Mel Antonen, "Rangers Rely on Pitchers to Keep Command in West," *USA Today*, August 13, 1966, C11.

13. Antonen, "Rangers Rely on Pitchers to Keep Command in West," C11.

14. Kevin Hargis, "So They Say," *Austin American Statesman*, March 10, 1996, C2.

CHAPTER 11

1. Dick Bosman, telephone interview by author, November 3, 2016. Unless specified otherwise, quotes by Dick Bosman in chapter 11 are drawn from this interview.

2. Tom Seaver and Lee Lowenfish, *The Art of Pitching* (New York: Hearst Books, 1984), 95.

3. Marc Topkin, "Rays Tales," *St. Petersburg Times*, March 3, 2002, C11.

4. T. R. Sullivan, "Rangers to Honor Cherished 1996 Team," *MLB.com*, June 21, 2016, http://m.mlb.com/news/article/185184858/rangers-to-honor-1996-team-before-game-tuesday/.

5. Mel Antonen, "Rangers Rely on Pitchers to Keep Command in West," *USA Today*, August 13, 1966, C11.

6. Mel Antonen, "Rangers Add Burkett to Their Rotation," *USA Today*, August 9, 1996, C5.

7. Antonen, "Rangers Add Burkett to Their Rotation," C5.

8. "Cardinals Activate a Healthier Lankford," *USA Today*, October 2, 1966, C6.

9. Denne H. Freeman, "October at Last: The Rangers Finally Turn Calendar Page to Postseason Berth," *Austin American Statesman*, September 29, 1996, C1.

10. Dave Anderson, "Rangers Hope It's Their Turn to Rally," *New York Times*, October 5, 1996, 33.

11. Anderson, "Rangers Hope It's Their Turn to Rally," 33.

12. Tom Boswell, "Young Arms Require an Old Head," *Washington Post*, April 1, 1992, B1.

13. Mark Maske, "Run of Stunning Pitching Elicits Praise for Bosman," *Washington Post*, March 18, 1992, D3.

14. Jeff Gordon, "Playing for Canaries Won't Be Feather in Guerrero's Hat," *St. Louis Post-Dispatch*, July 14, 1992, D3.

15. Boswell, "Young Arms Require an Old Head," B1.

CHAPTER 12

1. Dick Bosman, telephone interview by author, November 3, 2016. Unless specified otherwise, quotes by Dick Bosman in chapter 12 are drawn from this interview.

2. Mike Bernardino, "The Macho Appeal of the High Fastball," *Ft. Lauderdale Sun-Sentinel*, June 7, 1998, 6.

3. Joe Gugliotti, "1–2 Repunched," *Sporting News*, December 18, 1995, 47.

4. Bernardino, "The Macho Appeal of the High Fastball," 6.

5. Mel Antonen, "For Starters, They're Perfect; Change Is Good for Helling," *USA Today*, May 8, 1998, C13.

6. Dick Bosman, telephone interview by author, November 18, 2016. Unless specified otherwise, quotes from Dick Bosman in the remaining portion of this chapter are drawn from this interview.

7. Mel Antonen, "Helling Credits Teammates, Changeup for 20-Win Year," *USA Today*, October 1, 1998, C4.

8. Rick Helling, telephone interview by author, December 8, 2016.

9. Antonen, "For Starters, They're Perfect," C13.

10. "Sele's 4–0 Start Is First for Rangers," *Austin American Statesman*, April 22, 1998, D5.

11. T. R. Sullivan, "The Curveball Is Becoming a Lost Art," *St. Louis Post-Dispatch*, April, 24, 1999, 14.

12. Sullivan, "The Curveball Is Becoming a Lost Art," 14.

13. Helling, telephone interview by author.

14. Marc Topkin, "The Daily Report," *St. Petersburg Times*, June 2, 1998, 6.

15. "Names in the Game," *San Antonio News-Express*, November 10, 1998, C2.

CHAPTER 13

1. Josh Dubow, "Zimmerman Throws Surprise into AL Picture," *Austin American Statesman*, June 19, 1999, C4.

2. "Twins Notes," *Minneapolis Star-Tribune*, April 23, 1999, C10.

3. Dubow, "Zimmerman Throws Surprise into AL Picture," C4.

4. David Schoenfield, "Bullpen Revolution: Teams Continue to Emphasize Late-Game Relief," *ESPN.com*, Sweet Spot Blog, March 28, 2016, http://www.espn.com/blog/sweetspot/archive/_/month/march-2016.

5. "1999 AL Wins above Average by Position," *Baseball-Reference.com*, http://www.baseball-reference.com:8080/leagues/team_compare.cgi?year=1999&lg=AL.

6. Anthony McCarron, "Johnny Is Feeling His Oates," *New York Daily News*, June 17, 1999, 100.

7. Dick Bosman, telephone interview by author, November 18, 2016. Unless specified otherwise, quotes by Dick Bosman in chapter 13 are drawn from this interview.

8. Roger Kahn, *The Head Game: Baseball Seen from the Pitcher's Mound* (New York: Harcourt, 2000), 281.

9. Tom Weir and Mel Antonen, "Hurling Out of Control," *Baseball Digest*, December 1999, 58.

10. John Thorn and John Holway, *The Pitcher* (New York: Prentice Hall, 1988), 254.

11. Weir and Antonen, "Hurling Out of Control," 58.

12. Kahn, *The Head Game*, 48.

13. Ken Rosenthal, "Sam Lacy Not Slowing Down for a Second—Even at 94," *Los Angeles Times*, April 26, 1998, 3.

14. T. R. Sullivan, "Juan Gone, Rangers Deal Star," *San Antonio News-Express*, November 3, 1999, C1.

15. T. R. Sullivan, "Rangers Seeking That Perfect Pitch," *San Antonio News-Express*, May 2, 2000, C4.

16. "Rangers Go from First to Last; Pitching Woes Doom Season," *San Antonio News-Express*, October 3, 2000, D4.

17. "Around the Majors: Rangers Dump Pitching Coach," *Los Angeles Times*, September 30, 2000, 6.

18. Rod Beaton, "Griffey Denies Whining Call to ESPN," *USA Today*, July 7, 2000, C5.

19. Mike Shropshire, "Sports Man behind the Miracle," *D Magazine*, May 1997, https://www.dmagazine.com/publications/d-magazine/1997/may/sports-man-behind-the-miracle/.

20. Randy Galloway, "After Others Have Faded, Oates Still Going Strong after Five Years," *Pittsburgh Post-Gazette*, September 9, 1999, D5.

21. Tom Boswell, "Built from Ground Up," *Washington Post*, May 9, 1992, G1.

22. Shropshire, "Sports Man behind the Miracle."

CHAPTER 14

1. Mike Shropshire, "Sports Man behind the Miracle," *D Magazine*, May 1997, https://www.dmagazine.com/publications/d-magazine/1997/may/sports-man-behind-the-miracle/.

2. Dick Bosman, telephone interview by author, December 1, 2016. Unless specified otherwise, quotes by Dick Bosman in chapter 14 are drawn from this interview.

3. Marc Topkin, "Bosman Has Chance to Teach Series," *St. Petersburg Times*, January 7, 2001, C14.

4. Topkin, "Bosman Has Chance to Teach Series," C14.

5. John Romano, "Thanks Vince, but Your Time Is Up," *St. Petersburg Times*, April 12, 2005, C1.

6. Marc Topkin, "Hall, Rays Move Even Further Apart," *St. Petersburg Times*, November 5, 2006, C11.

7. Eduardo Encina, "Easy Path Wrong One for Shields," *St. Petersburg Times*, March 12, 2007, C1.

8. Angela Duckworth, *Grit: The Power of Passion and Perseverance* (London and New York: Penguin/Random House, 2016), 317.

9. Ron Darling, *The Complete Game: Reflections on Baseball and the Art of Pitching* (New York: Vintage, 2010), 5.

10. Marc Topkin, "The Good Stuff: Rays Get Strong Pitching, Clear Up Any Doubts with a Return to Form," *St. Petersburg Times*, October 24, 2008, C1.

CHAPTER 15

1. Dick Bosman, telephone interview by author, January 4, 2017. Unless specified otherwise, quotes by Dick Bosman in chapter 15 are drawn from this interview.

2. Chris Shebby, telephone interview by author, January 23, 2017.

3. Roger Kahn, *The Head Game: Baseball Seen from the Pitcher's Mound* (New York: Harcourt, 2000), 167–68.

4. Kahn, *The Head Game*, 167–68.

5. Kahn, *The Head Game*, 167–68.

6. Tom Boswell, "Stars for the Gazing," *Washington Post*, July 9, 1993, C1.

7. Ron Darling, *The Complete Game: Reflections on Baseball and the Art of Pitching* (New York: Vintage, 2010), 12.

8. Darling, *The Complete Game*, 67–68.

9. Dave Baldwin, *Snake Jazz* (Bloomington, IN: Xlibris Corporation, 2007), 97.

10. Rick Helling, telephone interview by author, December 8, 2016.

11. Helling, telephone interview by author.

12. Kahn, *The Head Game*, 17.

13. Dave Baldwin, e-mail, May 9, 2016.

14. Tom Seaver, with Lee Lowenfish, *The Art of Pitching* (New York: Hearst Books, 1984), 192.

15. Bob Gibson and Lonnie Wheeler, *Pitch by Pitch: My View of One Unforgettable Game* (New York: Flatiron Books, 2015), 47.

16. "Oates' Life Was Happy, Complete," *Pittsburgh Post-Gazette*, December 27, 2004, E2.

17. Dale Voiss, "Dick Bosman," *Society for American Baseball Research*, Biography Project, https://sabr.org/bioproj/person/0a88eccf.

Bibliography

NEWSPAPES AND MAGAZINES

Austin American Statesman

Baseball Digest

Chicago Tribune

Cleveland Press

Ft. Lauderdale Sun-Sentinel

Hannibal Courier-Post

Kenosha News

Los Angeles Times

Minneapolis Star-Tribune

New York Daily News

New York Times

Pittsburgh Post-Gazette

San Antonio News-Express

Sporting News

Sports Illustrated

St. Louis Post-Dispatch

St. Petersburg Times

Tampa Bay Times

USA Today

Washington Post

INTERVIEWS BY AUTHOR

Dave Baldwin

Dick Bosman

Jim Hannan

Rick Helling

Don Loun

Dave Marran

Chris Shebby

Fred Valentine

BOOKS

Achorn, Edward. *Fifty-Nine in '84*. New York: Smithsonian Books, 2010.

Baldwin, Dave. *Snake Jazz*. Bloomington, IN: Xlibris Corporation, 2007.

Bradlee, Ben, Jr. *The Kid: The Immortal Life of Ted Williams*. New York: Little, Brown and Company, 2013.

Brock, Lou, and Franz Schulze. *Stealing Is My Game*. Englewood Cliffs, NJ: Prentice Hall, 1976.

Darling, Ron. *The Complete Game: Reflections on Baseball and the Art of Pitching*. New York: Vintage, 2010.

Duckworth, Angela. *Grit: The Power of Passion and Perseverance*. London and New York: Penguin/Random House, 2016.

Gibson, Bob, and Lonnie Wheeler. *Pitch by Pitch: My View of One Unforgettable Game*. New York: Flatiron Books, 2015.

———. *Stranger to the Game: The Autobiography of Bob Gibson*. New York: Penguin, 1994.

Helyar, John. *Lords of the Realm: The Real History of Baseball*. New York: Villard, 1994.

Holtzman, Jerome. "Players, Umpires, Books, Lawsuits." *Official Baseball Guide 1970*. St. Louis, MO: Sporting News, 1970.

Kahn, Roger. *The Head Game: Baseball Seen from the Pitcher's Mound*. New York: Harcourt, 2000.

Leavengood, Ted. *Ted Williams and the 1969 Washington Senators: The Last Winning Season*. Jefferson, NC: McFarland, 2009.

Lowenfish, Lee. *The Imperfect Diamond: The History of Baseball's Labor Wars*. Lincoln: University of Nebraska Press, 1980.

Roberts, Robin, with C. Paul Rogers III. *Throwing Hard and Easy: Reflections on a Life in Baseball*. Lincoln: University of Nebraska Press, 2014.

Seaver, Tom, with Lee Lowenfish. *The Art of Pitching*. New York: Hearst Books, 1984.

Thorn, John, and John Holway. *The Pitcher*. New York: Prentice Hall, 1988.

Walker, Stephen J. *A Whole New Ballgame*. Clifton, VA: Pocol Press, 2009.

Whitfield, Shelby. *Kiss It Goodbye*. New York: Abelard-Schuman, 1973.

Index

About the Authors

Ted Leavengood is the author of several books on Washington, DC, baseball history, and his articles have appeared in numerous publications and on many websites. His career spanned three decades as an urban planner for local governments before he retired from the U.S. Department of Housing and Urban Development in 2011. He lives with his wife, Donna Boxer, in Chevy Chase, MD. He has two daughters, Julia Leavengood-Boxer and Claire Leavengood-Boxer, who live and work in Brooklyn, New York.

Dick Bosman is the minor-league pitching coordinator for the Tampa Bay Rays. His career as a major-league pitcher began in 1966, with the Washington Senators, and spanned 11 seasons. He complied 82 wins and a 3.67 ERA with the Senators, Texas Rangers, Cleveland Indians, and Oakland Athletics. Highlights of his career include leading the American League in ERA in 1969 and pitching a no-hitter against the world champion Oakland Athletics in 1974. His coaching career began in 1986, with the Chicago White Sox, and he has been affiliated with a major-league team in a coaching capacity continuously since then. Bosman's stints as a major-league pitching coach include with the White Sox (1986–1987), Baltimore Orioles (1992–1994), and Texas Rangers (1995–2000). He resides in Palm Harbor, Florida, and Irmo, South Carolina, with his wife Pam. They have three daughters, Michele, Dina, and Amanda, who live and work in Florida and South Carolina, and three grandchildren, Lucas, Landon, and Lola.

From left, Brent Honeywell—ranked as the second overall minor-league prospect for Tampa Bay—Dick Bosman, and Ted Leavengood on practice field at the Tampa Bay Rays spring training complex, 2017.